**SIMON & SCHUSTER**

New York London Toronto Sydney Tokyo Singapore

# IN THE FAST LANE

## A True Story
## of Murder
## in Miami

•

# Carol Soret Cope

SIMON & SCHUSTER
Simon & Schuster Building
Rockefeller Center
1230 Avenue of the Americas
New York, New York 10020

Copyright © 1993 by Carol Soret Cope

Designed by Karolina Harris
Manufactured in the United States of America

1  3  5  7  9  10  8  6  4  2

Library of Congress Cataloging-in-Publication Data
Cope, Carol Soret.
In the fast lane: a true story of murder in Miami/Carol Soret Cope.
p.    cm.
A John Boswell Associates/Herman Klurfield book—T.p verso.
1. Murder—Florida—Miami—Case studies.  2. Cohen, Joyce.
I. Title
HV6534.M6C67    1993
364. 1 ' 523 ' 09759381—dc20                          93-3932
                                                        CIP

ISBN  0-671-73026-6

A John Boswell Associates/Herman Klurfield Book

PHOTO CREDITS
1, 6, 7, 11: Courtesy of Art Trapani; 2, 3, 10, 12, 15, 29: Author's Collection; 4, 5, 19, 20, 25: Author's Photo; 8: Courtesy of Dr. Fred Wasserman; 9, 13, 14, 16, 17, 18, 23, 24: Trial Exhibit; 21, 30: Miami Herald; 22, 28: Miami Herald/David Walters; 26, 31: Miami Herald/Al Diaz; 27: Miami Herald/Albert Coya; 32: Courtesy of Raquel Navarro.

*For Cara and Jerry*

# Contents

●

# *Prologue*

T he old man awakened with the first shot. He was alone in an unfamiliar bed in the dark. Then he remembered—he was spending the night at his friend's condominium in Coconut Grove. There was a pause, then more shots, each like a sharp bang. He counted them automatically. Then it was quiet. After checking the glowing red numerals of the digital clock on the nightstand next to the bed, he got up and crossed the bedroom to the sliding glass door, which he had left slightly open. He peered down through the leafy darkness into the empty street below and listened intently. The gunfire had come from the left, he was certain. There was a crunching sound, then silence. The old man went back to bed and soon slept soundly again. After all, this was Miami.

The first call was logged by the Miami 911 emergency operator at 5:25 that Friday morning, March 7, 1986. A woman's voice was screaming, hysterical, nearly unintelligible. "Please, somebody, help me!" she begged. A burglar alarm shrilled in the background.

The Miami Police Department dispatcher radioed all units: a three/thirty-two, woman shot, at 1665 South Bayshore Drive, Coconut Grove. Correction, a three/thirty-two, *man* shot, QTH [same address]. A twenty-five [audible alarm], QTH.

Miami Patrol Officer Catherine Carter, a two-year veteran, was riding alone in Sector 70, Coconut Grove, the affluent Miami neighborhood that meanders gracefully along Biscayne Bay, just south of the city. The address on South Bayshore Drive was an enclave of historic mansions set on a small limestone cliff called Silver Bluff, overlooking the bay. Officer Carter took the call and within three minutes she arrived at 1665 South Bayshore Drive: a large old native limestone house looming above the cliff, screened from the street by huge trees and heavy tropical undergrowth—a perfect setting for a murder mystery.

Officer Carter parked her patrol car in the gravel driveway behind a new white Jaguar and a tan Bronco. The license tag on the Jaguar was SAC-1 and on the Bronco, SAC-7. Carter approached the rear of the two-story house, using her heavy Kell flashlight to pick her way past an open gate and through thick foliage. She could hear the alarm still ringing throughout the dark house. She turned a corner and found herself in a small paved courtyard with a reflecting pool at its center. Playing her flashlight along the stone walls, she found an open door, its glass pane smashed out and a large chunk of limestone lying nearby.

Beyond the door, in the dark kitchen, stood a large Doberman pinscher, teeth bared, growling. Carter froze, then approached the dog slowly, speaking softly. Somehow she persuaded the big dog to let her pass.

There was no light inside the cavernous old house. Flashlight in hand, Carter worked her way cautiously through the kitchen and into the shadowy dining room beyond. Suddenly the police radio on her belt came alive with sharp static. Patrol Officer Snow had arrived at the house and was trying to get in through the front door.

As Carter crossed the dark living room, she was startled by a figure bolting down a narrow stairway near the front door. It was a small white woman with thick, disheveled dark hair swirling about her face. She was sobbing hysterically. The frantic woman threw open the front door, and Officer Snow stepped into the foyer. Babbling incoherently, she raced ahead of the two officers up the steep stairs to the master bedroom suite on the second floor. The Doberman pinscher trailed behind. At the top of the stairs was a large room dominated by a huge brass bed against a smoke-mirrored wall. Clothing was strewn everywhere. An overturned brass table lamp lay on the hardwood floor next to the bed. In the faint light the officers could see a husky white man lying face down on the bed. He was nude, the pale yellow bedclothes pulled up just to the crease of his buttocks. A blood-soaked towel covered the back of his head.

He's dead, Officer Carter thought. She didn't touch him.

The sobbing woman ran to the bed. "Is he dead? Is he dead? Let me touch him! I know if I touch him I can wake him up!"

She's going nuts on me, Carter thought. I've got to get her out of here. Firmly she led the hysterical woman back down the steep stairs. Officer Snow radioed for the paramedics, then followed the two women into the living room. Lamps now glowed softly in the large room, illuminating a limestone fireplace on one wall, a luxury in South Florida. There were candles in a candelabra on the mantel. Dark oak wainscoting lined the walls and heavy, dark wooden beams traced the ceiling. Three banks of french doors led from the living room to the rear courtyard, to a separate wing of the house, and to an enclosed sun porch filled with television and stereo equipment.

The dark-haired woman sat cross-legged on a damask sofa facing the stone fireplace. With paramedics on the way, Officer Carter's immediate priority was to get enough information to put out a BOLO, be on the lookout for suspects. She eyed the woman curiously. Probably mid-thirties, not much older than Carter. Luxuriant, shoulder-length dark hair. The face was a mask of grief: red and puffy from crying, large dark eyes brimming with tears.

But even though the woman was disheveled and sobbing, Carter could see that she was attractive. The dark eyes had an exotic tilt, the generous mouth was full and soft. She was wearing expensive-looking hot pink sweats and socks but no shoes. There was a gold Rolex on her left wrist.

Officer Carter spoke to her softly, and the young woman finally calmed down. Haltingly she told her story. She was Joyce Cohen, thirty-five, wife of Stanley Cohen, the man in the bed upstairs. Her fifty-two-year-old husband was a builder, owner of SAC Construction Company in Miami. Although the names meant nothing to Officer Carter, she could see the Cohens were rich: the big old house in the fancy neighborhood, a new Jaguar in the driveway, the gold Rolex watch.

Joyce Cohen and her husband had been alone in the house that night, she told Officer Carter. While Stan slept upstairs, Joyce was in the downstairs bedroom of her son Shawn (who was away at school), sorting clothing for a garage sale. Mischief, the Doberman pinscher, was with her in the bedroom. Suddenly she was startled by a noise, Joyce said, a loud, banging noise. The dog bolted toward the kitchen and Joyce followed. A rock had been thrown through the kitchen door, which was standing open. Joyce found her heavy brass key ring with the key to operate the burglar alarm, and she set off the alarm. She knew the alarm company would call the police.

Then Joyce said she heard somebody running down the stairs from the bedroom. She saw two shadowy figures rush out the front door. She hurried upstairs and found her husband lying on the bed, blood seeping from his head. She tried to rouse him but he didn't answer. She panicked. She ran to the master bathroom for a towel to stanch her husband's bleeding head. Then she waited for help to arrive. That was all she remembered.

"Two shadowy figures" isn't enough for a BOLO, Officer Carter thought. But she still had some questions for Mrs. Cohen. Why was the home's alarm system turned off that night? Because, Joyce said, she was moving around the house gathering clothes for a garage sale and she didn't want to set off the alarm system's motion sensor accidentally. Why didn't the Doberman pinscher catch the intruders as they broke into the kitchen? Because Joyce had kept the dog with her as she worked in her son Shawn's room on the other side of the house. She didn't want Mischief to bark and awaken her husband.

Suddenly Joyce Cohen was on her feet, darting restlessly around the house. She wanted to show Officer Carter her son's room. She wanted a drink of water from the kitchen. Then she needed to use the bathroom. Officer Carter waited patiently in the hall outside the downstairs bathroom, then led Joyce Cohen back to the living room. Finally Joyce settled down again and sat with legs crossed Indian-style on pillows near the windows at the front of the house. She seemed calmer now and sat quietly, rocking back and forth, staring into the distance. Finally she began to talk aloud to herself, as if she had forgotten Officer Carter sitting next to her, listening. "What am I going to tell the kids?" she muttered. "Stan's daughter, Gerri—she's getting married on Saturday. I don't know what I'm going to tell the kids . . ."

Then she said something else, something startling, as she gazed ahead unseeing. Officer Carter heard the words clearly, but she wasn't sure what Joyce Cohen meant. She leaned forward to ask her. Just then, the phone rang. Distracted, Carter answered the call. The moment passed.

Abruptly, the Cohen home filled with noise and strangers. Joyce Cohen was no longer in control of her own life. The phone rang repeatedly, and Officer Carter answered each time, telling callers that Mrs. Cohen was unavailable. Odd, Carter thought, that several of the calls came from someplace in Colorado, where it was two hours earlier than Miami time. Who would be phoning Joyce Cohen at 4 A.M.?

Officer Snow stood outside the front door, calling directions to paramedics trying to find their way up from the street through the dense undergrowth at the front of the house. Three paramedics from Miami Station 8 burst in with Miami homicide detective Sergeant Tom Waterson right behind them. The four men followed Officer Snow to the upstairs bedroom, the paramedics lugging their heavy equipment up the narrow stairway.

The paramedics rolled Stanley Cohen onto his back on the bed and immediately attached electrocardiogram leads to his chest. "I think there's some action! We're going to have to move him, so take a good look!" a paramedic yelled at Officer Snow and Sergeant Waterson.

The cops knew what he meant. The crime scene was about to be irremediably altered in the effort to save Cohen's life—if there was any life left to save. They tried to fix a mental picture of the victim's position on the big brass bed. Blood soaked the pale yellow bedding and pillowcase. The designer signature "Diane von Furstenberg" showed on the pillow beneath Cohen's head.

The paramedics rolled Cohen over twice across the bed, then laid him on his back on the hardwood floor, to the left of the bed where the light was better. They needed a hard surface to support Cohen as they worked over him. Once more they monitored the leads—and got nothing but a flat line.

"He's gone."

Silently the paramedics repacked their equipment and headed back down the narrow stairs.

"Watch your head on the stairs," someone called out.

Sergeant Waterson ducked beneath the rough limestone edge on the low ceiling and headed downstairs. For Waterson, with two years as a homicide detective, the first few minutes at the scene of a crime were the most exciting part of an investigation because you never knew what you might find. He enjoyed the uncertainty, the action, the sense of time racing. And he liked being in charge. His adrenaline was pumping.

Downstairs Waterson walked over to Joyce Cohen and Officer Carter.

"Is he gone?" Joyce asked.

Yes, Waterson nodded.

Joyce began to scream.

Waterson watched her silently for a moment, then launched into his standard speech. Although this was a difficult time for her, she had to pull herself together because what she could tell him now might make a big difference in finding out who had done this to her husband.

Finally Joyce calmed down enough to repeat for Sergeant Waterson what she had already told Officer Carter. She added that earlier in the evening she and her husband had investigated a noise in the backyard but found nothing. Joyce walked Sergeant Waterson through the house, showing him where she had been sorting clothing in her son Shawn's bedroom in a separate wing of the house, how she crossed to the kitchen with the dog after she heard the banging noise.

As they walked, Waterson noticed mousetraps scattered about the old house. How peculiar, he thought—polished hardwood floors, expensive carpets, and mousetraps everywhere. He listened to Joyce intently, asking few questions. Then he excused himself to use the kitchen telephone to call the Miami homicide commander, Lieutenant Edward J. Carberry. It was nearly 7 A.M., time for the shift change. "Just hold the scene," Carberry told Waterson. "We're going to call in the day shift on this one because it's going to be too much overtime for you guys."

Waterson had mixed feelings about relinquishing the case to the day shift. The three/thirty-two call had come in near the end of his 11 P.M.-to-7 A.M. shift, the "midnight shift," while he was cruising nearby on Southwest 17th Avenue, wishing it was time to go home and get some sleep. He was exhausted, not ready to take on a fresh homicide at that hour. But this was an interesting case by Miami standards—not a run-of-the-mill druggie murder, but the slaying of a good-looking wealthy man, a man of substance. The case would attract attention. This kind of case could make a detective's reputation.

Joyce Cohen was still sitting in the living room when Waterson answered a knock at the front door. A man identifying himself as an attorney asked to see Mrs. Cohen. "She's not available at the moment," Waterson responded. These lawyers, he thought. How do they show up so quickly? Can they smell blood?

Next, technicians from the Identification Section, midnight shift, arrived to begin the tedious job of processing the scene for evidence. Waterson explained that day-shift homicide detectives would be handling the case. Since each shift has its own team of technicians, that meant the day-shift ID people would be working the scene. The midnight-shift ID techs could go home.

Waterson sent officers to interview the Cohens' maid, who lived in a small cottage about ten feet from the main house. She was still asleep when they knocked on her door. She heard nothing unusual during the night, she told them. No shots. No screams. No breaking glass. No barking dog. Even the ringing alarm hadn't awakened her.

Lieutenant Edward Carberry, homicide commander, arrived at the Cohen home with Major William Starkes, who was in charge of all investigations. Near the pinnacle of the police department hierarchy, Starkes reported directly to the assistant chief of police. Eyebrows raised and pulses quickened when he appeared at an investigation. Waterson promptly guided the lieutenant and the major on a VIP tour of the crime scene.

A perimeter of bright yellow crime scene tape was set up around the grounds of the Cohens' house. Dark blue–uniformed Miami police officers kept the curious outside the tape. The roadway began to fill with people and television station mobile units. Sergeant Waterson came outside looking for relatives and friends of the dead man.

• • •

Across town, the phone rang in the darkened bedroom of Gerri Cohen, Stan Cohen's twenty-seven-year-old daughter by a prior marriage. Still half asleep, she mumbled and picked up the phone. It was a
co-worker at Miami's Channel 10 television station. Gerri Cohen was
a well-known news reporter for Channel 10. Someone had contacted
the station, the caller said, asking for her home telephone number.

"Who was it?" she asked sleepily.

"Somebody named P. J. Carroll. He says he's a friend of your father's. Something about an accident involving your father. He wants
to talk to you. Shall we give him your number?"

"Yes, yes, give it to him." P. J. Carroll. Gerri Cohen was instantly
awake. Of course she recognized the name. P. J. Carroll was indeed
an old friend of her father's, a prominent Miami attorney. She hung
up the phone and waited, apprehensive in the dark, for someone to
call her back.

The phone rang again.

"Hello?"

It was P. J. Carroll. Something about her father. He had been shot.
Gerri Cohen couldn't seem to make any sense of the words. She only
knew that she had to get to her father, had to get there. Please, don't
let him be dead, she prayed silently. I have to talk to him! I have to
tell him . . .

When Gerri Cohen pulled up in front of her father's house in a
Porsche driven by her fiancé, Steve Helfman, Sergeant Waterson recognized her immediately as the attractive news reporter he saw regularly on Channel 10. She always looked great on television, he
thought. But now, as she stepped out of the Porsche, her face was red,
swollen, blotchy from crying, and her thick, dark hair was disheveled. She ran toward him. "What happened to my father?" she
asked frantically.

"He was shot. He's dead. I'm sorry," Waterson replied. "His wife
saw two men run out of the house."

"Oh, no! No! No!" Gerri Cohen collapsed, sobbing, and fell heavily against her fiancé. Steve Helfman caught her and held her close.

Suddenly Gerri recognized Barney Haddad, a television cameraman for Channel 4, the Miami station where Gerri had begun her

broadcasting career years before. He must be filming the crime scene for a live broadcast. "Barney! Barney! Please, don't run that film! My grandmother's alone—she'll see it—it'll kill her!" Gerri implored him.

But Barney Haddad didn't recognize the distraught young woman shouting at him. He tried to ignore her.

"Barney! Please! It's me—Gerri Cohen!"

Haddad was shocked at Gerri's distraught appearance. He wouldn't have believed she could look like that.

Just then the front door of the house opened, and Joyce Cohen ran down the steps to Gerri Cohen, her dead husband's daughter. The two women fell into each other's arms, clinging together, hugging, sobbing, Joyce babbling incoherently.

Downtown at the headquarters of the Miami Police Department, homicide detective Jon Spear parked his 1985 silver Thunderbird in the personnel parking garage and headed up the walk to the building's rear door, the cops' entrance. He was about ten minutes early for the beginning of his 7 A.M.-to-3 P.M. shift, the "day shift," and he was already deeply preoccupied with unsolved homicides he was investigating. Before he reached the door, he ran into an officer he knew.

"Hey, Jon, Vinson's looking for you."

"What? Already? Where is he?"

"Vinson and Rosello are at a scene. There was a homicide at five-thirty this morning in the Grove. It's your case."

"No way! If it happened at five-thirty, it's midnight's case! What's going on?" Spear felt frustration rising within him.

As he hurried on into the building, Spear thought about the homicide cases already on his roster. Just two weeks earlier, the bodies of two young Latin males had washed up on the Julia Tuttle Causeway, the highway that runs from downtown Miami to the long, narrow sand strip of Miami Beach. Spear and his partner were "hot" that week, meaning that they were on call for any homicides discovered during their shift. The other day-shift team was "cold"; they could devote their week to running down leads on their pending cases without having to answer calls on new cases.

The Dade County medical examiner who examined the bodies on the Tuttle Causeway couldn't find any trauma marks. Maybe the floaters were illegals who simply drowned while trying to swim ashore from one of the many ships in the area, he suggested. Spear marked the deaths "unclassified" and waited for autopsy results. Bad news—the medical examiner eventually found gunshot wounds in the young men's heads, giving Detective Spear a double homicide to work.

Since the victims were Latin, Spear had another problem. He didn't speak Spanish and needed a Spanish-speaking partner to conduct witness interviews. When Sergeant Steven Vinson, supervisor of the day-shift homicide teams, assigned Pablo Rosello to work with him, Spear gritted his teeth. He liked Rosello, but the guy was a brand-new detective. Spear would have to break him in, show him the ropes. With a more experienced partner, Spear could cover twice as much investigative territory.

Then, before that week was out, he had picked up two more homicides to work, bringing the week's total to four new cases in addition to the several unsolved old cases on his list. And the following week, when he was "cold," he had made little progress on his four new "whodunits," or "WDIs," as they are designated by detectives. Now Spear was "hot" again. And just as the week was drawing to a close, it looked as if he would get this new case in the Grove, even though it wasn't on his shift. Five new WDIs in two weeks—a crushing burden.

Still seething, Spear hopped into a department car, an unmarked white Ford LTD, and sped toward 1665 South Bayshore Drive in the Grove. Like most Miami cops, Spear didn't like the Grove. It was a place where people with too much money could buy lots of trouble—mostly drug trouble. It seemed the lovely old neighborhood was now full of swaggering drug dealers wearing open shirts and gold chains—and probably concealed weapons, too. Spear was not impressed by the so-called artistic ambiance of the Grove. Too funky. Everyone knew the movie *Deep Throat* had been filmed in an old Grove mansion.

As Spear drove up to the Cohen house on South Bayshore Drive, he whistled under his breath. He recognized the impressive old place immediately. *I never thought I'd be investigating a murder here,* he thought. He parked on the street outside the yellow tape perimeter and stomped up the stone steps to the front door, still grumbling under his breath about his workload. Inside the house, Sergeant Waterson greeted Spear briefly, introduced him to Mrs. Cohen, and then gave him a quick tour of the house. As they walked, Waterson summarized Joyce Cohen's account of the murder. Spear asked few questions. Despite his anger and frustration, he was becoming intrigued by the case.

Finally they headed upstairs. Stan Cohen's nude body still lay spread-eagled on its back, next to the bed. Blood from his head wounds made deep pools on the polished wood floor, running off into little rivers in low spots.

Spear stood silently at the right side of the bed, where the killer must have been standing when he pumped bullets into Stan Cohen's head. He gazed at his own reflection in the smoke-mirrored wall behind the bed. The killer must have come face-to-face with his own image as he stood over his victim. Did he watch himself kill Stanley Cohen?

Spear stared at the lifeless body still bleeding on the floor. After nearly seventeen years as a Miami cop, and more than a decade as a homicide detective, he never really got over this moment. It wasn't so much the blood; he had learned to handle the sheer horror of the sight. It was something else—a sense of the fragility of life, the finality of sudden, violent death.

As always at a homicide scene, Spear thought about the victim, trying to imagine his life as well as his death. He found himself wondering what Stan Cohen had planned for that day, for the weekend, for the rest of his life. He had never met Stan Cohen. But he knew he would have to learn everything he could about the man's life to unravel the mystery of his death.

Outside on the street, stunned friends and neighbors of the Cohens gave quotes to reporters.

"Stanley was a very strong, fair person and an excellent businessman," said Marvin Sheldon, Cohen's business partner for more than two decades. "This is a terrible shock."

"He was one of the most well-thought-of people in town." Miami lawyer A. J. Barranco, a neighbor, shook his head sadly. "He was just a prince."

A friend described the Cohens' eleven-year marriage: "They were devoted to each other. It was a Cinderella marriage."

When the press contacted Stan Cohen's ex-wife Martha, she said, "I just have no idea why anyone would do this. I can give you no reasons why or wherefore."

But someone had wanted Stan Cohen dead.

# I.

# Rich—
# and Dead

# *One*

*O*ne sunny Sunday in the spring of 1981, a small group of Miamians and their guests arrived at Miami International Airport to catch an Air Jamaica flight to Montego Bay. The trip was in celebration of the host's thirtieth birthday and his graduation from the University of Miami Law School. He had been offered a friend's elaborate oceanfront estate in the Ocho Rios section of Jamaica for a week's visit. There would be a full staff of cooks, maids, and housekeepers to serve them—and an armed guard on patrol after dark. The party was on.

Somehow, the Air Jamaica flight left without them. What to do? The young host's response was automatic. He chartered a private Learjet for the trip. And why not? This was Miami in the 1980s. All it took was a phone call and an American Express Gold Card. Easy.

Soon the group was chauffeured to Miami's Executive Airport, while the jet was stocked with Dom Perignon and caviar, and a pilot and copilot whose celebrity passengers had included John Lennon and Yoko Ono. The slender jet felt like a rocket on takeoff. Champagne-induced euphoria settled over the leather-paneled cabin as the plane soared over the sparkling turquoise waters of Biscayne Bay.

Champagne flute aloft, a young woman offered a toast—to the host, to Miami, to the decade of the '80s: "To extravagance!"

"Extravagance!" Her friends applauded, their laughter streaming behind them like the jet's contrail.

It was a fitting invocation of the '80s, the decade of excess, Miami-style.


Joyce and Stan Cohen were a couple whose philosophy meshed perfectly with Miami's. As former Miami mayor Maurice Ferre put it, "Miami is a town where people are awed by money as a status symbol of achievement." In Miami, rich always meant nouveau riche. There simply was no "old money" and few "old families" to set any standards of restraint or taste. Life was an acquisitive race, with success measured strictly in material terms. A popular maxim embossed on designer T-shirts and smug little wall plaques in fancy Miami homes said it all: HE WHO DIES WITH THE MOST TOYS WINS. It was a game Stan and Joyce were eager to play—and win.

By 1980 Miami was awash in money—some of it profits of legitimate commerce, but much from the illicit drug trade. Geographically and culturally the northernmost capital of the Caribbean, Miami was the port of entry for most South American drug traffic. It was a wholesale market that spewed money like a geyser. Drug money flooded South Florida banks and fueled lavish consumer spending: pricey imported cars, enormous houses, huge yachts, even personal jets. After busting a "respected" Miami businessman for smuggling, federal marshals were astonished to discover a fully equipped nightclub on a subterranean floor of his lavish Coral Gables home—complete with a stage, professional lighting, a bar, a full kitchen, and men's and women's bathrooms with three stalls each.

Inevitably, the lucrative smuggling trade spawned a new breed of Miami criminal defense attorney—the "drug lawyer." It began in the heyday of marijuana. Everyone who was busted needed a lawyer. Most of the arrests took place in South Florida, port of entry for an estimated 80 percent of America's imported grass. Sometimes they were made further up the distribution line, in southern states through which pot was transported to retailers in big cities up north. But wherever the busts went down, it was usually a Miami drug lawyer who got the call to defend the arrested. Their names became talismans on the lips of pilots, drivers, off-loaders, "mules," "smurfs," and their bosses. Soon there was a certain cachet to being represented by a premier Miami drug lawyer, and they dominated drug trials throughout the Southeast.

As their legal reputations grew, so did their fees—always up-front, always cash. To pay their lawyers' fees, clients sometimes had to throw in property, too—deeds to houses, titles to expensive boats, luxury cars, even airplanes. But the clients didn't complain. Legal defense fees were just a small cost of doing business in the enormously lucrative smuggling trade.

Attorney Alan Ross was a founding father of the Miami drug lawyer clique. Shortly after he graduated from the University of Miami Law School in 1976, he established his reputation with one big win in Key West. Ross's law firm sent him there to represent a small-timer—a man who was picked up with a semi loaded with something like 35,000 pounds of marijuana, driving north on U.S. 1, the only artery between Key West and the Florida peninsula. The defense: the driver didn't know what was in the trailer. The cops were not impressed, especially since the man's clothing was covered with what looked like marijuana residue, most likely obtained when he helped load the bales into the trailer.

Alan Ross tried the case before a jury in Key West. He asked the arresting officers whether they had actually smelled the odor of marijuana in the "alleged marijuana residue" on the defendant's clothing. No, they hadn't. When the jury was sent into the tiny jury room to deliberate, Ross made sure a bale of the grass that had been seized in the arrest went with them. Look at it, touch it, smell it, Ross urged the jurors. Then you decide whether my client could possibly have been covered with marijuana residue if the officers didn't smell it on him.

As the jurors deliberated, Ross pondered his gambit. Fresh marijuana, he knew, has little scent. But the seized bales had been moldering for months in custody. The marijuana now reeked with an unmistakable, pungent odor. He could have negotiated a plea for his client, but he thought this was worth the gamble.

The jury returned. Verdict: not guilty. Of course, this being Key West, some of the marijuana disappeared from the evidence bale in the jury room during the deliberations. There was an investigation into the jury's conduct, but the verdict stood, and Ross's client went free. He returned to the community in which he lived and worked and spread the gospel of Alan Ross to his friends and colleagues. Suddenly Ross was a big-gun Miami drug lawyer—at age twenty-seven, one year out of law school.

Soon Ross was getting drug trials all over the Southeast, along with his colleagues from Miami. The trials usually started on Monday and lasted most of the week. By Friday night, the Miami lawyers who had tried cases in places like Green Pond, South Carolina, were back in Atlanta, catching the last plane home to Miami. Any Friday night at the Atlanta airport, Ross inevitably met up with several of his colleagues from the Miami drug lawyers clique. They all wound up in the first-class section of the last Eastern Airlines flight back to Miami, swapping war stories, having a few drinks, joking with the flight attendants—and usually celebrating victories.

But much as Alan Ross enjoyed his practice, he followed one invariable rule: never get involved with your clients. To Ross this meant no business deals with clients, no entertaining clients, not even having dinner with a client. Even though Ross actually liked some of his clients, he knew any involvement could lead to big trouble for a criminal defense lawyer. The only sure way to avoid problems was to follow that ironclad rule.

One Miami lawyer who followed no such rule was Frank Lino Diaz. Frankie, as he was known, not only socialized with his clients, he went into business deals with them. Diaz helped drug trafficker Joe Rodriguez buy into a Miami auto agency that imported expensive Jaguars, Porsches, BMWs, Audis—and Diaz bought himself a piece of the deal while he was at it.

Diaz also set up Jamboni, an offshore corporation, for the infamous Laney Jacobs Greenberger, a Miami cocaine trafficker known by the Spanish nickname La Rubia for her blond hair. Diaz represented Greenberger and Hollywood producer Robert Evans in a failed movie deal. Later Greenberger was convicted of ordering the murder of promoter Roy Radin, the so-called Cotton Club murder. She was also a suspect in the slaying of her drug-trafficking husband, Larry Greenberger, in Okeechobee, Florida.

Eventually Diaz himself was indicted in Miami federal court on a long string of charges including conspiracy, perjury, mail fraud, bank fraud, and witness bribery. Shortly before he was scheduled to appear and plead guilty to at least some of these charges, Diaz faked his own kidnapping and simply disappeared. Alan Ross, meanwhile, kept his nose clean and his reputation as one of Miami's top criminal defense lawyers intact. But both Ross and Diaz, like Stan and Joyce Cohen, were traveling in Miami's fast lane, and it was perhaps inevitable that their paths would cross.

The Miami drug scene changed radically during the 1980s when cocaine replaced marijuana as the favored smuggling commodity. Coke is less bulky, easier to conceal, much more lucrative. But the coke traffickers were a different breed from the laid-back marijuana smugglers of the 1970s. A local maxim was that grass deals are done on a handshake, but coke deals are done in blood. Not coincidentally, Miami became the murder capital of America. In 1980–81, a record 1,180 murders were committed in Dade County, many related, directly or indirectly, to the vicious turf wars of rival gangs of Colombian cocaine cowboys.

Although innocent bystanders occasionally got caught in the crossfire, the extraordinary crime wave didn't touch the lives of most Miamians. For Stan and Joyce Cohen and their friends, life was good. Summers were spent cruising the warm waters of Biscayne Bay in Stan's fifty-five-foot boat, or at tony Ocean Reef Resort on Key Largo, or partying in the Bahamas. There were trips to the Caribbean, sometimes on Stan's own jet.

The annual Good Friends Party marked the beginning of the Cohens' winter social season. The organizers, well-heeled pals of the Cohens, sent out hand-drawn invitations. They always lined up a great band, good food, and plenty of liquor. In 1985, the Good Friends Party was held at the Grove Isle Club, a luxurious private club on exclusive Grove Isle in Biscayne Bay. Window walls provided a fabulous view of the southern end of the Miami skyline and the lights of the Rickenbacker Causeway, a sparkling strand across the bay to Key Biscayne.

The Cohens arrived at the party late—their social calendar was crowded—and they made a dramatic entrance. Wearing a tuxedo, Stan looked prosperous and distinguished, his graying temples contrasting nicely with his perpetual Florida tan. Joyce was an absolute knockout in a sinuous, glittering, white floor-length gown. With her glossy black hair, dark almond eyes, and dazzling smile, she looked like an exotic Polynesian beauty. A photographer snapped them together. Holding hands, the smiling couple strolled among their friends until it was time to move on to the next party.

After the festivities, the Cohens flew to Wolf Run Ranch, their 650-acre vacation retreat in Steamboat Springs. Their Colorado winters were filled with skiing, parties, dinners, friends, and family.

The Cohens, it seemed, had a perfect life.

# Two

"One-oh-one to one-oh-two. One-oh-one to one-oh-two. Where are you? What are you doing?"

The CB radio in Ben Abernathy's car crackled to life. It was the boss at SAC Construction Company, Stan Cohen, one-oh-one, checking on his young assistant, Ben, one-oh-two. It was 7 A.M. in Miami.

"Heading for the job site, boss," Ben replied.

"Listen, be sure you—" Stan reeled off reminders, orders, instructions, advice. Ben just smiled—it was the unvarying morning routine. The boss always hit the road by 7 A.M., and his first act was to check on his crews. God help them if they weren't on the job.

"One-oh-one to one-oh-three. What's up?" Stan moved on to another young employee, Jack Jamme. Like a cowboy riding the range, Stan Cohen rode his Bronco from one job site to another all over South Florida, checking on supervisors in the field, watching subcontractors, always pushing, sometimes bullying. His mere physical presence exuded power and control. Although he stood only five feet ten, his barrel chest and strong build made him seem taller. Stan was not really a handsome man. His sandy brown hair, streaked with gray, was an unruly bush to which he gave only casual attention. He had a smirky smile and squinty brown eyes that could be friendly or cold in turn. But he dominated every room he entered through the sheer force of his personality. Even those who didn't like him agreed that Stan Cohen had charisma.

"One-oh-one to base." Time to check in with the secretary at the SAC Construction Company office. "Any calls? Yeah? Call him back and tell him to call me on the car phone." SAC Construction Company was the epicenter of Stan Cohen's empire. He was a self-made man and proud of it. Like many Miamians, Cohen's family came to Miami seeking a better life. Stan, the eldest son, had made that dream come true.

It was 1948 when Julius Cohen, a New York furrier known as Julie, moved his family to Miami: wife Frances, sons Stanley, fourteen, Arthur, three, and daughter Barbara, called Bobbie, ten. Since there was little demand for a furrier in Miami's steamy climate, Julie and Frances Cohen opened a women's clothing store, The Little Cotton Shop, in downtown Miami. The store provided a bare living for the Cohens.

But for young Stan, after growing up on Long Island, Miami was a delight, an exotic, subtropical seaside city. Stan loved outdoor sports, and in South Florida's eternal summer, the games overlapped seamlessly. Stan made friends, mostly the sons of middle-class Jewish families like his own. And they played something—baseball, football, basketball—nearly every day in the city's public parks.

The Cohens had little money, but Stan and his friends always had some cash because they worked hard at after-school jobs—delivering newspapers, sweeping floors, washing dishes, stocking shelves. On Saturdays, they rode the bus downtown to the movies. On Sundays, another bus took them across the causeway to Miami Beach, the narrow strip of sand where they swam in the Atlantic's warm blue surf and roughhoused on the golden beach.

When Stan graduated from Miami High in 1951, he had one goal: the tree-shaded, red-brick-colonial campus of the University of Florida in Gainesville, a small town in the rolling hills of Alachua County in rural Central Florida. Fraternities dominated life on campus, and as soon as he enrolled, he pledged Pi Lambda Phi, the Jewish fraternity favored by Miamians. The Pi Lamb brotherhood included Arthur Sheldon and his brother, Marvin, who later became

Stan's business partner at SAC Construction Company; Bob Shevin, president of the fraternity and later attorney general of Florida; Fred Wasserman, who became a successful Miami dentist; Len Levenstein, a future Miami attorney; and Bob Salzman, a Miami physician. Theirs was an especially close-knit group. Decades later, as middle-aged men in Miami, they worked together, referred business to each other, still called each other by fraternity nicknames, and treasured their friendship. Their sons pledged Pi Lamb.

Stan Cohen's fraternity nickname, which followed him all his life, was Crusher. It was, the brotherhood agreed, the most appropriate nickname they ever dreamed up for anybody. Stan had a habit of sneaking up behind a buddy and squeezing the breath out of him in a massive bear hug, rabbit-punching an arm, or chopping his neck. Just his way of showing affection.

At the university Stan met a girl, a nice Jewish girl from New York named Martha. She was dark-haired, quiet, reserved—and probably the first girl he ever dated, his friends thought. Martha was content to follow Stan's boisterous lead. The couple married while they were still in school. Stan graduated in 1956 with a degree in civil engineering and was commissioned a second lieutenant in an army transportation corps stationed in Kansas. By then, Martha Cohen was already pregnant with their son, Gary Jay Cohen, who was born on November 3, 1956. By the time daughter Gerri Sue Cohen was born on February 6, 1959, Stan's army hitch was up, and the Cohens were ready to come home to Miami.

Stan took a job at Fidelity Construction, a company located in an industrial area northwest of the city. By coincidence, his old Pi Lambda Phi fraternity brother Marvin Sheldon, who had earned a building construction degree, worked only three blocks away at Web Construction. Marvin had also married a University of Florida coed, pretty, blond, vivacious Anne, and the couple had two little daughters. Anne had known Martha slightly in the women's dorm at the university and liked her. Now the Cohens began to socialize with the Sheldons, playing cards together on Saturday nights in their small apartments while their young children slept nearby. There was no money for baby-sitters or restaurants or movies. They were young and poor—but they optimistically planned successful futures in Miami. Stan and Marvin began to talk about going into business together someday.

Then, in 1963, Stan saw the opportunity he had been waiting for. His boss at Fidelity Construction decided to go out of business. Stan found an investor and scraped together enough money to form a new firm: SAC Construction Company, Stanley Alan Cohen's initials. As soon as he got some work, he asked Marvin Sheldon to join him as a partner. Marvin was delighted. They were ready to build Miami.

Theirs was a partnership that worked. Stan was the hustler, the hard-charging front man who brought deals in the door. Marvin, a quiet, amiable, easygoing guy despite his burly appearance, was the conscientious detail man who priced the jobs and negotiated the contracts. Once the contracts were signed, Stan made sure the job got done. He liked riding herd over the men in the field. And Stan kept track of the money.

Their timing had been good. Miami was growing rapidly. The early 1960s saw the beginning of a trickle which would turn into a flood: immigrants. It started, of course, with Castro's takeover of Cuba. Thousands of Cubans fled to Miami, and the strain threatened to rupture the young city's infrastructure of health care, housing, utilities, and schools. But where others saw problems, Stan Cohen saw opportunity. Over the next twenty years, SAC Construction built schools, car dealerships, hospitals, warehouses, strip shopping centers, all kinds of commercial buildings. The company prospered.

One of SAC's most celebrated projects was the new courthouse for the Third District Court of Appeal, a $1.6 million project at the edge of the Florida Turnpike, in western Dade County near the Florida International University campus. The handsome building was contemporary in design, with the plans calling for a large semicircular courtroom styled as an amphitheater: tiers of upholstered, theater-type seats sloping down to a massive judicial bench on an elevated platform. The high, cantilevered ceiling was specially designed for acoustics, and some of its sections had to be shipped all the way across the country. But Stan Cohen was confident that he could deliver the project on schedule and within budget.

Judge Thomas Barkdull of the Third District Court of Appeal

worked closely with Stan during construction of the new courthouse and was impressed by his competence and enthusiasm. Stan was on the job site early every morning, cheerful and friendly. And, as he had promised, he made sure the job was done right. When the building was finished, it won the Florida Governor's Award for architectural excellence. Stan Cohen was proud of that courthouse.

But as his career gained momentum, Stan's marriage deteriorated. Finally, Martha filed for divorce. The children, Gary and Gerri, continued to live with Martha in a modest house in the suburban Whispering Pines development, and Martha went to work as a bookkeeper.

After the divorce, Stan moved quickly into the singles scene in Miami's bars. He went through a string of sexy young girlfriends, one of whom he claimed was a former Playboy bunny. There was a brief, tumultuous second marriage, a third that none of his friends knew about, and then another frenetic bachelorhood. Stan and a buddy, Charlie Wilmont, established a bachelor pad at 2120 Tigertail Avenue, an aptly named thoroughfare that twists languidly through the lush Miami suburb of Coconut Grove. They put a big stone sign out front that read Stan & Charlie's, and it became a social landmark of sorts in the Grove.

Stan and Charlie fell in with a group of about twenty single guys in the Grove, mostly new bachelors with at least one marriage behind them and enough money to enjoy the single life—guys like Ed Smith, a self-made man who rose to success at the Poole & Kent Company, a mechanical contracting firm in Miami. Smith was recently divorced from his wife, with whom he had three children. A slightly paunchy guy with a booming voice and a boisterous sense of humor, he was an avid skier and partier who sometimes wrote letters to the editor of *The Miami Herald* on community matters. Stan helped Ed Smith renovate his bachelor quarters just down the street from Stan & Charlie's.

The bachelors in the Grove were joined by Len Levenstein, an old Pi Lamb buddy from Stan's college days. Also divorced, Levenstein had a successful law practice in Miami, but like nearly everyone else in town, it seemed, he wanted to get into real estate development. Stan built a strip shopping center for Len, and a bar named the Checkmate Lounge, which became a hot spot for live jazz. Hanging out at the bar, listening to jazz as they talked and shared beers, Stan and Len renewed their college friendship. Soon Len recruited Stan as a partner in his favorite sport: big-time gambling.

With Len's tutelage, Stan caught on quickly. They played only blackjack, taking over the table and running several hands at once. They always played in partnership and they called each other by movie-star nicknames: Stan was Butch Cassidy and Len was the Sundance Kid. Together they gambled all over the world—Las Vegas, the Caribbean, Monte Carlo. They went on gambling junkets regularly, all expenses paid, and they usually took dates.

Then Stan finally found someone who made him happy again: Joyce, the lovely young woman who became the fourth Mrs. Cohen. His life was back on track.

By the 1980s, Stan Cohen was an established Miami success story, a version of local boy makes good. SAC Construction Company had made him rich, and he rode SAC to the pinnacle of the Miami construction industry—first he was vice-president, then president of the South Florida Chapter of Associated General Contractors, the most prestigious professional organization for contractors. He also served as trustee for the organization's pension plan.

Inevitably, Stan made some enemies in the rough-edged Miami construction trade. He first drew fire as a union buster when he made SAC Construction a nonunion shop. And there were always disgruntled owners, developers, and subcontractors with whom Stan clashed, sometimes violently. Some of his competitors grumbled that Stan made his money by cutting corners and manipulating construction draws. But nothing seemed to worry Stan. He was riding high and life was good.

Project managers Ben Abernathy and Jack Jamme had come to work for SAC Construction in 1979. Ben tried hard to be just like Stan. If the supervisor was having problems getting men to work on the job, Ben would yell at them to get them moving, just like Stan did. He even dressed like Stan—polyester pants or jeans and a sportshirt. And he volunteered to do personal favors for the boss, like taking Joyce Cohen to the airport or to pick up her car somewhere. Ben liked the glamorous Mrs. Cohen, but he never felt he really knew her. She was friendly but reserved, not as outgoing as Marvin Sheldon's wife, Anne, who always laughed and joked with everyone when she dropped by the SAC Construction office.

Like everyone else, Ben Abernathy knew Stan Cohen was just crazy about his wife. The boss hung a large, gilt-framed photo portrait of her in his office. Taken when she was a bride, it was an evocative portrayal. Shoulder-length dark hair full around her face, Joyce Cohen gazed pensively into the distance over her bare left shoulder, a diamond pendant on a thin gold chain circling her neck. Her dark, wide-set eyes had an exotic tilt; her full, sensual lips curved slightly in an enigmatic Mona Lisa smile. The photographer, Becker Studios in Miami, had used a dark background, dramatic lighting, and a soft-focus lens to create a romantic mood. But despite the artistry, Joyce's face seemed curiously closed, a mask that concealed rather than revealed. Who was this woman, Ben Abernathy often wondered when he gazed at her picture in the boss's office.

In fact, Joyce Cohen was a woman who had everything: beauty, style, plenty of money, a career as an interior decorator, a husband who loved her, and a comfortable family life. When Stan met her in 1974, she had been Joyce Lemay McDillon, a secretary at a SAC Construction project, a divorcée struggling to support her five-year-old son, Shawn. No one knew much about Joyce. "She just seemed to drop into our lives," Anne Sheldon commented. But Stan's friends had never seen him so happy.

One night Stan arranged a dinner at Chez Vendome, an elegant French restaurant in Coral Gables patterned after Maxim's in Paris. It was an engagement party of sorts—Stan wanted his friends to meet the woman he had decided to marry. She was attractive, charming, affectionate, obviously devoted to Stan. His friends liked her immediately.

A few weeks later Stan called his pal Len Levenstein and told him he was ready to marry Joyce McDillon. Len was delighted. She's not a JAP, he thought, but a nice little shiksa. And she made Stan happy. "Great!" Len exclaimed. "Let's do it!"

Len took charge of the wedding plans for his friend. He called his casino connections in Las Vegas and got a two-bedroom penthouse suite at the Dunes Hotel. Just the four of them were flying out—Stan and Joyce, Len and his girlfriend, a tall, pretty, vivacious blonde whom everyone called C.J. instead of her given name, Cheryl Jane. C.J. was outgoing and friendly, and she liked Joyce immediately. It was a happy group.

Once they arrived in Las Vegas, Len got a marriage license for Stan and Joyce and then found a preacher to perform the wedding ceremony in the lavish Dunes Hotel suite. He was the Reverend Bob Richards, whose name was the same as that of a famous athlete, a pole-vaulter. The phallic symbolism suited Stan's ribald humor. He and Len laughed uproariously about it.

Len's next project was a ring for Joyce. "You've got to get her a diamond," he told Stan. Stan agreed, and they all went shopping. Joyce chose a traditional wedding set: a gold engagement ring with a modest diamond and a plain gold wedding band. When the rings were worn together, they made a design like a little *J*, which appealed to Joyce. It was her first diamond. Stan didn't want a wedding band for himself. He always wore two favorite gold rings: his college class ring and a ring made with the initials *SAC*.

Len Levenstein planned the wedding ceremony and the party afterward in the suite. He ordered acres of flowers, groaning platters of food, and cases of Dom Perignon champagne. By coincidence, a gambling junket from Miami was in Las Vegas at the time, a group that included a former Miami Beach mayor and Len Levenstein's mother and two aunts. Len invited all the Miamians to Stan's wedding, and the guest list climbed.

Joyce was delighted. It was more like a big, glamorous party than a wedding. "There were a hundred people at my wedding I didn't know," she later reminisced happily. "It was exciting!"

The wedding was pure Las Vegas: a penthouse hotel suite, a civil ceremony performed by a preacher with the name of a pole-vaulter, uniting a divorced Catholic and a thrice-divorced Jew, attended by gambling junketeers. The beautiful young bride wore a long pink three-piece knit ensemble. The stocky, middle-aged groom wore a rust-colored leisure suit and a loud print shirt. No tie.

It was, Len Levenstein thought, a nice little ceremony. Following Jewish tradition, he put a wineglass at the couple's feet.

"Stan, you've got to break the glass," he said.

Stan did.

That was December 5, 1974. Stan Cohen was forty. The fourth Mrs. Cohen was twenty-four. She was, Stan's friends thought, just what he needed. And they knew Stan would be good to her. Stan wrapped his big arms around Joyce and said, "Babe, I'm going to take care of you."

Stan adopted Joyce's young son, Shawn, the child of her prior marriage. That gave him a total of four children: Gary Jay Cohen and Gerri Sue Cohen, the children from his first marriage, to Martha; Michael Cohen, the adopted son of his second wife; and now Shawn Cohen.

Stan found an impressive house for his new family, a Miami landmark at 1665 South Bayshore Drive, a prestigious address in the suburb of Coconut Grove. In the Grove, one of Miami's oldest neighborhoods, small wooden cottages and huge old Spanish stucco mansions nestled together in dense foliage along narrow, winding, tree-canopied lanes with names like Leafy Way and Bayhomes Drive. Exotic subtropical foliage flourished. But the real ambiance of the Grove was its bohemian nature. Once an artists' colony, it retained a funkiness that even the recent gentrification of the neighborhood couldn't entirely obscure. And the Grove had always had a reputation for tolerance of the drug scene.

Stan was fascinated by antiques and old houses, and 1665 South Bayshore Drive suited him perfectly. The house was large and, by Miami standards, very old, built in 1916–18 when Miami was only twenty years old, a small town on Biscayne Bay near the mouth of the Miami River, and Coconut Grove was just a cluster of homes farther south on the bay. Looming above the busy intersection of South Bayshore Drive and Southwest 17th Avenue, the house was built entirely of limestone, which locals call coral rock, its foundation melded into the exposed limestone ridge of Silver Bluff. But despite its size and solidity, there was something romantic and mysterious about the old place.

When the house was finally released for sale by the previous owner's estate, Stan bought it for $125,000. The price seemed like a bargain, but the interior was in terrible shape—cobwebs everywhere, broken windows, gaping holes in the hardwood floors, antique wiring and plumbing, and leaks in the roof. Stan's friends joked that there was so much to be done in the house that only a contractor could afford to buy it.

As soon as basic repairs were completed, Joyce set about decorating her new home. It was a daunting task, but she learned fast. She had an eye for rich, soft colors and subtle patterns, and she chose the very best in fabrics, furniture, and carpets. When she was finished, a thick, luxurious cream-colored area rug covered the polished hardwood floor in the formal living room. Two love seats and a matching sofa in a soft floral design were arranged before the stone fireplace. Lladró porcelain figurines and candelabra adorned the mantel. There were antique clocks in the living room and foyer. The crowning touch was a baby grand piano, which neither Joyce nor Stan knew how to play.

Upstairs, smoked mirrors covered the master bedroom wall behind a huge brass bed. Small oriental rugs accented the hardwood floor. The french doors leading to the outdoor terrace facing Biscayne Bay were hung with custom-made heavy brocade valances and drapes in a rich blue and gold pattern that matched the bedcovers. Joyce's small white bath with a tub opened off a sitting room, while Stan's large white-tiled bath with a shower was adjacent to the master bedroom.

The total effect was quaint, charming, rather country-French—relaxed and comfortable, yet elegant. Everyone who saw what Joyce had done with the old house agreed that she had a flair for decorating. Buoyed by her success with the house, Joyce decided to enroll in interior decorating classes at Miami-Dade Community College.

Shawn Cohen loved the big house on South Bayshore Drive. His bedroom was on the first floor in a separate wing, and there was a small room attached to the old garage behind the house where he played army games. Beyond a big stone wall in the backyard was a field where he could throw a softball or football with Stan. And there were secret places in the house—a tiny cupboard in his mother's bathroom where she hid his Christmas gifts; and a little room behind a door under the stairs to the master suite. There were stories about treasures or bodies buried beneath the house. Sometimes strangers stopped by to ask if they could dig in the front yard or under the foundation for treasure. Stan always laughed and said no.

Stan loved what his wife had done with their new home. Together with Joyce, he spent even more money to fill it with antiques and knickknacks picked up on their travels in the Bahamas, the Caribbean islands, Mexico, and Colorado. To keep the big house running, a housekeeper and groundskeeper were hired and quartered in the cottage next to the main house. The housekeeper cooked most of Shawn's meals. At Joyce's urging, Shawn was enrolled in Gulliver Academy, an expensive private school in Miami.

Once installed in her beautiful new house, Joyce settled easily into the life of an affluent Miami wife. She learned where to shop for gourmet groceries, expensive trinkets, and designer clothes. She was right at home in the Grove, which had become a mecca for the trendy nouveau riche. Chic sidewalk cafés and expensive boutiques with names like La Dolce Vita lined the Grove's Main Highway. Well-heeled young professionals congregated on the outdoor patio at the Taurus Restaurant on Friday evenings, guzzling Coronas with lime slices and checking out the yuppie traffic. The club scene moved constantly—one week Faces in the Grove was hot, the next week it was Suzanne's or Ensign Bitters. When Regine's opened at the top of the elegant Grand Bay Hotel, the Grove was on the map for international celebrities. Even Princess Caroline of Monaco came to town.

But the Grove was also home to some of Miami's most desperately poor. The trendy new boutiques rubbed shoulders with old neighborhood establishments like the Krest 5 & 10, which had been run by the same Grove family since 1933. Because nearly all of the Grove was a high-crime area, the Krest stocked some unusual items. Alongside the T-shirts and toiletries was a rack of hand-held stun guns that delivered 120,000 volts of electricity from a 9-volt battery. The store had a hard time keeping the guns in stock at $89.95 apiece.

Like nearly everywhere else in the Grove, the Cohens' neighborhood was plagued with break-ins and robberies, and Joyce was afraid to be alone in the big house at night. She heard noises—creaking floorboards, branches rustling against the roof. Even Stan's grown son, Gary, felt the spookiness of the old house. Whenever he stayed there alone, he always kept a baseball bat next to his bed at night.

At his wife's insistence, Stan ordered a sophisticated alarm system for the house. There was a perimeter alarm and separately controlled motion and sound sensors. Panic buttons could be reached from the Cohens' big brass bed upstairs. If there was a break-in, an audible alarm would ring, and a call was sent to the 911 emergency operator automatically. The system was monitored twenty-four hours a day. Finally, the Cohens added a big Doberman pinscher to their family, as pet and protection.

As Stan's wife, Joyce was quickly swept up in the social life of Miami's affluent. Her winter scene revolved around snow—the hard-packed base and deep powder of ski slopes in the Rockies. She and Stan belonged to the Miami Ski Club, which boasted 2,500 members and was said to be the largest snow ski club in America—ironically located in subtropical Miami. Fit, strong, and naturally athletic, Joyce became an excellent skier. Stan was pleased and proud of his pretty young wife's prowess. Because of numerous accidents and injuries to his ankles and knees, he could barely turn on skis. But he was absolutely fearless, barreling downhill at breakneck speed.

The Miami Ski Club sponsored seven ski trips each year, one a month from October through April, and chartered a jet for each trip. The destinations: Aspen, Vail, Snowmass, Snowbird, Sun Valley, Steamboat Springs—all the big resorts. Many ski club members had vacation homes in Aspen, Vail, and Steamboat Springs, where they hosted après-ski parties during the trips.

At the start of ski season each year, the club put on a fashion show in which members modeled the latest upscale skiwear and fur jackets, coats, and hats. The show was always near-professional quality, with flashy dance routines choreographed to the pounding beat of current rock hits. In one year's show, Joyce modeled a form-fitting black ensemble as she danced, clutching prop manacles in both hands, to the strident "Manhunt" number from the *Flashdance* movie sound track. A photographer captured her sultry pout.

The ski club parties continued during the summer months. Members took their boats out to Stiltsville, a unique collection of party houses on tall stilts in the middle of Biscayne Bay, which could only be reached by boating through a narrow channel across the flats—a very shallow area which was nearly dry at low tide. The parties at

Stiltsville usually started around 10 A.M., but preparations began much earlier. All the party supplies were brought out by boat: long submarine sandwiches, barbecued chicken, hot dogs, hamburgers, kegs of beer, coolers of wine and soft drinks. Sometimes there was live music, a combo or steel-drum band, which had to be ferried out with all its equipment. When the guests arrived and the music started, there were always contests and games: dance contests, limbo contests, tube races, swimming races, with ski club T-shirts awarded as prizes. Sometimes, when everyone had had enough to drink, there were wet T-shirt contests.

One South Florida event that Stan, Joyce, and their pals never missed was the Columbus Day Regatta, the largest floating party in Florida. From its rather sedate beginning in 1954 as a race for twenty-five sailboats in honor of Christopher Columbus's discovery of the New World, the event swelled to 700 racing boats and an additional 1,500 spectator boats. It was organized chaos.

Like most of their friends, Stan and Joyce motored down to watch the race and party—they were power boaters, not sailors. Beginning early on the second Saturday in October, up to twenty separate fleets of sailboats crossed the starting line and raced south along a zigzagging course to the finish at Elliott Key, nearly twenty-five miles to the south. Each fleet had a separate start time and an individual course from marker to marker down the bay. The fleets were made up of classes organized by size and type, from light, serious racing boats like J-24s, to big, fast boats which campaigned in races throughout the Caribbean, to comfortable pleasure craft designated "Dowager" or "Gunkhole" class, with names like *Aphrodite* and *The Big Easy*. The entire fleet anchored overnight in the shallow water off Elliott Key and then raced back up the bay on Sunday.

For serious racers, it was an important event. But most of the Columbus Day crowd was anything but serious. Binoculars were indispensable equipment on every boat, not just to find the race markers along the way but to check out nude sailors, sometimes an entire crew of men and women, a staunch Columbus Day tradition some called "sailing barracuda." Another tradition was pelting unwary competitors with water balloons during the race. Each year the barrage escalated, with elaborate launching systems called "funnelators" and even high-impact frozen water balloons. Fearing serious injury, the race committee finally outlawed water balloons entirely.

Hundreds of spectator boats of every conceivable size and shape waited to hail the racers across the finish line. One year hula-skirted men wearing nothing beneath their skirts danced and swayed atop a cruiser. Every year music blared from elaborate sound systems, and sometimes there were steel-drum bands. Spinnaker-flying was a popular sport—riding in a rope seat attached to the lower corners of the huge, brightly colored spinnaker billowing from the top of a sailboat's mast. When the ride was over, the rider simply dropped into the warm water below.

After the race, spectators and racers anchored their boats in the lee of Elliott Key and tied up together in huge rafts to party and spend the night. If the wind came up and anchors dragged, the rafts could come apart, throwing sleepy sailors into a wild melee of boats thrashing in the dark. But most nights at Elliott Key were peaceful. A small city of lights twinkled from sailboat masts, the boats swayed softly on the gentle swells, and spent sailors slept like happy children after a busy day at the beach.

The next morning, they got up early and did it all again.

Stan loved water sports and decided to organize a special event for his buddies, something he called "The Jews Versus the Christians Spearfishing Tournament." Stan was the captain of the Jews, and his pal Ed Smith led the Christians. The Jews team thought they were culturally disadvantaged as fishermen, so they were out to prove their mettle.

Stan's team comprised his SAC Construction partner Marvin Sheldon, Marvin's brother Arthur and son Eric, and Dr. Fred Wasserman, another Pi Lamb fraternity brother. Wasserman, now a successful Miami dentist, was a happily married family man with two children and a large, tasteful home in suburban Miami. Although his hair was now prematurely white, Wasserman had kept his rangy, athletic build and his engaging sense of humor. He stayed in close touch with his fraternity buddies, especially Stan Cohen, with whom he skied in the winter and fished in the summer. Wasserman still fondly called Stan Crusher, his old fraternity nickname.

For his team, the Jews, Stan ordered T-shirts emblazoned with each member's initials. When the team members lined themselves up, enlarged red letters on their T-shirts spelled J-E-W-S. The team used Arthur Sheldon's fishing boat, with Stan as driver and Fred Wasserman's dental practice partner, Dr. Larry Stein, as lookout.

After three years, the spearfishing tournament ended in a draw. Wasserman kept the final tournament photograph of his teammates, squinting into the sun, arms around each other's shoulders, white shirts with red letters spelling J-E-W-S against the blue backdrop of sky and Biscayne Bay. Team captain Stan Cohen grinned into the camera. So strong, so vital, he looked as if he would live forever, Fred thought.

The photograph was taken in May 1984.

# *Three*

•

*T*he Ute Indians were the first visitors to Steamboat Springs, Colorado, but it was early-nineteenth-century fur trappers who gave the town its name. The trappers thought they heard a steamboat chugging out of sight around a bend in the Yampa River. Instead they discovered hissing, bubbling mineral springs that sounded like a steamboat. The town eventually became a major ski resort, famed for its "champagne powder." Although the Indians had long since gone, they left behind the legend of the Yampa Valley curse: If you are afflicted by the curse, you'll lose your heart to the valley and never be able to stay away.

Stan Cohen had a bad case of the Yampa Valley curse.

He loved Steamboat Springs from his first ski trip there. Less sophisticated and more rustic than Aspen or Vail, Steamboat Springs cultivated a casual western atmosphere. The ski lift attendants and locals all wore cowboy hats on the mountain. Boots and jeans were de rigueur, and the town itself was a real community with parks and softball fields, not a manufactured resort like Vail. There were sleigh rides through town and a Winter Carnival with horse-drawn ski races. Stan looked great in his cowboy boots and jeans. He loved the place—and he recognized its commercial possibilities. He could become a player in Steamboat Springs.

Stan bought two condos in Yampa Valley, one near the Steamboat ski slopes and one in nearby Stagecoach. Following his lead, Marvin Sheldon took his wife, Anne, to Steamboat to look at condos. "I can pick this up for a song if you want," he told her.

"No, thanks. I don't want to be in Steamboat," Anne replied firmly. She preferred the more sophisticated atmosphere of Vail, where they already owned a vacation place. Even the Sheldons' Miami home resembled a Vail ski chalet, with its wood paneling and big fireplace. Besides, their Miami friends all congregated in Vail when they skied, not in Steamboat. It was a different crowd.

In Steamboat, Stan made friends with the Mosers, who lived there year-round. Bill Moser was a real estate broker and property manager, and his attractive, dark-haired wife, Kathy, worked for the ski resort management company. One day Bill called Stan with a problem. He had been appointed receiver of a condo project in Steamboat after the builders were killed in an automobile accident. Now Bill needed someone to finish the construction. Was Stan interested?

Stan was delighted. He and Marvin sent a SAC Construction crew to Steamboat with Frank Wheatley, a SAC supervisor, and they completed the condos. As soon as the work was finished on that project, Stan was ready for the next one: Riverside Shopping Center, on the banks of the Yampa River. The shopping center included a bar, Riverside Suds, which catered to young adults. By Colorado law, beer with a reduced alcoholic content can be sold to minors aged eighteen to twenty. Called "three-two beer," it had a legal limit of 3.2 percent alcohol rather than 5 percent as in most beers. Stan became a hero to the town's teenagers, not only because he built the popular watering hole but because he provided well-paying construction jobs for them. Frank Wheatley was a part owner of Riverside Suds, and Stan kept a piece of it for himself.

Then Bill Moser put together a big development project for Stan: a 2,000-acre parcel of land that Stan purchased with Julie Belcher, the wealthy young heiress to the Belcher Oil fortune. The plan was to divide the land into parcels of sixty acres each, to be sold as exclusive home sites. But the project didn't go, and they managed to sell only one or two sites.

Finally Stan decided to take 650 acres of the land for himself, a parcel called Wolf Run Ranch. It was to be his own personal show-place—barns, a caretaker's house, a stable for horses, a show ring, and a big house with a spectacular view of the mountains across the valley. Near the road, a large, open gate and log fence framed the entrance to the dirt road leading up a hill. A carved wooden wolf ran above the crosspiece of the gate. A wooden sign swung on chains beneath: Wolf Run Ranch.

On the property's first hill, facing the road below, Stan and Joyce built a beautiful, rustic, cedar-sided ranch house in the California contemporary style. It was a warm, spacious, casual house with large windows and decks, but curiously there were only two bedrooms and two separate living rooms, each with a fireplace. The heart of the house was the Great Room, the larger living room, with a beamed cathedral ceiling and huge stone fireplace. Light streamed into the comfortable room from enormous, uncurtained windows reaching to the high ceiling.

Joyce spent much of the summer of 1982 at Wolf Run Ranch, decorating and furnishing the new vacation home. She had finished with the big house in the Grove and was ready for another challenge. Joyce had developed a certain flair, which translated well to the casual lifestyle of Steamboat Springs. In the Great Room, she grouped russet-accented sofas and love seats in front of the fireplace. Carved, spindle-backed wooden chairs were pulled up to a large, rustic wood dining table. An antique clock and carved wooden animals adorned the mantel, and a big copper tub served as a scuttle for fire logs on the wide hearth. Lamps with Tiffany shades were scattered about, and leaded glass panes hung from chains at the windows. The effect was cozy, casual, informal, very Colorado.

Then Joyce was ready for her own interior design company. She wanted a part-time venture, more like a hobby than a business, really. She had her eye on a ready-made clientele: her husband's clients. Joyce would design interiors for buildings built by SAC Construction. She and Stan formed a company—SAC Interiors—and Joyce recruited a partner, Toni Pollack, a woman she had met in her interior design classes at Miami-Dade Community College. Like Joyce, Toni Pollack was married to an older man. She was small, attractive, and dark-haired. But where Joyce tended to be reserved, Toni was usually animated and vivacious, her Spanish-accented words pouring forth in a rapid, excited torrent. The two women were close friends as well as partners.

Soon Stan decided that SAC Construction should buy a plane to ferry friends and employees back and forth between Colorado and Miami. It was the ultimate toy for a man who loved toys. Marvin Sheldon went along with the idea, and with another investor, a businessman from Boca Raton, Florida, SAC bought a brand-new Cessna Conquest turboprop. The price was steep, $1.3 million, but it was fairly economical to operate at $650 per hour for fuel and a pilot.

Stan hired an executive pilot named Elmer and paid him $45,000 a year just to be available to fly the plane whenever Stan and his friends wanted to go somewhere. Elmer dressed well and sported a gold Rolex watch with a diamond bezel. "Honey, we look like we're the crew," the outspoken Anne Sheldon joked to her husband when she met Elmer.

But Stan wasn't entirely happy with his new toy. The Cessna Conquest took nearly seven hours to fly from Miami to Steamboat Springs. Stan wanted to get there faster. In a Sabreliner 60, a small jet, the ride was only about four hours. Because the Sabreliner Stan wanted was used, the plane cost only about $900,000. But there was a substantial trade-off in expenses. This one burned a bundle in fuel and required two pilots instead of one.

Stan talked Marvin into the idea, and SAC traded up for the Sabreliner, still with the same partner. They had the plane painted beige with an orange stripe, reupholstered in orange, cleaned up, and repaired. They took the Sabreliner out to Steamboat and to Gainesville for University of Florida football games.

The planes fascinated SAC Construction project manager Ben Abernathy. He was a licensed pilot, but he wasn't rated to fly either the Cessna or the Sabreliner. He knew the planes were a big ego boost for Stan—"I have my pilot fly me out to Steamboat," and so on. But soon the Sabreliner was costing a tremendous amount of money. Ben estimated it at $20,000 a month, well above what was prudent for SAC Construction Company. And the fuel charges were eating them alive. Finally even Stan agreed that the plane had to go. He and Marvin sat down with the third owner of the Sabreliner and told him they didn't want to be partners in the plane anymore. He agreed to take them out of the deal—he wanted a larger plane, anyway. Marvin was relieved to be out from under the planes, and SAC Construction never bought another one.

But soon Stan was back in business with another Sabreliner. He just couldn't get planes out of his system. The idea this time was to outfit the jet as an air ambulance for transporting organs for transplants around the country. The price looked good—around $300,000 or so—but the jet was in terrible condition. Stan had it repaired, but when his pilot saw the bill, he told Stan it was a rip-off. Stan refused to pay the repair bill, and he stopped paying on the purchase-money note and mortgage held by the sellers. After defending two lawsuits filed against him—a foreclosure suit brought by the sellers and a suit to collect for repair charges—Stan finally decided to sell the plane. But then he couldn't find a buyer, and the plane sat on the ground for months.

Although SAC was out of airplane ownership, the company continued to buy cars for Stan and Marvin to drive. They always bought themselves Blazers or Broncos, something practical for visiting job sites on rough terrain. But in addition to the field cars, the company bought an after-hours car for each of them, which became the wife's car.

One evening Marvin came home from work and asked Anne, "Do you want a new car?"

"Why would I want a new car?" she responded. "I love my Datsun 280Z. Why do you ask?"

"Well, Stanley is going to get Joyce a new company car and he wanted to know if you want a new Z."

"What kind of car is Joyce getting?" Anne asked.

"A Jag."

"Wait a minute," Anne replied. "Let me be sure I understand this. Joyce is going to get a new *Jaguar* and I'm going to get a new *Z*?"

Marvin nodded.

"I want a Porsche," Anne stated flatly.

"Are you crazy?"

"No. I want a Porsche. I like fast cars, I like sporty cars."

"You *are* crazy," Marvin responded. "I'm not spending that kind of money."

"Marvin, this is really stupid," Anne countered. "If you can spend $15,000 on a car for me and $30,000 on a car for Joyce, why can't you spend $30,000 on a car for Joyce and $40,000 on a car for me? That makes sense."

"I'm not going to discuss this anymore," Marvin retorted. "Take a Jaguar or nothing!"

"Okay, I'll take it, but it's not what I want."

Anne was certain her new Jaguar knew she didn't like it. The car died in traffic for no apparent reason. It was in the repair shop frequently, but it never got fixed. She was disgusted.

Anne wasn't really surprised at Joyce's taste in cars. It was obvious that her lifestyle had become more lavish. But the change had come on gradually. And as the years went by, Joyce herself seemed to change. She became more self-assured, more her own person, no longer content to stand in Stan's big shadow. She was, after all, an interior designer with her own company now. And she was a rich man's wife. She had acquired a certain presence. People remembered her.

Joyce cultivated an exotic look. With her shiny, straight dark hair in a long, sleek bob and her slightly almond dark eyes, people often thought she was Oriental, maybe Chinese or Polynesian. She was vague about her ethnic background. "French," she usually said with a smile.

Joyce dropped some weight. When she first married Stan, Anne recalled, she hadn't spent much money on herself. Now she was spending a small fortune. There was, of course, plenty to spend. SAC Construction provided an excellent income for both Stan and Marvin. And Stan had obviously loosened his purse strings for Joyce. She had an eye for accessories—jewelry, purses, belts, scarves, hats, boots, shoes—and her taste was excellent. She always chose the best—and most expensive—of everything.

When Joyce shopped for skiwear now, she bought sweaters, ski pants and parkas three or four at a time. She quickly accumulated furs: a short mink jacket, a full-length red fox coat, a long ranch mink, another jacket, plus assorted fur hats and muffs. One day she asked Anne, "How come you have only one fur coat? And why don't you go to New York to shop, like I do?"

Joyce had chosen her first mink from a furrier in New York, an uncle of Stan's. Next came the red fox. "We started skiing a lot and spending time in Colorado, and I wanted a long coat," she told her friends. "And so Stan got me a red fox coat, a full-length one, because I was always so cold. I was freezing!" She smiled and shivered. Then she found the full-length ranch mink at a Denver furrier favored by her Miami Ski Club pals.

Stan encouraged Joyce's conspicuous consumption. He liked to see her dressed, jeweled, a showpiece. "He buys me one fabulous present a year," Joyce would say, showing off the latest gift. Diamond stud earrings. A diamond necklace. The gold Rolex. Another fur coat. He was Pygmalion adorning a willing Galatea.

In addition to Stan's gifts, Joyce shopped continually for herself: clothes, jewelry, boots, purses, whatever struck her fancy. She became well known in the Grove's expensive boutiques. Sometimes she took Shawn on her shopping sprees. He despised those trips. While she tried on outfit after outfit, Shawn pleaded, "Yeah, that looks good, let's go, let's go!" The big closets in the master bedroom were filled with Joyce's clothes. And there were even more clothes in the closets in Steamboat Springs.

"Your mother's going to shop me to death," Stan joked to Shawn.

But occasionally Joyce's spending aggravated her indulgent husband, and they quarreled. Stan proposed a budget. One day he asked Marvin how much Anne spent annually on clothes. Marvin had no idea. It simply was not an issue between them. Marvin suspected that Stan and Joyce must be arguing about her spending sprees. But Stan never confided in Marvin about personal matters.

"How much money do you spend a year on clothes?" Marvin asked Anne at home that night.

"I don't know. Whatever is required, I spend," she replied. "Why?"

"Well, Stanley is complaining about how much money Joyce is spending on clothes."

Anne just shrugged. She knew that no matter how much Stan complained, he was proud of his elegant wife. She had become the trophy he wanted her to be: beautifully groomed, polished, attired, accessorized, bejeweled. Joyce was the perfect consort for Stan Cohen, Miami millionaire.

One May morning Joyce called her friend Sharon Johnnides to suggest a weekend trip. Sharon and her husband, George, were a handsome couple closer to Joyce's age than to Stan's. The Cohens had met the Johnnideses through mutual friends, and a warm friendship developed. A beautiful blonde, Sharon was a former flight attendant; George ran a wholesale seafood business. Years of hard work had paid off, the business was successful, and the Johnnideses moved into a big house on the Coral Gables Waterway—an exclusive address. As a surprise, George had recently bought Sharon a red Mercedes to replace the little red Honda she had driven for years. Sharon was delighted—it was her first expensive car. The Johnnideses had enough money to travel and party with the Cohens and their crowd. Because they were attractive, sociable, and friendly, they were popular companions.

That morning Joyce asked Sharon whether she and George would like to fly to Mexico for the long Memorial Day weekend. But Sharon was hesitant. She was pregnant and didn't want to take a chance on getting sick in Mexico, she said. "Well, how about Martinique?" Joyce suggested cheerfully. "We have our plane and we can fly to Martinique."

Sharon was still reluctant, but she promised to discuss the invitation with George. "I don't want to go," she told him later. Lately Joyce had seemed different—flamboyant, a little bit "hyper." Sharon just wasn't as comfortable around Joyce anymore. She couldn't really explain why.

"Well, look," George said, "I'm going to be with you. You're not going to be stuck alone with her. Don't worry about it. We'll get some sun and just relax."

As it turned out, Stan's Sabreliner wasn't available for the trip. So they chartered another plane and headed down to Martinique, stopping to refuel in San Juan, Puerto Rico. The island of Martinique was somewhat disappointing—not as pretty as Jamaica, Sharon thought. But the trip went well.

One afternoon the foursome walked up the side of a mountain to view a religious site. Suddenly someone yelled, "I don't believe they let Jews in here!" Sharon and George stared at each other apprehensively, then at Stan. Stan ran toward the man who had shouted—and hugged him. Then he introduced them to Frankie Diaz, a lawyer he said he knew from Miami. It seemed like a chance meeting, pure co-incidence.

They all settled in for lunch together at a nearby restaurant. Frankie was accompanied by a pretty, dark-haired woman he introduced as his wife, Maggie. Sharon and George enjoyed Frankie's company very much. He was outgoing, friendly, fun, an infectious personality.

After Frankie and his wife left, Sharon asked Stan, "How do you know this guy? He's so funny and outgoing. What's he do?"

"Well, he does a lot of things." Stan laughed. "He's a lawyer. When I met him, he was representing this bedspread company that Joyce and I were suing."

Back in Miami, Sharon and George occasionally asked Stan about his friend Frankie Diaz. Perhaps they could all get together for dinner sometime. But Stan always replied that he hadn't seen Frankie recently. Frankie Diaz was making a name for himself around Miami, and Sharon and George never saw him again. But Stan did.

Like the Cohens, Frankie was a regular patron of Buccione's, the trendy Italian restaurant in the Grove in which Stan had acquired an interest a few years earlier. The restaurant had a reputation for excellent, if expensive, cuisine. The decor was elegant, the service attentive—the atmosphere was what Miamians think of as New Yorkish, the highest accolade. Buccione's was a favorite of chic Grovites.

When Stan bought out his partners in the restaurant, he and Joyce began to spend more time there. The waiters thought Stan was a good boss. He watched the quality of the food carefully and insisted on fresh ingredients. He rarely complained, never yelled at the help. Before customers came in, the waiters often congregated in the back of the restaurant, chatting and joking. Stan would walk in the front door and through the empty dining room without a word. Then as he passed the cluster of waiters, he would mutter, "If they threw a bomb in this place, they'd get you all!" Raucous laughter.

When the restaurant was really busy, Stan helped out in the kitchen, working "the line" between the pasta cook and the grill. The waiters put in their orders, or "dupes," and Stan would read them. "One veal parm! Is the veal ready?" he yelled out. "Is the steak ready?" He was a pretty good line man, the waiters thought. When the rush was over, Stan would just say good-bye and leave.

If the restaurant's hostess didn't show up, Joyce sometimes took over until someone else could be found. Favoring longish skirts or culottes (the length made her look taller than her five feet) with silk blouses or sweaters and high-heeled boots, she always looked terrific. She loved boots and seemed to have dozens of them—gorgeous, high leather boots, snakeskin boots, hair-on calf boots that looked like the hide of a black-and-white pinto pony. She wore the hair-on calf boots with a long black skirt and a black-and-white sweater, a striking ensemble with her shiny dark hair, exotic eyes, and dazzling smile.

"Boy, you really look nice," the waiters told her.

"Oh, do I? Do I?" Joyce always asked eagerly.

They all noticed her vast collection of beautiful sweaters—bulky sweaters, often with patterns or designs, unique sweaters like pieces of art. Whenever someone complimented Joyce on a sweater she was wearing, she always mentioned where she got it—"I got this at Saks," "I got this in Colorado," "I guess this was when I was in Mexico."

Near the restaurant's front door was a glass display case filled with chilled vintage champagnes. Whenever Joyce came into the restaurant, it was her first stop. She peered into the case, trying to make up her mind which champagne she would tell the waiters to bring her. Should I drink the Dom Perignon? The Perrier Joie? The Cristal? One night there was a bottle of pink Cristal in the case. As Joyce stood pondering before the glass, one of the waiters came up behind her and said, "Aw, drink the pink champagne!" And she did. But she didn't share her champagne with the waiters. If she didn't finish a bottle, she just corked it and took it with her.

Buccione's became a stopover for visiting celebrities like Cheryl Tiegs, who always came in when she was in Miami promoting her clothing line. Zsa Zsa Gabor and Peter Allen, Liza Minnelli's former husband, ate there, and Don Ameche, Maureen Stapleton, and the entire cast of the movie *Cocoon II* frequented Buccione's while filming in South Florida. Finally the waiters began to keep a celebrity autograph book, which they asked famous guests to sign.

Then there was the Grove celebrity crowd, people locally well known like developer Monty Trainer, attorneys P. J. Carroll, Alan

Ross and his partner Jeff Weiner, Frankie Diaz, and a string of developers, doctors, lawyers, businessmen, politicians. Dade County circuit judge Mary Anne MacKenzie sometimes ate at Buccione's, as did Dade County's chief prosecutor, State Attorney Janet Reno. Most of Stan's friends were regulars—the Sheldons, the Johnnideses, the Wassermans.

Every Sunday night, Stan's younger brother, Artie, and their widowed mother, Frances, came to Buccione's for dinner. Artie Cohen had muscular dystrophy and was confined to a wheelchair. Joyce rarely stopped by on Sunday nights, but Stan usually breezed in to say hello and sometimes stayed to eat. He always took good care of his brother and mother. There was never a check for their dinner. Even if Stan wasn't there, Artie would just sign a chit.

Stan and Joyce had their special table at Buccione's—number eighteen, against the back wall by the window, where they could see everybody who walked in. When they entertained six guests or more, they used number three, a big round table near the front of the restaurant. But even when the Cohens had dinner with friends, the waiters never saw Joyce eat a meal. She asked for a half-order of pasta or a salad or soup, but never an entree. She just picked at her food.

A frequent dinner guest of the Cohens was Myra Wenig, Joyce's good friend. She got to know Myra at the Miami Ski Club, where she usually choreographed the ski fashion show. Although Myra worked as a legal secretary, she always described herself as a dancer. She was attractive, trim and athletic, graceful and creative. Myra had a good sense of style. Her hair, which changed color and style frequently, was often some shade of blond. People were usually surprised to learn that she was Cuban. She spoke English without a trace of accent.

Myra had lived with a friend of Stan's, in a kind of affluence she could not afford on her own. When the relationship ended, she was devastated. She had turned to Joyce and Stan for comfort, and Joyce invited her to move into their house for a while. When Myra couldn't sleep, Joyce stayed up with her, drinking tea and talking far into the night. Joyce was usually up late anyway—she always had trouble sleeping. The two women became close confidantes. They were almost like sisters.

Joyce often invited Myra to come to Buccione's for dinner, especially when she knew Myra was alone. And she, too, noticed that Joyce rarely ate a meal. She must be starving herself to keep her weight down, Myra thought. But she looked great, very thin, toned and tan.

Myra was fascinated by the stream of well-heeled Grovites who stopped by the Cohens' table to say hello. Everyone knew Joyce drove the white Jag and Stan the tan Bronco, and people noticed when their cars were parked right in front of Buccione's, a sign that the Cohens were in and receiving guests. Myra was impressed—Joyce and Stan had become celebrity-restaurateurs in Coconut Grove, the trendiest spot in Florida.

Joyce and Stan Cohen had it all, Myra thought.

# Four

**A**mong Stan Cohen's many blessings were his children. Daughter Gerri had graduated in 1981 from Florida State University in Tallahassee with a degree in journalism. She was a very attractive young woman—slender, with glossy dark hair and large, rather soulful brown eyes. Like her father, Gerri was smart and strong-willed. With her good looks and poise, she projected a competent, authoritative image on camera and soon found her niche in the world of television journalism.

Gerri started as a reporter with WCTV, the small CBS affiliate in Tallahassee, and after five months, she was lured to the Tallahassee bureau of Miami's Channel 4. The bureau was a small outpost—just a cameraman and a reporter-producer—so her official title was Tallahassee bureau chief. She was twenty-one years old.

Gerri quickly developed a reputation as a reliable, hardworking journalist who was serious about her career. After a year and a half, she was ready to return home to Miami. But Channel 4 refused to transfer her—she was doing a great job in Tallahassee. So Gerri took an offer from a rival station, Channel 10, and finally made it back to Miami. At Channel 10 she hosted a Sunday morning public affairs talk show for a while, then became a reporter. After five years she was hired back by Channel 4 as weekend news anchor in Miami.

Stan Cohen was proud that his pretty daughter had become such a success.

He was just as proud of his son Gary. A Pi Lamb like his father, Gary graduated from law school at Stan's alma mater, the University of Florida in Gainesville, and returned to Miami to practice. He joined the respected Miami law firm of Fine Jacobson Schwartz Nash & Block (Fine Jacobson, for short), which occupied several floors of CenTrust Tower, the I. M. Pei–designed office tower in the heart of Miami that had become the signature building of the city's skyline. Specializing in tax law, Gary was regarded as a smart, careful lawyer who got along well with colleagues and clients. His legal future looked bright.

Although Gerri and Gary had grown up together, Stan's only natural children, the two weren't close. Their personalities were near-polar opposites. Gerri was outspoken and assertive, her father's daughter, friends often commented, while Gary was more easygoing. There was mutual respect and affection, but there was also a distance between brother and sister. It seemed they had little in common, except their love for their father. Both Stan's children adored him.

While Stan's grown son and daughter were bounding up their separate career ladders, his adopted son, Shawn, was beginning to have a classic 1980s problem—drugs. His first experience, as a twelve-year-old, was with some marijuana he found hidden in his parents' bedroom. He took it, although he didn't know what it was. He showed it to one of his friends, who said, "Oh, I know what this is. It's grass. You roll it into cigarettes and smoke it. Here, I'll show you how. I've seen my brother do it." They smoked the joint, not really inhaling but just puffing at it. And they decided they liked it.

His parents never asked Shawn about the pot missing from their bedroom. Shawn didn't know whom it belonged to, but he guessed it might have been his mother's. Stan lectured Shawn constantly about the evils of drugs. Shawn couldn't believe the dope was his father's.

Soon Shawn found other opportunities to get pot. At Buccione's Restaurant, Stan paid him $1 an hour to wash dishes and scrub out pots and pans with the other dishwashers in the kitchen. There he soon discovered that among his co-workers was a Jamaican dishwasher who liked strong island ganja and had a good supply of it. Soon Shawn started sneaking upstairs in the restaurant with the dishwasher to smoke thick joints stuffed with ganja. One night the cook caught them at it.

"Well, I'm not going to tell your dad about this," the cook said to Shawn, but he fired the Jamaican dishwasher on the spot. Shawn felt bad about that. But it didn't diminish his appetite for pot.

During the summers Shawn earned $1 an hour working for SAC Construction, helping the carpenters or just cleaning up. Stan put him to work at the Galloway Medical Center project, which SAC was building in the Miami suburb of Kendall. The supervisor on the job, Jimmy Grubb, noticed that Shawn was coming in to work high most mornings and had a bag of pot in his pocket. Shawn was thirteen years old. Grubb took the pot away from him and angrily complained to Ben Abernathy, his project manager.

"I don't know what to tell you," Ben replied uneasily. "I don't want to say nothing to Stanley. It's none of my business. Call Marvin. Talk to Marvin about it."

Finally Grubb called Marvin Sheldon, and Marvin agreed to talk to Stanley. "Stan, I think you'd better hear what Jimmy has to say," he told him. Reluctantly, Stan listened, and the incident seemed to mark the beginning of his problems with Shawn.

Soon Shawn was smoking dope every morning before going to Palmer School, the expensive private school in South Dade where Joyce and Stan sent him after he was kicked out of Gulliver Academy. Shawn really liked Palmer and wanted to stay there. He had lots of friends, and the teachers were nice. He especially liked playing on Palmer's varsity football team. Because he was only a freshman, he played on the special squads like the kickoff team and the punt team. He idolized the older players.

One afternoon football practice ended early, and Shawn took off into the woods with a couple of friends from the team to smoke a joint. Then he went to the parking lot to meet Mrs. Consuegra, a teacher who gave him a ride to and from school. On the drive home, Mrs. Consuegra kept staring at Shawn suspiciously. Suddenly she shouted, "You're high! You're high! I'm taking you back to school!"

"No, you're not taking me back to school!" Shawn yelled back at her. "I'll jump out of this car right here!"

Mrs. Consuegra drove on to the Cohens' house, marched Shawn inside, and told Joyce and Stan exactly what he had done.

"No, no, no, I didn't!" Shawn shouted.

"Okay," Stan told Mrs. Consuegra. "We'll look into it."

After the teacher left, Stan confronted Shawn. Joyce stepped back and let her husband handle the situation, just as he handled most situations in their lives.

"Okay, I smoked a little pot with the guys on the football team," Shawn admitted sheepishly.

"Well, if you want to be a star, you don't do that," Stan admonished.

"Well, look at these guys," Shawn replied. He rattled off the names of several good players, starters on the team, who had been smoking with him.

Stan wasn't impressed. "You won't get anywhere that way," he said. "Drugs are a dead end. Don't do it again."

Shawn was grounded for a month.

Finally Shawn was kicked out of Palmer, not for smoking dope but for cheating on a science test. One of his favorite teachers, Mr. Motter, noticed him diligently copying answers from another student's test paper. He took Shawn to another room by himself and handed him a clean test paper.

"Take this test," he said.

Of course, Shawn failed. Joyce and Stan were called to school for a conference, and it was agreed that Shawn would leave Palmer. He had already been kicked out of Gulliver Academy. Where could Joyce and Stan send him this time?

Unknown to his parents, Shawn had been sneaking out of the house at night for years. He had learned to circumvent the elaborate alarm system by leaving one of his first-floor bedroom's french windows open while the other was closed to make the necessary contact for the alarm system. As soon as his parents were upstairs and the house was quiet, he merely jumped out the open half of his bedroom window.

Shawn headed immediately for Peacock Park down by the bay to rendezvous with his pals and assorted drifters, druggies, drinkers, and gamblers. He learned to shoot a good game of pool—and he had easy access to booze and drugs. Soon he was snorting cocaine as well as smoking grass and drinking beer.

Finally one night Shawn got caught. Stan discovered he was missing from his room. He called the police, filed a missing person report, and then went looking for Shawn himself. He found him in a pool hall, holding his own with men twice his age.

Shawn was grounded again, and this time Stan put locks on his bedroom windows.

When Stan caught him smoking pot in his own bedroom, he and Joyce faced the fact that something had to be done about Shawn. They couldn't keep him in school, and they couldn't even keep him home at night. It was obvious he was into drugs and booze. He was fourteen years old. Stan really loved Shawn, but he just couldn't seem to get through to the kid. But he wouldn't give up on him; the boy needed serious help.

Eventually they found a place for Shawn: Rocky Mountain Academy, a year-round boarding school in northern Idaho near the Canadian border. The place was strict—no smoking, no booze, no drugs. Lots of sports and supervised study. The campus was isolated— about six miles from the tiny logging and farming community of Bonners Ferry. There was nowhere to go even if students left the school. And the staff provided a strong program of group therapy and individual counseling. Although many of the students had problems like Shawn's, it wasn't a drug rehab center, exactly. It sounded ideal.

It would be expensive, of course. The cost was about $1,500 per month, twelve months a year, a grand total of nearly $20,000 annually. Stan was willing to pay.

In September 1983, Shawn was sent to Rocky Mountain Academy, and once he adjusted, he got along well there. He began to make friends and earned a spot on the football team. Most important, Shawn participated in the school's counseling program. For the next two years, he would see his parents only twice—once for a brief vacation in Hawaii and then at his graduation from Rocky Mountain Academy in December 1985.

Shawn was effectively out of Joyce's life. She felt ambivalent about that. Certainly she loved Shawn. She always said he was her first responsibility, the center of her life. But he had been so difficult for the past few years—skipping school, sneaking out at night, the drugs, the booze. With that problem solved, Joyce and Stan didn't have a worry in the world. And all Joyce had to think about was herself.

# *Five*

•

Joyce Cohen had time on her hands, and old friends began to notice another change in her. She became more . . . *social*. Suddenly, it seemed, she had to be the center of attention everywhere she went.

Joyce's friend Myra Wenig dated the change precisely: April 1984, when the Miami Ski Club had its big Spring Fest bash to mark the end of ski season. The party was held at Miami's open-air Bayfront Auditorium, overlooking Biscayne Bay. The food and decorations were elaborate. A Michael Jackson impersonator was hired to entertain. The party theme: Hooray for Hollywood. Each guest was to come dressed as a favorite celebrity, the more elaborately, the better.

Myra went to the Cohens' house to consult with Joyce and Stan about their costumes. Myra decided to go to the party as Joan Crawford because she had the perfect dress for the part. Stan chose his favorite tough guy, Al Capone. And Joyce? She would become actress Joan Collins in her "Dynasty" television role, the bitchy, manipulative Alexis Carrington.

"I really want to do this. It's going to be so out of character for me," she told them excitedly.

For the party, Joyce planned to wear a body-hugging black suit and a little red hat with a veil perched on the side of her head. She had a long, elegant cigarette holder, which she could brandish in dramatic gestures. Her hairdresser, Tyrone of Grove Isle, and her makeup artist, Terry Jacobs, were hired to give her professional finishing touches right before the party.

Joyce was a regular client who used Terry Jacobs's services often for parties and special events. And she was a big tipper; she always handed Terry $20 in addition to the $50 bill for her usual makeup job. Joyce and Stan made a fuss over Terry when she came into Buccione's—some special appetizers, perhaps, or a drink on the house. Terry was fond of Joyce and used a glamorous picture of her in a makeup advertising brochure.

Well-heeled socialites in the Grove all agreed that Terry Jacobs was a true artist who achieved amazing results for her clients. One woman clutched Terry's hands in her own, raving, "What's in these hands? It's magic!" But even Terry Jacobs was startled at what she achieved for Joyce Cohen that spring evening. With her shiny black hair, dramatic makeup, and elegant costume, Joyce was a dead ringer for Alexis. And she was absolutely gorgeous.

Everyone noticed Joyce at the Spring Fest party. People came up to her all night, saying, "My God, you are so beautiful! Why don't you wear that makeup all the time? Your hair . . ." She was the star of the show. And she loved it. Not only was she dressed for the part, Joyce flaunted a personality to match the grasping, manipulative character of Alexis Carrington. But some thought her new bitchiness wasn't just an act. There were whispers: cocaine.

Joyce's hairdresser, Tyrone, had heard all the rumors. Joyce was a favored client at his salon in exclusive Grove Isle, a tiny island of expensive condominiums and shops. Tyrone always cut Joyce's hair himself. She was a perfectionist who wanted every strand precision-cut in her habitual french bob style—blunt cut, shoulder length, absolutely straight, with heavy bangs. If she thought even one hair was out of place, she would march back into the shop for a recut.

When Joyce came into Tyrone's shop, she was always bubbly, effervescent, "up." Tyrone's other clients enjoyed talking to her. But sometimes she seemed to be a little high, Tyrone thought. Probably cocaine. After all, coke was the social prop of the '80s.

In fact, Joyce was doing some coke. Even Stan did a little now and then, as did some of their hip friends. After a party at the Cohens' one night, several couples snorted a line, just as a lark, an experiment. Like a glass or two of wine, coke took the edge off. Joyce felt more self-confident after a few toots, more social, more outgoing. It was no big deal in Miami.

In the summer of 1984, the nighttime scene in Coconut Grove was struck by lightning: Biscayne Baby, a hot new disco. Myra Wenig's friend Diana Shapiro and her husband opened the club in the second story of a wooden building on Virginia Street, a quiet side street in the heart of the Grove near the boutiques and cafés. It was an instant hit. Oriented to the young, chic set, the club quickly became *the* late-night spot—music, drinking, and dancing until 5 A.M. And it had the best sound system in Miami. By 10 P.M. at The Baby, as it was known, there were long lines waiting to get IDs checked and pay the $5 cover charge. But insiders knew how to get in fast. One way was to go with someone from Miami's premier Greenberg Traurig law firm, where Diana Shapiro's husband was an attorney. Another way was to be recognized by the doorman on duty downstairs. Or to have reservations for the club's Champagne Room, a small, private room with an additional $20 cover charge per person.

Diana Shapiro, the owner, gave Myra Wenig carte blanche at Biscayne Baby, and Myra brought Joyce and Stan. Although at thirty-four she was older than most of the Biscayne Baby crowd, Joyce instantly fell in love with the place and became a regular. Stan was less enthusiastic. After working since dawn at SAC Construction projects, then supervising at Buccione's, he usually preferred a good night's sleep to dancing all night at Biscayne Baby. Since his heart bypass surgery a few years earlier, he had started to slow down a little. Stan tried to get some regular exercise and plenty of rest each night. But Joyce wanted to party. She began to drop by The Baby with Myra Wenig occasionally, without her husband. Stan didn't seem to mind.

Joyce was particularly fond of the Champagne Room, an intimate, dimly lit alcove with space for only twenty people. The motif was yellow and black: yellow walls and black leather sofas arranged to form a pit, with zebra-striped pillows scattered about. A private bartender manned a small bar set up on a cart. At the door to the Champagne Room, a velvet rope kept the curious out, while a handsome young doorman checked reservations against a list on his clipboard. The doorman wore a sort of trendy uniform: tuxedo shirt, red bow tie and cummerbund, dark trousers and sneakers. The Champagne Room quickly acquired the cachet of a laid-back version of New York's Studio 54.

Joyce established a reputation as a generous tipper in the Champagne Room and was a favorite with the doorman and bartender. Sometimes alone, always immaculately groomed and stunning in the dramatic black-and-white outfits she now favored, she still affected the Joan Collins/Alexis persona. She usually arrived late—about eleven o'clock or so—and she drank only champagne. Joyce was always recognized at the door and quickly ushered upstairs. People noticed her.

Joyce made a new friend: Lynn Barkley, fortyish, a tall, lanky, attractive man with longish blond hair and a languid air. He had worked at Studio 54, he told Joyce, and had once managed a rock band. Now Barkley worked occasionally as a professional photographer and lived on and off with various friends in the Grove. Barkley was cool.

Joyce and Barkley saw each other occasionally, sometimes at Biscayne Baby. They discussed going into business together and came up with a product they called Cool Aids, plastic, fluid-filled wrist- and headbands that could be chilled and worn by athletes to stay cool during sports. Joyce took the idea to Stan's attorney, Richard Hays, to see about getting a patent.

But nothing came of the Cool Aids venture, and Lynn Barkley seemed to drift out of Joyce's life. It was like that in the Grove. People came and went. New night spots and shops opened and closed. It made life more interesting, and Joyce couldn't imagine living her life any other way.

# Six

$T$he Cohens planned another busy winter social season at Wolf Run Ranch in Steamboat Springs. The first event on the calendar was Shawn's graduation from Rocky Mountain Academy on December 7, 1985. After graduation, he planned to bring a classmate back to Colorado to join his mother and father for some holiday skiing, snowmobiling, and partying at the ranch.

Every year Stan and Joyce invited Miami friends to spend Christmas with them in Colorado. Joyce especially liked to entertain over the holidays, and she always made elaborate preparations. One year the Cohens invited Patty and John Bartell, who handled Stan's life insurance, and Patty was amazed by Joyce's strenuous hostessing. Some days Joyce skipped the skiing to stay at the ranch while the others were out. When they returned from the mountain one evening, the Bartells found their laundry in their rooms, washed, ironed, and folded, and a wonderful dinner awaiting them. The huge, shimmering Christmas tree Joyce decorated was the most beautiful Patty had ever seen. There were thoughtful gifts for all the guests. Patty talked about that vacation for years.

This year the Cohens invited their Miami friends the Sampsons to spend ten days with them over Christmas. The Cohens and the Sampsons had been friends for years. Skip Sampson worked with Ed

Smith at the Poole & Kent Company, a mechanical contracting firm, and his wife, nicknamed Shu, taught at a Miami Christian school. The Sampsons weren't stuffy—they liked to ski and party with the Cohens and their friends—but they took their religion seriously. And they didn't do drugs, not even as a lark. Their son was about Shawn's age, and the two boys had spent time together as children. When Shawn was young, Joyce was reluctant to leave him home alone with the housekeeper so often while she and Stan traveled. Sometimes she arranged for Shawn to stay with the Sampsons while they were out of town. If he was going along on a trip, Joyce usually invited the Sampsons' son or another child to be company for Shawn. Shu Sampson, an intelligent, straightforward woman, thought Joyce was a very good mother, and they grew to be close friends.

With so much company coming, Joyce had a lot to do at the ranch, and she flew from Miami to Steamboat alone to begin preparations for the holidays. Stan would join her there, and then they would travel together to Idaho for Shawn's graduation. But something odd happened at Wolf Run Ranch while Joyce was there alone. Late in the evening of December 2, she frantically telephoned the ranch's new resident caretaker, Scott Flower, asking for help. She told Flower she had just returned from partying in town and discovered a break-in at the house. Flower promptly called the Routt County Sheriff's Office in Steamboat Springs, and then dashed from the caretaker's cottage over the hill to the main house.

When Sheriff's Deputy David Gilmore arrived to investigate, he made careful note of what he found. Fresh snow blanketed the ground. There was only one set of tire tracks up the winding driveway to the ranch house—tracks made by Joyce in the Subaru when she returned home. A fire log had been thrown through the glass pane in a first-floor bedroom door.

But the only footprints in the powdery snow around the woodpile outside were small, like a woman's boot. And the log that had been thrown through the door still bore unmelted snow, despite the warm temperature of the room inside. Nothing was missing from her home, Mrs. Cohen confirmed. Deputy Gilmore checked out the house but found no intruder.

Gilmore wasn't sure what had happened at Wolf Run Ranch that night, but it didn't look like an attempted burglary. He marked his incident report "no further action to be taken" and filed it away.

Shawn graduated from Rocky Mountain Academy on December 7 as planned, with Joyce and Stan beaming in the audience, and after the ceremony, the Cohens and Shawn's guest flew back to Colorado. That year, as every year, a towering twenty-foot Christmas tree adorned the Great Room of the ranch house. By the time the Sampsons arrived from Miami, all was ready. As usual, Joyce had found thoughtful Christmas gifts for her guests and family. It was an idyllic holiday.

Joyce proudly showed Shu Sampson the large diamond ring Stan had bought her for their eleventh wedding anniversary on December 5. She had picked out the ring herself. She saw it pictured in a magazine—*Vogue,* she thought, or *Vanity Fair*—and she loved it. The large center stone was surrounded by a spiral of baguettes set in heavy gold. Although she had pointed the ring out to her husband, she wasn't sure he was going to buy it for her. But Stan had come through for her again.

Shawn teased his mother about her new ring, which looked huge on her small, perfectly manicured hand. "When you die, Mom, are you going to give me that ring?" he asked her repeatedly.

"Oh, no," Joyce always replied with a laugh. "I'm going to be buried with this ring!"

The Cohens made a videotape of their holiday with their friends and family at Wolf Run Ranch. It seemed to Shu Sampson that Stan and Joyce were happier than ever that Christmas.

After the holidays, Shawn started school at Tennessee Military Institute in Sweetwater, Tennessee, and Stan and the Sampsons returned to Miami. Joyce stayed behind to prepare for the next event on their schedule, the Miami Ski Club trip to Steamboat in February. The Cohens would host parties for their ski club buddies during the trip.

When the Miami Ski Club arrived in Steamboat Springs, Stan flew up from Miami to join in the fun. Fred Wasserman was in charge of the trip that year, and Joyce and Stan hosted a party for 120 club members at Riverside Suds, the three-two bar that Stan and his partners owned at the Riverside Shopping Center. Everyone remembered it as a great party—thick, juicy steaks cooked to order by Stan, plenty of beer and booze, a great country-western band, a good time for good friends.

Stan and Joyce skied with their Miami friends nearly every day during the ski club trip. Ed Smith was there with his second wife, Claudia, nicknamed Sam, a strong-willed, athletic woman who was an excellent skier. Sam and Ed had gone together for years, off and on, until Sam's four children from her first marriage were grown. Finally she issued an ultimatum: Either marry me or get lost. Ed married her. Although Sam was older than Joyce, the two women had become particularly close friends. Sam seemed almost protective of Joyce. Joyce knew she could count on Sam.

Fred Wasserman liked Joyce. They often rode up on ski lifts together, with Joyce chatting happily about how well Shawn was doing. It seemed the kid had really straightened out. Ed Smith wasn't quite so happy to be around Joyce. One night the Smiths, the Cohens, and several friends agreed to meet for dinner at Mattie Silk's restaurant in Ski Time Village. Joyce showed up late, without apology. Ed was irritated. Then at dinner he noticed that Joyce was fidgety, up and down all night, giggling and whispering, "Let's go to the ladies' room!" She got on his nerves.

The Miami Ski Club's Steamboat trip culminated in a big banquet at the Sheraton Inn. Since the dinner roughly coincided with Stan's fifty-second birthday, Fred Wasserman had a cake for Stan and a raucous birthday serenade. When all the festivities were over Stan went back to Miami, but Joyce again stayed on at Wolf Run Ranch alone. She had made some new friends in Steamboat, an affluent crowd that included ski slope celebrities like Peter Brewster and Billy Kidd, former Olympic racer, and the locals who skied by day and partied by night. She had also gotten to know Kathy Dickett, who was part owner of Cafe Blue Bayou, a casual hangout that Joyce frequented. Kathy was blond, very thin, an attractive young woman. Although she was considerably younger than Joyce, the two seemed to hit it off.

Like most people in Steamboat, Kathy Dickett liked to ski. She also liked to party, particularly with a crowd of young, single guys. She seemed to have plenty of time and money for fun. Joyce often stopped by Cafe Blue Bayou around closing time. Then she and Kathy would move on to late-night party spots like Tugboat Annie's, for a drink and dancing with Kathy's young friends.

A few of Joyce's women friends came out from Miami for the season. Geri Carroll was staying at the Steamboat Springs condo she owned with her husband, prominent Miami attorney P. J. Carroll. Geri and P.J. had recently separated, and a messy divorce seemed imminent. The Carrolls' grown daughter, Kimberly, accompanied her mother to Steamboat. Geri was a strking redhead who managed to look more like Kimberly's sister than her mother. Mother and daughter skied together by day and partied together at night. They often met their friend Joyce on the slopes or in the bars, partying until early morning. Kimberly Carroll had a well-known penchant for calling friends during these late-night parties, after everybody had had a few drinks. But she knew Stan Cohen wouldn't tolerate that. He didn't like to have his sleep disturbed. Kimberly liked Stan, but like all the Cohens' friends, she didn't want to cross him.

One February night after Stan had returned to Miami, Joyce wound up at the Rendezvous Lounge in Steamboat Springs. There she ran into the blond country singing star Tanya Tucker, who came to Steamboat every winter and was popular with the locals. The two women began to chat, and Joyce invited Tucker to spend the night with her at Wolf Run Ranch. Tucker accepted.

That night they sat together before the fire, exchanging confidences about their lives as they drank champagne and snorted a few lines of coke. The next morning Joyce caught up with Tucker at the airport in Steamboat to return a jacket she had left at Wolf Run Ranch. As they said good-bye, Tucker gave Joyce her home phone number in Nashville. A few days later, Joyce called Tucker, awakening her at home in the middle of the night. "I've called all the stores and ordered all your albums," Joyce gushed happily. She had just bought Tucker's new cassette, *Girls Like Me*. Joyce told everybody Tanya Tucker was her personal friend.

The next big social event in Joyce's life awaited her in Miami. Gerri Cohen had become engaged to Steve Helfman, a handsome young lawyer at her brother Gary's Miami law firm, Fine Jacobson. The Helfmans were prominent in Miami society, and Stan had promised his daughter a beautiful wedding. The date was set: March 29, 1986. Stan and Gerri were planning the wedding together, but those plans had caused some family friction.

The Helfmans were not like most of Stan's crowd, the self-made men who started with nothing and wound up rich—and perhaps still had a few rough edges. Steve's father was a well-respected physician, and Steve's upbringing had been one of ease and privilege. His mother was a charming, elegant woman who moved in the best social circles, and the family's close friends stood at the pinnacle of Miami Jewish society, people like Norman Braman, the automobile millionaire who was part owner of the Philadelphia Eagles. If Stan was not entirely comfortable with his daughter's choice he never mentioned it to her. It was Joyce who seemed somehow uneasy about the prospect of socializing with the Helfmans.

And there was the subject of wedding finances. Stan and Gerri had agreed on a budget in the neighborhood of $28,000, nothing outrageous by Miami standards. But why couldn't Gerri and Steve pay for at least part of their own wedding, Joyce asked. After all, they were adults, financially independent, successful in their high-paying careers.

One evening when Joyce was in Miami, Gerri came to the house on South Bayshore Drive to discuss wedding plans. They were sitting around the dining table, eating pizza and talking, when Gerri announced that she wanted to invite 250 guests to her wedding.

"Gerri, there's no way your father will let you have so many guests," Joyce said bluntly.

Gerri turned to her father expectantly. But Stan said nothing. The guest list was pared to 125.

In fact, the Cohen-Helfman wedding attracted attention beyond their families and friends. It was the romantic union of two attractive, successful young professionals—a real 1980s love story. *The Miami Herald* mentioned Gerri Cohen's upcoming wedding in an article about sophisticated career women searching for the perfect bridal gown. The story, which ran just before Valentine's Day, led with a description of Gerri, a reporter at Miami's Channel 10, shopping for a gown "befitting her station in life." According to the article, she finally selected an elegant contemporary design by Frank

Masandrea for the Diamond Collection: a full-length mermaid-shaped dress of white lace over a nude-colored lining, with a deep, plunging back.

"It's the perfect combination. It's sophisticated, sexy, and traditional. I'll be the bride in it. And who cares if you can wear the dress again, anyway?" Gerri Cohen was quoted in the article.

Steve Helfman's colleagues at Fine Jacobson were dazzled by his glamorous bride-to-be. And when they met her, they liked her even more. Despite her professional success, they found, Gerri Cohen was down-to-earth, warm, and genuine. Her career was important to her, she said, but family was even more important. She and Steve planned to have children, and Gerri was determined that her career wouldn't interfere with raising her family. Stan Cohen would be a doting grandfather, Gerri knew. She happily anticipated sharing her children with her father.

The wedding would take place at the elegant Grand Bay Hotel, just down the street from the Cohen home on South Bayshore Drive. Prenuptial plans included an elegant luncheon shower to be given by Dr. and Mrs. Helfman at the Grove Isle Club in late February. The Helfmans invited Joyce and Stan and Gerri's mother, Martha.

Joyce returned to Miami just before the Helfmans' luncheon shower. It was a great success, elegant and sentimental. Gerri was radiant in a simple black-and-white silk dress, her luxuriant dark hair gleaming. The Helfmans offered an affectionate toast to their son's future wife, and their distinguished guests followed suit. One after another, Miami's elite complimented Gerri and warmly welcomed her into their circle.

But Joyce had seemed edgy and ill-at-ease from the moment she walked in the door of the exclusive club. She and Stan were seated at a rear table with Gary Cohen and his date, Carol Norris, who couldn't help noticing as Joyce toyed nervously with the silverware at her place. Watching from the head table, Gerri began to worry about her stepmother, but then she relaxed. She was marrying the man she loved. Her wedding, just a month away, would be beautiful. Nothing could spoil it.

# Seven

•

The weekend of March 1, Shawn Cohen came home for a visit from his first semester at Tennessee Military Institute. Although Joyce and Stan didn't know it, he was already getting into trouble at the school, sneaking out of the dorm at night and buying booze, just as he had done as a rebellious teenager in the Grove. It was Shawn's first trip back to Miami since he had left for Rocky Mountain Academy in September 1983, and life seemed about the same in the big house on South Bayshore Drive. But he did notice that now even the closets in his own bedroom—in fact, all the closets in the entire house—were crammed with his mother's clothes, many with price tags still attached. Guess she hasn't slowed down in the shopping department, he thought. What the hell did she need with so many clothes?

But there were outward manifestations of change in the Cohens' lives. The house on South Bayshore Drive was up for sale. Stan said he was tired of the old place, and Joyce was ready for a change. Asking price for the landmark old home: $450,000. The Cohens planned to move to the luxurious penthouse condomimium they owned at Port By-Water, right on Biscayne Bay, overlooking Grove Isle. Stan's pal Len Levenstein had built the six-story Port By-Water project in 1979, and Stan and Joyce had taken title to one penthouse. Len and

C.J., who was now his wife, took the other. Of course, SAC Construction was the contractor.

That sunny Saturday morning in March, the phone rang in the bedroom of the Levensteins' penthouse condominium. Len answered. It was Stan, just calling to chat. "Why don't you join us for dinner?" Len suggested. "We're going out with George and Sharon." It was to be a small celebration, just the Levensteins and the Johnnideses. Sharon Johnnides had just learned she was pregnant with her third child.

"Let me check with Joyce and I'll call you back," Stan replied. A while later, he phoned Len and said they would be happy to go.

That afternoon, Joyce and Stan participated in a suburban Miami ritual: the sidewalk art show. Streets in South Miami were blocked off so that exhibitors from around the country could set up little outdoor booths displaying their work: watercolors, oils, multimedia creations, metalworks, ceramics, photographs, wood carvings, leather works, handmade paper collages, handmade jewelry, straw hats with nosegay headbands of dried flowers—and plenty of just plain junk. Food and drink vendors jammed the sidewalks with ordinary fast food, liberally laced with dishes from Miami's rich ethnic stew: spicy Jamaican meat pies, Bahamian conch fritters, ceviche, fried calamari, Cuban black beans and rice with fried plantains. And delightful tropical fruit drinks: piña colada, goombay punch, guava coolers, papaya and passion fruit. The outdoor art show was a community happening, a place to see and be seen while dodging the endless parade of strollers, roller skaters, skateboarders, and cyclists who weaved through the scene. Friends saw the Cohens strolling along, hand in hand, waving, smiling, chatting.

As planned, the Cohens met C.J. and Len Levenstein and Sharon and George Johnnides at Sassafras, a trendy bistro in the Grove's elegant Mayfair shopping plaza. Sassafras was a festive spot, just the place to stop in for a predinner drink. The waiters and waitresses, recruited heavily from the University of Miami performing arts departments, zoomed around the small restaurant on roller skates, taking orders, delivering food and drinks, and sometimes joining in impromptu renditions of Broadway show tunes. At Sassafras, the Cohens and their friends shared a bottle or two of champagne and toasted the Johnnideses on their good news before moving on to Cafe Tanino, a new Italian restaurant in Coral Gables that was garnering good reviews.

Stan sat at the head of the table at dinner that night. Everyone there noticed Joyce's affectionate attention to her husband. It was "Honey" this and "Honey" that all night as she petted his arm or stroked his hand. The conversation drifted casually from one topic to another. Joyce later recalled that Stan mentioned Frankie Diaz, the Miami attorney that the Cohens and the Johnnideses had met on the island of Martinique a couple of years earlier. Diaz was now a fugitive from the law, but Stan said something about being able to get in touch with him whenever he wished.

Dinner finished around midnight, and Stan suggested that George and Sharon Johnnides stop by the SAC Construction office the next day to see the new gym he had put in there. He was exercising at the gym three nights a week, pumping iron with his young project manager Ben Abernathy. He felt great, Stan told them, as strong as he had been in college. The friends went their separate ways.

Later that night, Stan, Joyce, and Shawn were watching television together in the family room at home when they heard a knock at the front door. Stan answered and then ushered in a good-looking dark-haired man and an attractive young woman. Joyce recognized the man immediately.

"Shawn, this is Frank Diaz," Stan said, introducing him to his son. Shawn shook Diaz's hand. Then Stan asked Shawn and Joyce to leave the room, and later, after his guests had left, he called them back. "Well, son, tonight you just met your first international fugitive," Stan told Shawn with a smirk. He didn't explain his late-night visit from Diaz, who had faked his own kidnapping to escape federal charges involving conspiracy, perjury, fraud, and witness bribery. Shawn, who had no idea who the mystery man was, found his father's behavior curious, but he asked no questions. He thought no more about the strange late-night visitor. The next morning, he went back to school at Tennessee Military Institute in Sweetwater.

The following evening, Joyce invited her friend Myra Wenig and Myra's new boyfriend to have dinner at the Cohens' home. The meal was simple and casual—burgers grilled on the Jenn-Air in the kitchen. After dinner they watched television together in the family room. A perfectly ordinary evening.

On Wednesday, March 5, Joyce and Toni Pollack, her partner in SAC Interiors, worked together preparing a bid for a job in Tampa. That afternoon, Stan met with his attorney, Richard Hays, about various business matters. When the meeting concluded, Stan chatted happily about working out at his new gym. "I'm pumping more iron than ever," he bragged. "I'm in great shape!"

Then Hays asked for Stan's advice. "Stan, I need some help on a slip-and-fall case in Bal Harbour." As a favor to an inexperienced young lawyer, Hays had agreed to try a personal injury case involving a woman who had fallen on the stairs at the exclusive shopping arcade. "I don't know if there's any liability. I don't have measurements on the stairs, but I do have pictures."

"How soon do you need this?" Stan asked.

"Yesterday," Hays replied ruefully. "I'm going to trial in two weeks and I can't settle."

"Okay," Stan said. "I can't go tomorrow, but I can meet you out there Friday afternoon." Stan promised to look the site over, bring along the Dade County Building Code, and take some measurements. If there was any stairway construction that violated the building code, Stan Cohen would find it. "I'll meet you at two o'clock Friday," he promised.

Later that day, Stan had a meeting in his SAC Construction office with two young accountants from Jay Rossin's firm. Just routine stuff, but the meeting lasted into the evening. While the accountants were there, Joyce called her husband several times. Each time he patiently took the call. Hi, Babe. See ya later, Babe. Bye, Babe. Love you. He was pleasant, affectionate. After the last call, Stan turned to the accountants with a grin. "You know, some people say our marriage is in trouble. Does that sound like we're in trouble?"

It certainly didn't, they agreed.

On Thursday, Joyce and Stan flew from Miami to Tampa together, Joyce to make the presentation on the interior design bid and Stan on other business. Joyce took a midafternoon flight back to Miami. Stan had left earlier and arrived back in the SAC Construction office about two or three o'clock in the afternoon. How did it go? Marvin

Sheldon asked his partner. Fine. Business as usual.

Stan left his office at the end of the day. Later Marvin couldn't remember what they had said to each other. It was a day like any other day. It was just so—*ordinary*.

Late that afternoon Joyce ran into her old friend Lynn Barkley, and they decided to stop for a drink at the outdoor bar at Monty's Bayside Restaurant in the Grove. Then Joyce went on to Scotty's gourmet grocery to pick up something for dinner.

About 8 P.M., Joyce and Stan dined at home alone together. After dinner, Stan called Scott Flower, his resident manager at Wolf Run Ranch, to see how things were going out in Steamboat Springs. Flower's wife, Trish, was expecting the couple's third child. "If she gets any bigger," Stan joked, "we'll have to move her with a truck."

Shortly before 10 P.M., Stan stepped into the shower in the white-tiled bathroom—his bathroom—behind the master suite on the second floor. The phone rang. It was Tyler Arroyo, one of Stan's employees at Riverside Suds, the three-two bar in Steamboat. Joyce answered the phone. There was casual small talk. How's the weather down there? Arroyo wanted to know. Good, Joyce replied. Arroyo asked to speak to Stan. Joyce said no, he's busy right now.

"I really need to talk to him about the Miami Ski Club party," Arroyo said. He needed funds from Stan to pay the bar bill the skiers had run up at the party.

"Stan, Tyler's on the phone," Arroyo heard Joyce yell. Then she said, "He's in the shower. Do you want me to have him call you back?"

"Yes, would you please have him call me." Arroyo hung up, expecting to hear from Stan, but no call came.

At 10:00, Stan watched his favorite television show, "Hill Street Blues," and lounged on the big brass bed reading the paper. The local news came on at 11:00. Former Miami Dolphins star Eugene "Mercury" Morris had won a new trial on his 1982 conviction in Miami for cocaine trafficking. A financial dispute between Universal Studios in Hollywood and the NBC television network had erupted into a threat to relocate filming of Miami's cops-and-cocaine series, "Miami Vice," to Southern California. The weather in Miami was sunny and breezy, with more of the same expected next day—highs in the 70s, lows in the 50s. Good sleeping weather.

Around midnight Stan drifted off to sleep. Joyce, a frequent insomniac, read for a while: *Love Is Letting Go of Fear,* by Gerald G. Jampolsky, M.D.

That night in Steamboat Springs, Miamians Geri Carroll and her daughter Kimberly were partying late. It was after 2 A.M. in Colorado—after 4 A.M. in Miami—when they ran into Joyce's friend Kathy Dickett at the Tugboat Lounge. The three women decided to return to the Carrolls' condominium in Steamboat for a nightcap. When they arrived at the condo, it was 3 A.M. in Steamboat Springs, 5 A.M. in Miami.

"Has anybody heard from Joyce lately?" Kathy Dickett asked.

"Let's call her right now!" Kimberly suggested. She dialed Joyce's Miami number, then passed the phone to Kathy. "Stan will kill me if he answers and recognizes my voice. It's so late," Kimberly explained.

Kathy Dickett took the phone. Joyce answered, they had a brief conversation, and then Kathy hung up. "It's okay—it was Joyce, not Stan," she said.

"What? I wanted to talk to her," Kimberly said. She redialed the Miami number, and again Joyce answered the phone. "Something's happened," she said suddenly. "I hear a noise. I've got to go now."

The phone went dead.

Concerned, Kimberly called again.

When she answered this time, Joyce Cohen was screaming.

# II

•

## Avenge
## Thy Father

# *Eight*

·

**T**he bedroom telephone rang in Marvin and Anne Sheldon's suburban Miami home. The phone was on Anne's side of the bed, and she picked it up automatically, struggling out of sleep.

It was Friday, March 7, 1986, shortly after 5:30 A.M.

Dr. Bob Salzman, Stan's fraternity buddy from their college days in Gainesville, was on the line. He was the family physician for the Sheldons, the Cohens, and most of their friends. "I think you'd better go to Stanley's house," he said. "He's been shot."

"What?" Anne asked, still groggy from sleep. "What hospital are they taking him to?"

"I don't think they are, Anne," Bob Salzman replied. "I think he's dead."

"It's Stanley," Anne repeated to Marvin as she hung up the phone.

"Who?"

Still half asleep, Marvin had no idea what had happened, or even which Stanley his wife was talking about. Anne and Marvin knew lots of Stanleys—Anne even had a brother named Stanley. Anne tried to collect her thoughts. She couldn't seem to remember exactly what Bob Salzman had said. Finally she decided he must have meant Stanley *Cohen*. Maybe he said so, she just couldn't think.

Anne called the Cohens' number. A stranger answered the phone.

"What's happened?" she asked. "Is Stanley dead?"

"I don't know," someone replied before the line went dead.

Thoroughly alarmed, Anne and Marvin threw on their clothes, jumped in the car, and raced to the Cohens' home on South Bayshore Drive. As they hurried through the cool predawn darkness, the Sheldons had no idea what to expect. Anne tried again to recall what Bob Salzman had told her. Maybe he said something about a robbery, but she couldn't be sure. They rushed on.

Just across the street from the Cohens' house, the phone rang in the Levensteins' penthouse condominium. C. J. Levenstein was already in the kitchen making coffee. Len was still in bed, half asleep. Both picked up extension telephones.

It was a friend, Miami attorney P. J. Carroll, whose wife Geri was out in Steamboat Springs at their vacation condominium with their daughter Kimberly. Geri and Kimberly had phoned P.J. frantically from Steamboat after that last terrifying call to Joyce Cohen.

Now, Len Levenstein struggled to understand what P. J. Carroll was trying to tell him. "Stanley's dead!" P.J. shouted, or, maybe, "Stanley's been murdered!" or "Stanley's been shot!" The words seemed to make no sense to Len. C.J., listening from the kitchen, dropped the phone and rushed into the bedroom.

"What? What?" Len said. "How could this happen? How did this happen?" He was aghast. P.J. said something about a break-in, a robbery, somebody shot Stan. Len couldn't be sure. Then P.J. hung up.

When Len understood that Stan Cohen was dead, he grew hysterical. Stan was such a dear friend, and just down the street from him at that very moment. It couldn't be true!

Len slammed down the phone and ran to the bathroom window. It overlooked South Bayshore Drive, and he could see down through the leafy darkness, gray dawn just lightening the sky. Emergency vehicles, vans, and police cars were clustered along the roadside. There were uniformed officers everywhere. Yellow crime-scene tape wound along the road. As C.J. raced behind her husband to the bathroom window, she rounded the corner of a mirrored wall too closely, slicing her toe open. She never felt the pain, never noticed the blood.

Dazed, C.J. and Len hastily threw on clothes and dashed across the street. The Cohen house and grounds were completely cordoned off. Len raced up to a uniformed officer. What had happened to his friend? But Len couldn't get much information. All he knew for certain was the unthinkable: his buddy Stan Cohen was dead.

Just then, Gerri Cohen and her fiancé, Steve Helfman, drove up in Helfman's Porsche. When the Sheldons pulled up a moment later, uniformed officers and lines of yellow tape barred their way. The police wouldn't let anyone in the house. Joyce Cohen was nowhere in sight.

"I'm Stanley's business partner," Marvin Sheldon told Sergeant Steve Vinson, a homicide detective already on the scene. "Tell me what happened."

"Well, there's been an accident," Sergeant Vinson replied.

"Is he dead?"

"I don't know." Sergeant Vinson refused to tell Marvin anything else.

"Well, can we wait here?"

"Yeah."

By then both friends and strangers had filled the roadway in front of the house. A sinister aura pervaded the very air: the eternal fascination with violent death. Small clumps and crowds began to form. Anne and Marvin Sheldon recognized Joyce's friend Myra Wenig.

Suddenly Marvin recalled that Stan had had the entire SAC Construction payroll with him— checks totaling $9,000, ready to be delivered on Friday as usual. Where was the payroll? Had it been stolen? What would Marvin do about getting the payroll checks to the waiting employees? But the police were unsympathetic. Marvin couldn't go into the house to search. No one knew anything about the payroll.

Inside the house, Miami homicide detective Jon Spear completed his tour of the scene and reached his first decision: He had to get Joyce Cohen to the homicide office downtown for a private interview. He had some questions about what Joyce had already told homicide detective Sergeant Tom Waterson, and he wanted a more detailed statement from her as soon as possible. Like all homicide investigators, Spear adhered to the "golden rule" that most leads in an investigation develop during the first twenty-four hours after the murder. After that, as Miami detectives put it, you're waiting for "the magic phone call" from an informant, and as each day passes, that prospect dims.

Joyce seemed dazed but calm, and she agreed to let Sergeant Waterson drive her to Miami Police Department headquarters. Waterson led her out the front door of the house, and as Joyce stumbled down the stone steps toward his department car she saw Gerri Cohen, anguished, distraught, weeping. The two women threw themselves blindly into each other's arms, moaning, sobbing, shaking, clinging, old tensions swept aside by their shared grief.

C. J. Levenstein hurried up. She, too, threw her arms around Joyce. "Joyce, my God, what happened?" she cried.

"Sorry, you can't talk to her now," Sergeant Waterson interrupted.

"Where are you taking her?" C.J. asked.

"To the homicide office downtown."

"But why?"

No response.

"Well, she can't go alone! She's been through enough! Can't I go with her?" C.J. persisted.

"All right," the detective replied.

C.J. clasped Joyce in a strong hug and walked her down to the car.

"Please, do me a favor," C.J. asked Waterson as they settled into the back seat. "Please take me back to my apartment for a minute. I need some shoes and my purse." For the first time, C.J. had noticed that she was barefoot, and her cut toe was bleeding badly. Later, a homicide detective asked her suspiciously, "How did you get that blood on your foot?"

As he drove his unmarked department car back downtown to the police station, Detective Spear pondered the task before him. He knew he had to isolate Mrs. Cohen and interview her immediately. Like all seasoned homicide detectives, Spear approached his investigation with a simple premise: If you find two people in a house, one murdered and one alive, the survivor is a suspect. Automatically. It's just that simple, Spear thought. Mrs. Cohen was his first suspect.

Spear knew he would be able to establish some rapport with Joyce Cohen in an interview. A compact, powerfully built man who looked like a cop even in the street clothes he wore to work, Spear had a soft-spoken manner and friendly blue eyes that crinkled at the corners when he smiled. In a two-man homicide investigation team, he was the classic "good cop" half: approachable, reasonable, considerate, despite his slightly brooding, melancholy air. He looked like a cop who was saddened by all the misery he saw on the streets. He looked like a cop you could trust.

In fact, Spear was looking forward to the challenge of interviewing Joyce Cohen. Interrogation—especially when it led to confession—was his favorite part of the job. After more than a decade as a homicide investigator, he considered himself a human lie detector. He believed he could literally *feel* when someone was lying.

Six months earlier, Spear had demonstrated his interrogation skills for a reporter from *The Wall Street Journal* who followed the "real-life Miami Vice cops" around the city for several days. Miami was hot: murder capital of the nation, with 23.7 homicides per 100,000 residents in 1984, triple the national average. The reporter's adventures in Miami led to a front-page *Wall Street Journal* story on October 16, 1985, complete with portraits of Spear and his partner at the time, Antonio Rodriguez.

The *Journal* article detailed Spear's interrogation of a murder suspect as seen by the reporter through a two-way mirror. Spear held the suspect's hand in both his own, softly, gently, patiently coaxing him to tell his story. "The truth wants to come out," he said. "I can feel it running from your hand to mine. Let it out." The suspect confessed.

Shortly after eight o'clock that Friday morning, Detective Spear parked in the secured lot next to the looming, orange-brick Miami Police Department headquarters downtown. He crossed to the back door, then took the elevator up to the fifth-floor homicide office. It was one large room, bisected by rows of small metal government-issue desks with carrel-type dividers, one desk for each detective. The dividers and desk tops reflected the detectives' special affections: photographs of wives, sweethearts, babies growing into teenagers, jokes, drawings, mementos of their lives in the war against crime. Pictures of a pretty, dark-haired daughter were pinned to Detective Spear's divider. A nameplate that read INSPECTOR CLOUSEAU sat on his desk, a long-running joke with a former partner.

Large plate-glass windows faced north, overlooking shabby rooftops and the perpetual crawl of traffic on Interstate 95. There was a big clock on the wall, with hours from one through twenty-four, military-style. Time stood still at 23:30, the clock having long since broken. On a bulletin board littered with cop, judge, and lawyer cartoons was elaborate calligraphy: THOU SHALT NOT KILL.

When Spear arrived at his office, Joyce Cohen was already there waiting for him, with C. J. Levenstein and Sergeant Waterson. Gil Martin, a day-shift identification technician, arrived to take swabs of Joyce Cohen's hands.

"What's this for?" she asked.

"Just routine," Martin replied.

"But I've washed my hands. Twice," she said.

"That's okay."

Martin carefully swabbed Joyce's hands with cotton. He used a separate swab for each palm, another for the web between the thumb and the forefinger of each hand and the back of each hand. Each individual swab was placed in a separate plastic sleeve, which was labeled with the date, the time, the technician's initials, the location, the area swabbed, the subject, and the case number.

It was official. Stanley Cohen's murder had a number. And a suspect.

Detective Spear took Joyce Cohen into Interview Room Two. C. J. Levenstein waited outside. "Do you think Joyce Cohen is on drugs or stoned?" a detective asked her.

"No!" C.J. was upset. "The woman's husband has just been murdered, for God's sake!"

Someone asked C.J. if Joyce had an attorney. Why would Joyce have—or need—an attorney? C.J. wondered. She decided to call her husband, Len. After all, he had a law degree, even though he was no longer practicing. He would know what to do.

"C.J., I don't know what to tell you," Len replied. "Maybe you should call P. J. Carroll and see if he can get someone for her." She called P.J.

Interview Room Two was a small cubicle with a worn brown sofa, two armchairs, and some cheap prints hanging crookedly too far up the wall. The attempt at domesticity was unconvincing. Still, Spear always used Room Two when he interviewed females. He thought they were less intimidated there than in Room One, with its bare table, three chairs, and looming two-way surveillance mirror. And he wanted his suspect to be comfortable.

Spear motioned Joyce to the sofa and positioned himself directly across from her in a sagging chair. He leaned forward, elbows on his knees, hands clasped. He smiled slightly and began. "I need to talk to you now," he told her softly, "so that I can find out exactly what happened. You have to help us find the person who did this terrible thing to your husband. Tell me everything you remember. Tell me what happened."

"Where do I begin?" Joyce asked.

"At the beginning," Spear replied. He waited patiently.

She was Joyce Cohen, age thirty-five, born July 18, 1950. She and her husband, Stan Cohen, lived at 1665 South Bayshore Drive in the Grove.

"Did anything unusual happen there last night?" Spear prompted her gently.

Joyce continued. She and her husband had been upstairs in their bedroom together. Around 11:30 P.M. she went downstairs to get a glass of warm milk to help her sleep—she always had trouble sleeping. As she walked down the stairs, she heard a distinctive noise— the sound of the latch on the gate next to the house. She was frightened. She ran back upstairs and told Stan.

Joyce said Stan pulled on a pair of shorts and got his gun, a revolver he kept in a beige holster. Together they went out the kitchen door to the backyard to investigate the noise. They found the gate standing open but saw no one. After latching the gate, Joyce and Stan went back upstairs.

Detective Spear waited.

After that, Joyce resumed, Stan went to sleep. But she couldn't sleep, so she read for a while. Then she went downstairs to her son Shawn's bedroom to sort clothes for a garage sale. Her Doberman pinscher, Mischief, was with her. Joyce had deactivated the home's alarm system so that she wouldn't accidentally set if off and awaken her husband.

Joyce said she left her son's bedroom and walked toward the living room. The phone in the family room rang and she picked it up. It was her friend Kimberly Carroll calling from Steamboat Springs, Colorado. While she was talking to Kimberly, Joyce heard a noise. She hung up the phone. The dog ran into the kitchen to investigate the noise and Joyce followed. That's when she saw that the kitchen door was standing open, the glass pane broken out. She called 911 or activitated the burglar alarm, she couldn't remember which. Then she hurried toward the dining room. Suddenly she saw a shadowy figure running down the stairs, through the foyer, and out the front door. The figure had yelled, "Let's get the fuck out of here!" She thought it was a Latin accent.

Then Joyce said she ran upstairs and found her husband lying in bed. The back of his head was bleeding. She raced to get a towel and tried to stop the blood. She had been hysterical.

When Joyce finished her account, Detective Spear asked a few questions to clarify the sequence of events. Then he was ready to find out about Joyce's marriage, the quality of her relationship with her husband. Possible motive.

"When was the last time you had sex with your husband?" he began carefully. Spear considered sex a good barometer of a relationship.

"Like, in a three-week period." Joyce replied. Spear thought she seemed reasonably calm about the subject. He let it pass.

Spear moved on. Something else was bothering him. "I think there are some inconsistencies in your story," he began cautiously.

But Joyce was suddenly hysterical again. She leaped off the sofa, shoved open the door, and ran out of the room. Sobbing loudly, she ran to C. J. Levenstein, who was waiting in the hall. C.J. threw her arms around Joyce's heaving shoulders. "Hasn't she had enough?" she railed at Spear, who had followed Joyce out of the interview room. "Leave her alone a minute!"

"I just want to go home!" Joyce sobbed hysterically. "I just want to be with my husband! Get everyone out of my house! Don't touch his things!"

With those few words, Joyce Cohen threw the entire murder investigation into chaos.

Try as they might, neither Spear nor his supervisor, Ed Carberry, could persuade Mrs. Cohen to continue the interview. And now she had, in effect, ordered the police out of her house. Belatedly, the detectives asked Joyce to sign a consent-to-search form for the house, but she refused. That meant they would have to get a search warrant before they could investigate the crime scene—or remove Stan Cohen's body. The ID technicians already on the scene would have to be pulled out and the entire homicide scene held until a warrant was prepared, signed by a judge, and served at the house. Spear and Carberry knew it would take hours.

Spear gritted his teeth. If only Joyce Cohen hadn't had her friend there to run to, he thought, he could have handled her. Now it was a disaster.

Just then more friends arrived, Arthur and Carol Sheldon. Spear tried to persuade Arthur Sheldon to reason with Joyce, but it was obvious that his interview with her was over. Sheldon asked Spear to release Joyce Cohen to him. He would take her back to C. J. Levenstein's home so she could rest and calm down. They would be in touch.

Spear had no choice. As Joyce's friends escorted her out of the homicide office, Spear fumed. Then he picked up the phone and called the Cohens' home number. Get everyone out of the house, he ordered the cop who answered. Set up a perimeter and just hold the scene. No one is allowed in the house, not even Mrs. Cohen. (Especially not Mrs. Cohen, he thought.) We're going to have to get a warrant!

At the Cohens' house, Sergeant Vinson herded all the officers and technicians out the door. Mrs. Cohen, he told them, had decided she didn't want them in her house after all. He repeated the story Detective Spear had told him. Spear had asked Mrs. Cohen a question she didn't appreciate: "When was the last time you had sex with your husband?" Loud guffaws from the cops.

None of the cops could remember being thrown out of a homicide scene in the middle of their investigation by a grieving widow. They made the obvious assumption. There must be some reason Joyce Cohen didn't want them there. She must have something to hide. Mrs. Cohen's status as a suspect rose.

As she packed up her equipment and hauled it outside, Identification Technician Sylvia Romans felt frustrated by the interruption in her routine. A slender, attractive young woman who wore glasses and had a studious air, Romans was an FBI-trained technician who had been with the Miami Police Department about two and a half years. This was her first big case as lead technician—her chance to prove herself—and now her work had been interrupted barely an hour after she got started.

Romans's first task at the Cohen house had been a tour of the crime scene, inside and out, with Sergeant Vinson. Then she had begun photographing the exterior of the scene in sequence. Her photographs, assembled in order, would reflect each aspect of the outside of the Cohens' house and surrounding grounds. Then Romans had moved to the point of entry at the rear of the house, the kitchen door with the smashed pane of glass. She took close-ups of the door, the doorjamb, the smashed glass, the hunk of coral rock lying outside. She photographed the entire kitchen, right down to a rubber glove lying in the sink and a cup of milk sitting, forgotten, in the microwave. On the island in the kitchen was a paperback copy of *Love Is Letting Go of Fear,* the book Joyce Cohen told Detective Spear she had been reading that night. Next to it was a cassette tape: *Girls Like Me,* by Tanya Tucker.

Romans had begun to photograph the dining room when Sergeant Vinson stopped her. She had not yet reached the crime scene, the master suite upstairs where Stanley Cohen's body lay, still gently seeping blood into puddles and small rivers. There would be no photographs documenting the corpse's appearance at that hour of the morning.

With officers guarding the doors to the now-empty house, Sergeant Vinson, Sylvia Romans, and others gathered in the backyard to wait for the search warrant. In the meantime, the crime scene was secured. No one was going in, nothing inside the house would be removed or altered. It would all be there, just as they left it, when the cops were allowed back in to finish their work.

There was one crucial exception: something that would be changed irrevocably by the mere passage of time and the operation of natural laws—the body of Stanley Cohen. The cooling of the body after death, the chemical changes that cause rigidity of the muscles, the seepage of blood out of vessels and into surrounding tissues, the gravitational pull settling and staining tissues red at their lowest point—algor mortis, rigor mortis, livor mortis—all would continue their inexorable progress, forever altering the condition of the corpse. No one would be there to mark the changes. There would be no photographs or measurements from which to reconstruct the body's condition early that morning.

With each hour that passed, evidence faded forever on what would prove to be a central issue in the crime: the precise time of Stan Cohen's death.

That morning, Romans, Vinson, and the others sprawled comfortably in the shade of the red gazebo in the Cohens' backyard, passing the time, sharing speculation about the case. It looked like a home invasion robbery gone wrong, they thought. Hours passed. It seemed the search warrant was taking forever. At lunchtime someone brought submarine sandwiches and Cokes back to the troops. They waited patiently for the signal to resume their work inside the house.

Joyce Cohen's friend Lynn Barkley had gone to the beach on Key Biscayne early that Friday morning for a photo shoot. On his way back home, he drove past the Cohens' house and saw the yellow crime-scene tape. He pulled over, hopped out of his car, and spoke to a Miami police officer. I'm Lynn Barkley, he introduced himself, a friend of the Cohens. What happened? Is there anything I can do to help? The officer took Barkley's address and phone number. Homicide detectives invited him down to the station for an interview.

Officer Edward Golden, a uniformed cop, stood guard on the stone steps near the front door of the Cohen house, waiting, like everyone else, for the search warrant. As his gaze wandered down to the front yard, he saw something gleaming in the dense undergrowth. He stepped over and took a closer look. It was a blue steel revolver. Golden called out to Sergeant Vinson at the rear of the house. Vinson and Sylvia Romans raced around the corner, then cautiously approached the revolver, which was lying in a little nest of foliage. It must be the murder weapon: a .38-caliber Smith & Wesson, apparently tossed aside by the killer.

No one must touch it, they knew. Romans wouldn't even take a photograph of the weapon until the search warrant was served. There must be no mistakes, no slip-ups in handling this crucial piece of evidence. Officer Golden then stood guard over the weapon as well as the front door to the house. Vinson and Romans took up their vigil in the gazebo again, still waiting for the warrant.

Meanwhile, uniformed officers were dispatched on a door-to-door search of the Cohens' immediate neighborhood, looking for anyone who had heard or seen anything unusual that night or early morning. They got a few reports of a suspicious man ringing doorbells, apparently panhandling for money.

Then something more promising turned up. Neighbor Jerry Mandina, who lived directly across the street from the Cohens, told the officers he had been sitting near an open window from 3:30 A.M. until nearly 5:30 A.M. that morning, working on some accounts. Shortly after 5 A.M., Mandina had heard a strange noise. He said it sounded like a gunshot.

# *Nine*

·

A cross the street from the crime scene, at the Levensteins' penthouse condominium, friends and relatives of the murdered man began to congregate: Anne and Marvin Sheldon, Myra Wenig, George Johnnides, Gerri Cohen and her fiancé, Steve Helfman, and Helfman's parents. They clumped together in small, sad groups, trying to make some sense of the tragedy. No one was in charge. Joyce Cohen, of course, should be the one to make decisions about funeral arrangements. But everyone could see that Joyce was in no condition to handle the necessary details. Gerri, too, was in a state of shock. She had phoned her brother Gary, who was vacationing in Jamaica, but he hadn't yet returned her call. No one seemed to know what else to do.

C. J. Levenstein and Arthur and Carol Sheldon had brought Joyce back to the Levensteins' after the disastrous interview with Detective Jon Spear. They were still angry that the detective had upset Joyce so. She looked terrible, they thought. Her face was red and swollen, and she couldn't seem to stop crying. Everyone came to Joyce that morning, her friends, Stan's friends, Stan's family, all of them drawn together by their grief. They tried to comfort Joyce. But she was inconsolable.

At Joyce's request, C.J. called Dr. Lawrence Cohn, a psychiatrist

Joyce knew, and asked for an appointment. The psychiatrist couldn't see Joyce immediately, but he did speak with her by phone. Then he called in a prescription for her, to help her get through the next few days.

There was a call from an attorney, Alan Ross, who had been contacted through P. J. Carroll, the lawyer who was the Cohens' friend. An immediate appointment was arranged, and Anne Sheldon offered to drive Joyce to the attorney's office. In the car, Joyce told Anne about the interview with Detective Spear and how he had asked her that question: "When was the last time you had sex with your husband?"

Alan Ross was a partner in the law firm of Weiner Robbins Tunkey & Ross, which lawyers shortened to Weiner Robbins. The firm's expertise was in criminal law, and Ross himself had a well-earned reputation as one of Miami's premier drug lawyers. It was a specialty that paid handsomely, especially in the halcyon years of the 1970s and 1980s when "square grouper," plastic-wrapped bales of marijuana, bobbed in the current along Florida's coast and those who harvested the crop frequently found themselves in need of a criminal defense lawyer.

Weiner Robbins occupied two floors in a glass-walled high-rise near the Grove. Together Joyce Cohen and Anne Sheldon rode the elevator up to Ross's office. While Joyce went in to confer with Ross, Anne stayed behind in the client reception room, which was designed with the firm's particular clientele in mind. It was not unheard of in Miami for a client to attack his own lawyer, especially in the event of an unfavorable outcome at trial. A prudent attention to security was evident in the Weiner Robbins reception area. There was an alarm system with a glowing red light at the elevator door. The doors from the reception area into the attorneys' offices were securely locked. Entry was controlled by the firm's receptionist, who sat in an enclosed booth.

Lighting in the reception area was subdued, and seating for clients was discreetly arranged in little alcoves that afforded a semblance of privacy. In addition to newspapers and *Florida Trend* magazine, Weiner Robbins provided practical reading matter for its waiting clients, racks of brochures with titles like "What to Do if You Are Arrested in Florida."

Inside his private glass-walled corner office, Alan Ross studied Joyce Cohen. She looked, he thought, absolutely distraught. She was wild, sobbing uncontrollably. He had never met Mrs. Cohen before, never heard of her or her wealthy husband, never noticed the big stone house on the corner of South Bayshore Drive and 17th Avenue. Ross didn't really hang out in Coconut Grove with what he thought of as the Grovey types. And he never socialized with his clients. In his early thirties, he was very much the married young professional, with a pretty blond wife and two young childen. Ross's idea of a good weekend was taking the family out on his big sportfisherman, aptly named the *Knot Guilty*.

As Joyce Cohen haltingly told Ross about the tragedy she had just suffered, he watched and listened with few interruptions. Her ordeal had been so horrible, he thought, and her emotional state was so severe, perhaps a doctor should give her a shot of Valium or something to calm her down, just let her go to sleep for a while. Joyce told Ross that she wanted to cooperate with the police in their investigation. After all, it was she who had begged them to come to her house right after the murder. But then the police had been, as Ross thought of it, less than kind in their treatment of Mrs. Cohen, which upset her even more.

And now there was another problem. There might be illegal drugs in the house, Joyce said. Just recreational drugs, maybe some cocaine. She wasn't sure what her husband might have hidden in the house. But when she thought about that, she had been afraid to sign the consent-to-search form that Detective Spear gave her. She didn't know what to do, so she did nothing.

Mrs. Cohen was right not to sign the consent-to-search form, Ross told her. In fact, it was one of Ross's two golden rules for clients. Never consent to a search, and never talk to cops without a lawyer present. If you sign a consent-to-search form, you could be prosecuted for things you didn't know were even in your house. If the cops get a search warrant, on the other hand, they have to specify exactly what they are looking for and why. Then, with some exceptions, the cops can only seize what they have described in the warrant.

But still, Ross thought, this shouldn't be a big problem. In the first place, a consent-to-search wasn't really necessary. Mrs. Cohen herself had called the cops to the house, and they had already been inside. Clearly she had given them permission to search the crime scene. But Ross didn't know about his client's outburst—"Get everyone out of my house!"

Moreover, a small amount of recreational drugs should be inconsequential in the search of a house where a murder had taken place, Ross explained. Surely the Dade County State Attorney's Office would agree not to prosecute Mrs. Cohen for any recreational drugs that might be found in the house. He could probably straighten this out with a few phone calls, Ross said.

By the end of the conference, Ross had agreed to represent Joyce Cohen, and she trusted her new lawyer. A big, bearded man who exuded confidence, Ross was outgoing, friendly, reassuring. He told Joyce to go home with Anne Sheldon. He urged her to get some rest. He would let her know what he worked out with the cops. Like many clients before her, Joyce was relieved to leave everything to Alan Ross.

After his new client left, Ross picked up the phone and called the Miami homicide office. When he got Lieutenant Ed Carberry on the line, he explained that he was representing Mrs. Joyce Cohen and had heard there was some problem about searching the house. That's right, Carberry told him, we want a consent-to-search and your client refused to sign it.

"Ed," Ross began, "you don't need it. It's ridiculous. I don't understand why you need a consent-to-search."

"Well, you know, that's what we want," Carberry replied. "We're going to cross all the T's here. We want to do it right. Look, tell me what the problem is. Is it drugs?"

"Are we talking on the record or off the record?" Ross asked.

"We can talk off the record," Carberry answered.

"Yeah, so, the problem is drugs," Ross confirmed. "Let's assume you find drugs there."

"This is a homicide investigation," Carberry said. "We're not interested in drugs."

"Well, great," Ross responded. "Then you certainly won't have a problem getting the state attorney to tell me that Mrs. Cohen is immune from any drug prosecution."

"Yeah, okay, we could do that with regard to personal drugs for personal consumption."

"I have no idea what you might find in that house," Ross hedged.

The conversation ended and Ross expected to hear from Assistant State Attorney George Yoss, confirming his client's immunity from prosecution for any drugs found in the house. With that understanding, he could agree to the search of Mrs. Cohen's home. But that call never came. Instead, Ross had one more call from homicide: "We're going to get a search warrant."

"Go ahead, get a warrant," Ross replied curtly. As he banged the phone down, Ross was frustrated. He didn't understand why he and Carberry hadn't been able to reach an agreement. He knew the cops would think his client must be guilty of something, that she must have something to hide, or else she would consent to the search.

But Ross wasn't worried about what the cops thought. He was concerned about the specter of public perception. What would people think of a widow who wouldn't let the cops search the crime scene for clues to her husband's killer? A widow who "forced" homicide detectives to get a search warrant? But as long as the facts were reported accurately—that Mrs. Cohen herself had called the police into her home right after the murder and they had searched the house for at least three hours before the dispute arose—Ross didn't expect too much fallout.

Even if there was negative publicity for Mrs. Cohen, Ross thought, he really had no choice about the advice he had given her. No matter how he turned it over in his mind, he always reached the same conclusion. It was malpractice for a lawyer to advise a client to consent to a search when there was reason to believe something illegal would be found in the house.

Downtown at the police station, Ed Carberry walked over to Tom Waterson. "We're going to need a search warrant," he said. Waterson wasn't surprised. He had been standing in the hall when Joyce Cohen burst out of the interview room sobbing. With a sigh, Waterson sat down to draft the search warrant for the Cohen house. He carefully prepared the form, identifying the homicide and the premises and describing evidence the cops would search for: latent fingerprints, blood and tissue samples, weapons, projectiles, basically anything pertaining to the crime of murder. There was no mention of drugs.

Usually Waterson took his warrants straight to a judge for signature, but this one was special. He decided to have one of the assistant state attorneys look it over first, just to be sure he hadn't missed something. He called Assistant State Attorney David Waksman.

A seasoned prosecutor, Waksman was a particular favorite of the Miami detectives. He was always available to the cops, always ready to give advice about procedure or look over a warrant. The cops trusted Waksman. They felt he spoke their language, understood their concerns. With good reason. For six years, Waksman himself had been a cop, working the South Bronx in New York City, at the station known as Fort Apache.

Waksman carefully went over the search warrant. It was good. He had one minor revision, then the form was ready for signature by a judge. It took a while, but finally Waterson headed back to the Cohen house with a fully executed search warrant in hand. The examination of the crime scene could proceed.

ID Technician Sylvia Romans was relieved to resume her examination of the crime scene. First, she photographed a close-up of the search warrant at the scene, which was routine. Then she walked through the front yard to the spot where Officer Golden was standing guard over the revolver he had spotted in the brush. Romans photographed the weapon as it lay in the undergrowth. Then her partner, Gil Martin, lifted the gun gently, carefully, so that no fragments of evidence would be lost. Romans took more close-ups. Finally, Martin placed the gun in a brown paper bag and secured it in the crime scene van. They couldn't take time to examine the weapon. There was far too much work to do at the scene.

Romans walked back into the house and resumed her photographic record of the path that intruders would have taken from the kitchen to Stan Cohen's bedroom. She wouldn't venture upstairs to photograph the body, however, until someone arrived from the medical examiner's office. She couldn't take a chance on disturbing the scene until the medical examiner was finished.

It was nearly 2:30 P.M. when a medical examiner was summoned to the crime scene, a full nine hours since the murder was reported. Dade County deputy chief medical examiner Charles V. Wetli, M.D., took the call on his car phone as he drove north on Interstate 95. Dr. Wetli was headed to a television interview about the Dade County Medical Examiner's Office, his favorite subject. As far as he was concerned, it was the best job in Dade County—interesting, exciting, intellectually challenging work. No two cases were ever the same. And it was important work, Dr. Wetli believed. People really relied on his conclusions about a death, and he liked to get things right.

Dr. Wetli had been on "scene call" since 7 A.M. that Friday and would remain on the roster until 7 A.M. the following day. Scene call, in the parlance of the Medical Examiner's Office, meant that Wetli would examine the corpse at all homicide scenes reported in Dade County during that twenty-four-hour period. Since the county's murder rate was astronomically high, medical examiners usually took scene call in pairs, with one serving as backup, so that all scenes could be covered expeditiously.

Now Dr. Wetli's scene call partner for the day, Dr. Ken Warner, was on the line. He had just received a call from the Miami Police Department. "Another 'scene' has just happened," Dr. Warner said, referring, of course, to another Miami homicide. "Plus they want somebody at this homicide scene in Coconut Grove. They're ready for you now."

"It sounds like it might be kind of a touchy case," Wetli commented to Warner. "Why don't you go ahead to the other scene? And I'll just cancel my TV thing. I'm going to head south to Coconut Grove."

It was nearly 3 P.M. when Dr. Wetli drove into the driveway of the Cohen house. The cops were glad to see him arrive. After he completed his examination of the body, they could finish going over the murder site for evidence. It was the unwritten rule of homicide investigation that the scene "belonged" to the police investigators, but the body "belonged" to the medical examiner.

Dr. Wetli's car, a ten-year-old Checker Marathon, was referred to as "the hearse" by the cops. After years of performing autopsies on traffic accident victims, Wetli had concluded that from a safety standpoint, there were only five or six cars worth buying. So he bought the only one on the list he could afford, a Checker Marathon, a massive, ungainly, heavy machine built by the Checker taxicab company. He liked it so well that he bought another for his wife. Then he installed a special safety device, a series of overlapping mirrors on the windshield to eliminate blind spots in rear vision. Of course, Checker had stopped building the Marathon years ago, so Dr. Wetli stocked up on any parts he thought he might need on the road. His trunk was stuffed with spare parts, belts, and tools, in addition to the rubber gloves, lights, camera, flash, and other medical examiner equipment.

Dr. Wetli examined the nude body of Stanley Cohen lying in a pool of blood on the floor of the master bedroom. Cohen had died about 5:15 or 5:30 that morning, he was told. Fire rescue had arrived shortly before 6 A.M. and had found the victim face down on the bed, head on its right side on the pillow. No one reported rigor mortis that morning. There seemed to be no dispute as to time of death: approximately 5:15 to 5:30 A.M.

Dr. Wetli listened carefully to the observations reported by the police and fire rescue paramedics. Since so much time had already passed, his examination of Stanley Cohen's corpse was rather cursory. He noted the bullet wounds to the back of the head. Then he and Sylvia Romans located a projectile in the bloody pillow and removed it. Wetli took numerous photographs from all angles. The body was lifted slightly so that he could photograph the back. The photographs, sixty-eight in all, including those which would be taken at the autopsy, would be developed as 35-millimeter slides in the medical examiner's own photo lab. Now Stanley Cohen had an official medical examiner's case number: 86-626.

When he finished his examination and photographs, Dr. Wetli called for what medical examiners still refer to as "the wagon" to take Stan Cohen's body to the Medical Examiner's building at the outskirts of the Jackson Memorial Hospital complex in Miami. There the body would be refrigerated until the autopsy the following day.

After Dr. Wetli's departure, the examination of the murder site resumed in earnest. Once Sylvia Romans finished documenting the scene with photographs, the investigators began the tedious process of collecting physical evidence of the murder: latent fingerprints from the kitchen door and the bedroom, the bloody pillow and pillowcase from the bed, another handgun found in the bedroom, two holsters, blood samples from the bedroom and from a bloody spot on the low ceiling over the stairwell, and so on. Each item of evidence had to be separately photographed, collected, tagged, and listed on a duplicate set of inventories, one of which would accompany the evidence into the police van while the other was left at the Cohen house.

Careful examination of a murder scene can take ten or twelve hours, even with an experienced team of technicians. And the Cohen house and grounds were large. Sylvia Romans and her colleagues knew they would be spending most of the night there.


That afternoon at the Miami Police Department's downtown headquarters, Alan Ross accompanied Joyce Cohen back to Detective Spear's fifth-floor office to continue her aborted interview. Ross told the detectives that Mrs. Cohen was anxious to cooperate with the investigation, even though she was very tired and upset. This time his client would give a formal statement about the crime, under oath, in the presence of a court reporter. Detective Spear and Lieutenant Carberry settled in to listen to Mrs. Cohen's recollection of events.

Joyce recounted what she had already told them earlier that day. When she finished, Spear asked a few questions to clarify the exact sequence of events. Then he worked to establish the time of each occurrence.

Stan had watched the television program "Hill Street Blues" from 10 to 11 P.M. Then he watched the news. That made it 11:30 or so. By the time Joyce and Stan went out to investigate the noise and came back upstairs, it was about midnight. Is that right? Spear asked.

"Yes," Joyce replied.

Spear continued. Then they talked for a while, turned off the television, and Joyce read for a few minutes. She went down to Shawn's room, made one trip back upstairs carrying clothes, then went back to Shawn's room again. She had been in his room maybe five or ten minutes when the phone rang and she ran to answer it. The caller was Kimberly Carroll, Joyce said. Kimberly and her mother, Geri, had been partying at their condo in Steamboat Springs, Colorado.

"What makes you think they were partying?" Spear asked.

"Well, it was three o'clock in the morning," Joyce answered. "They are partying, I think. By Kimberly's voice. I can tell they were partying. She said, 'Hey, what's going on.' They don't usually call me that late."

"You just said three o'clock in the morning. Is that three o'clock their time or our time?"

"I think three o'clock our time," Joyce said. "It's later there—no, it's later here, so it was one o'clock their time, two hours earlier there. I guess that's about it, I think."

"It came out very quickly that it was three o'clock," Spear said.

"For some reason—I don't know why, but it seemed like three when Kimberly called," Joyce said. "You can verify that with them, what time they called me. You can check that time with whatever the operator says."

Spear moved on to other questions. But he tucked the topic away at the back of his mind. Time was becoming a problem in this case. A neighbor said he thought he had heard the sound of a shot around 5 A.M., but the time sequence that Joyce Cohen had just outlined didn't seem to add up, didn't jibe with what she had told them earlier—that her husband had been shot moments before she called 911 at 5:25 A.M.

What happened to the nearly three hours between midnight, when Joyce and Stan returned to bed, and 3 A.M.? And if Joyce heard the noise of the break-in or the shooting at 3 A.M. while she was on the phone with Kimberly Carroll, why was it nearly 5:30 A.M. before she called 911? What happened between 3 A.M. and 5:30 A.M.? There was just too much time unaccounted for, Spear thought. Could Joyce Cohen be confused about the times? Was she asleep part of the night? Was she high on something and afraid to mention it? Or was she lying?

Spear went back to the handgun that Stan took with him when they went outside to investigate the suspicious noise. Where was the gun when Joyce went downstairs to Shawn's room, he wanted to know.

"Well," Joyce said, "when we had come back upstairs—before, he had laid it on the nightstand next to the phone and I had picked it up, and I said why are you leaving this here? He said leave it here for now. And it was in a case then."

Spear was instantly alert. He knew the probable murder weapon had been found in the Cohen's front yard. Now Mrs. Cohen recalled that she had picked up her husband's gun that night. Was it possible that Stan Cohen had been shot with his own gun? And would they find his widow's fingerprints on it?

Ed Carberry took over with further questions about the shadowy figure Joyce had seen running out the front door. But she said she had seen very little—it was dark—and she really couldn't give any better description.

Spear concluded the interview with a final question: "Is everything you told us the truth?"

"Yes."

After slightly more than an hour, the interview was over, but by then, Detective Jon Spear, the self-professed human lie detector, had made up his mind: Joyce Cohen was lying. He didn't know why, didn't know which parts of her story were false, but he was certain he would find out. It was just a matter of time.

Across town, someone else was searching for leads in Stan Cohen's murder: Richard Hays, Stan's longtime lawyer. When Marvin Sheldon had called him that morning to deliver the terrible news, Hays was in the middle of a real estate closing in his office. He would never forget that conversation.

"Dick, you'd better sit down," Marvin began.

Hays sat abruptly. "What's the matter?"

"Stanley's dead. He was shot and killed at five-thirty this morning in his own bed."

Hays was overcome with chills. "Well, do you know who did it?" he asked after a moment.

"I have no further details," Marvin said. "The police are there. I'll tell you what develops."

Hays was in shock the rest of the day. But he knew what he had to do: he had to review all the files on the many matters he had handled for Stan Cohen over the years and prepare a list of enemies. There were those, he knew, who had it in for Stan—a lawyer who had threatened him once, real estate brokers who thought Stan had screwed them out of commissions, construction projects with angry owners, people involved in various business disputes that had led to hard feelings. Hays knew fugitive Miami attorney Frankie Diaz and was aware of some of his business dealings with Stan. And there was that whole mess with Stan's plane, the Sabreliner with all the defects that Stan had refused to pay for. The list would be a long one.

But the police never called Hays about Stan Cohen, never asked him for leads, never followed up on any of the names he would have given them. He couldn't understand it.

Richard Hays wasn't the only one to wonder whether Stan's murder was business-related. Late that night, Anne Sheldon suddenly turned to her husband, Marvin. "This doesn't have anything to do with business, does it?"

"No," Marvin replied. "It has nothing to do with business. Nobody's mad at us."

"Would you be offended if I asked you to sleep in the other room, just in case?" Anne was only half kidding.

That afternoon, while Joyce was being interviewed at the Miami Police Department, C. J. Levenstein called Shawn Cohen's school to ask them to send him home. When Shawn was summoned to the dean's office, he assumed he was in trouble again. Just another whacking, he thought. Big deal. But when he walked in the door, there was a priest. They told him that his father had been killed and he had to catch a flight home right away. Shawn was stunned. What about my mother, he asked. No one knew. No one had thought to ask when C. J. Levenstein called from Miami.

As he headed home on the plane that afternoon, Shawn was in turmoil. He had no idea what had happened to his family. It must have been a car accident, he thought. Until he was picked up at Miami International Airport by Myra Wenig, Shawn didn't know whether his mother was dead or alive.

• • •

Late that night prosecutor David Waksman stopped by the Cohen house for the second time. He had spent several hours there during the afternoon, then left to meet his wife for a wedding at Vizcaya, an Italian Renaissance–style mansion built on Biscayne Bay by industrialist James Deering in 1914. Now a museum open to the public, the villa and its formal gardens were the site of many Miami weddings. The Cohen house was only a few miles away, and throughout the wedding, Waksman couldn't help wondering what was going on there, what evidence was being discovered. After the ceremony, he hurried back to the crime scene.

It was nearly midnight when Waksman arrived, and the ID technicians were still hard at work. They hadn't seen any drugs in the house after all, although there was some drug paraphernalia in a bedroom drawer: a sieve, a grinder, seeds, some small containers with residue, nothing dramatic. David Waksman headed on home.

All that day, Gerri Cohen had been trying to contact her brother Gary, who was vacationing in Jamaica. When he finally returned her call that evening around 11 P.M., Gerri was exhausted, still half in shock herself. But she had to give him the terrible news of their father's murder.

Gary's first words stunned his sister. Did Joyce have anything to do with this? That thought hadn't even occurred to Gerri.

After she hung up the phone, Gerri called the Miami Police homicide office. When Sergeant Vinson answered, she asked him bluntly whether Joyce could have had anything to do with her father's murder. "I think you'd better come right down and talk to us," he replied.

It was close to midnight by the time Gerri Cohen and Steve Helfman arrived downtown at the fifth-floor homicide office. Sergeant Vinson and Detective Spear were still there. When they told her that parts of her stepmother's story sounded suspicious, Gerri made up her mind that her stepmother was somehow involved in her father's death.

"What can we do to help?" she asked.

# *Ten*

•

$O$n Saturday, March 8, *The Miami Herald* ran a front-page story on the Cohen murder under the headline PROMINENT BUILDER MURDERED IN HOME. But the subheadline set the tone of the article: Wife Keeps Police Outside for More Than Eight Hours. For many Miamians, that was enough—they knew Joyce Cohen had murdered her husband.

Alan Ross was furious. He thought the story gave the misleading impression that his client had met cops at the door and, after letting them have a quick look at her husband's body, barred them from the house. The misinformation, Ross guessed, probably came from the cops. The truth was that the cops had been all over the Cohen house for three hours before the search warrant dispute. That was hardly a quick look, Ross fumed. But he was afraid the damage was already done—and partly at his direction, since he had advised his client not to consent to the search.

Downtown at Miami Police Department headquarters, Jon Spear and Sylvia Romans were on the job early, despite having spent most of the night on the Cohen case. Stan Cohen's name went up on the homicide department's murder board, an expanse of white that covered nearly all of the office's west wall. Stanley A. Cohen was the twenty-ninth murder of the year to be investigated by Miami Police Department homicide detectives, the seventy-fourth murder in Dade County. Before year-end, the county total would rise to 438 homicides.

The murder board was lined in columns to provide quick information on the vital statistics and status of every Miami homicide: name of victim, date and location of homicide, victim's birth date, detectives working the case, name of suspect (if no suspect had been identified, "WDI" meaning "whodunit"), status of investigation ("open" or "arrest made"). As lead detective, Spear wrote in the information on the Cohen homicide. When he reached the "name of suspect" column, he wrote "WDI" in bold red letters, despite his suspicions about Joyce Cohen.

Down the hall from the homicide office, Sylvia Romans began to sort through the physical evidence taken from the crime scene at the Cohen house. She located the brown paper bag containing the handgun found in the front yard. She removed the gun and took more close-up photographs.

As she focused her camera on the weapon's serial number, Romans noticed something unusual: trace evidence on the gun itself. There was bark, probably from the trees in the Cohens' front yard, she thought. And there were two tiny pieces of what looked like paper tissue, Kleenex, caught at the edge of the handgrip. She took more close-ups of the tissue. Then she looked for gunpowder residue on the gun, called "blowback," and traces of blood, body tissue, or flesh. She found a speck of blood on the muzzle.

Romans decided to alert the homicide detectives before she went any further in her examination. Should she remove the tiny tissue bits for further analysis? Should the weapon be processed for latent prints, or should the blood on the muzzle get priority? Once she processed the weapon for latent prints, Romans knew, it might be impossible to analyze the tiny blood spot. Go for the latent prints, she was told. And remove the tissue first. And another thing. You'll have to go back to the Cohen crime scene to pick up samples of anything that looks like that tissue on the grip.

Romans removed the handgrip from the gun in order to retrieve the tiny pieces of tissue intact. She packaged the tissue separately and put it aside. The pieces were so small, it was unlikely they could be matched to any particular sample. Next she prepared the gun for latent print analysis. Since the gunmetal was dark, the usual method of dusting with black graphite powder to locate latent prints wouldn't work. There would be no visual contrast to show up the prints. The best method of processing this gun, Romans decided, was the "Super Glue fuming method."

First Romans carefully placed the gun inside a glass aquarium tank. She used a wooden dowel to prop it up, so that all surfaces would be exposed to processing. Next she put a few drops of Super Glue in a small container and set the open container inside the aquarium with the gun. Super Glue gives off caustic fumes, which leave behind a white residue that actually adheres to latent fingerprints. After correct processing, the residue makes latent prints visible in white against a dark surface. Once the prints are located, the technician processes them in the usual manner, dusting with the black graphite powder and a tiny brush, lifting off the powder with transparent tape, and then attaching the tape to a latent print card.

Romans covered the top of the aquarium so the caustic fumes wouldn't get in her eyes and nose. She checked the gun every fifteen minutes to see whether any prints were visible. Finally, whitish residue began to appear. But as the residue developed, there was no pattern of prints. The most Romans could identify was a smear of white. It looked like wipe marks, she thought. This gun must have been wiped down.

After she completed her processing, Romans sent the gun to the Metro-Dade County laboratories for further analysis. First the serology department would check for blood and tissue, then firearms would evaluate the ballistic pattern inside the barrel. And the barrel would also have to be analyzed for blowback gunpowder residue. Shortly after noon, Sylvia Romans and her partner Gil Martin headed back to the Cohen house to look for paper tissue samples.


That afternoon, Detective Spear met Dr. Wetli for Stanley Cohen's autopsy in the old Medical Examiner's building near Jackson Memorial Hospital. The small cement block–stucco facility was hopelessly inadequate to handle the virtual avalanche of corpses that descended on it in the 1980s. The Pit, as the autopsy room was called, held facilities for only three autopsies to be perfomed simultaneously, and the staff desperately needed more space. *The Miami Herald* reported that the Medical Examiner's Office was storing overflow corpses in a refrigerated Burger King truck it had leased, a story that was promptly picked up and repeated by national news media. Corpses were stored in the truck, Dr. Wetli confirmed. The bodies in the truck were unidentified. Sometimes it took months to track down identities, especially with the flood of foreign refugees to Miami. The truck was simply more convenient for long-term storage, according to Wetli.

Dressed for work in his surgical greens—drawstring pants, short-sleeved V-necked shirt, paper shoe covers—and rubber surgeon's gloves, Wetli chatted briefly with Spear and reviewed some basic information about Stanley Cohen. Although Cohen was Jewish, there was no request for a Jewish autopsy. If there had been, Wetli would have called in a rabbi and performed the autopsy according to rabbinical rules. In preparation for the autopsy, Stan Cohen's corpse had been washed and placed supine on the gleaming stainless steel tray table that had been pushed over to a low sink with hoses and a drain. The head and shoulders rested on a large wooden block. The skin was pallid and yellowish. The sightless eyes were open now, the mouth slack.

Dr. Wetli began with an examination and description of Stanley Cohen's external features: a five-foot-ten-inch, 205-pound, moderately obese Caucasian male consistent with the stated age of fifty-two; chest scar from heart bypass surgery; scars over the left hip, on both thighs, just below the right knee, and on both ankles; three gunshot wounds to back of head, plus a graze wound on top of the head—a total of four.

Dr. Wetli stepped to a worktable to make notes of his examination as he went along. He sketched in the visible scars and the head wounds on an outline form. There was a gold ring bearing the initials "SAC" on Cohen's finger. Because the fingers were so swollen, the ring had to be cut off the corpse.

Dr. Wetli inserted a hollow needle into each eyeball to withdraw ocular fluid, which was labeled and stored for later analysis. After examining the inside of the mouth and nose ("slight abrasions on the nasal alae," he noted), he was ready to open the body cavity. Using a surgical scalpel, he began with the traditional Y-shaped incision, which runs from the left and right clavicles, meets at the sternum, then continues down to the pubis. Just under the skin was a layer of bright yellow fat, contrasting sharply with the dark red muscles beneath. There was no odor of alcohol from the body tissues, no suggestion that Stanley Cohen had been inebriated when he died.

Using syringes, Dr. Wetli withdrew blood from the heart and urine from the bladder. The volume was recorded and samples labeled for further analysis. Samples in tubes with red tops would be sent to the Metro-Dade lab; tubes with gray tops went to the medical examiner's own lab.

After Dr. Wetli separated the fat and muscle from the rib cage, he was ready to enter the chest and examine the heart and lungs. It takes a surprising amount of strength to cut through the rib cage. Some pathologists use a bolt cutter or a linoleum knife to sever the ribs. Since cartilage is easier to penetrate than bone, Dr. Wetli preferred to use a scalpel to excise the cartilage that connects the sternum to the ribs.

Once inside the chest, Dr. Wetli examined, removed, and described the heart and lungs. Stan Cohen had healed well from his heart bypass surgery several years earlier. As he checked the coronary arteries, Dr. Wetli wondered, as he always did at this stage of autopsy, what his own forty-two-year-old arteries must look like by now. He methodically weighed each organ and took two tissue samples from each; one sample was placed in a container of formaldehyde for storage, another in a similar container for later histologic study. The carefully labeled containers were white plastic, the kind a deli uses. By the conclusion of the autopsy, both containers would be full of tissue samples.

Finally Dr. Wetli was ready to investigate the gunshot wounds on the back of Stan Cohen's head. He designated them "A," the graze wound creasing the top of the scalp; "B" and "C" on the left side of the head; and "D" on the right. He made an incision below the wounds, then incised the scalp, carefully reflecting it off the skull and forward over the face. When he was finished, he signaled to a laboratory assistant wearing surgical greens and a large plastic face shield. The assistant removed the top of Stanley Cohen's skull in one piece with a large hand-held vibrating saw. The removed portion bore all three bullet holes.

Then Dr. Wetli carefully excised the brain. He carried the organ to a work table and began meticulous serial sectioning of the brain tissue. He knew just what he was looking for, and he found it: several small, misshapen lead fragments from the bullets that killed Stanley Cohen. He could see that the bullets had traveled from the back of the skull toward the front, but he couldn't trace the individual paths because they were so close together. He noted his findings, but even his dry professional prose in the autopsy report couldn't diminish the devastation those bullets had wreaked in Stan Cohen's brain: "These gunshot wounds are associated with extensive pulpification of the brain."

The medical examiner's photographer, an attractive, dark-haired young woman wearing a white lab coat, took official autopsy photographs at each stage of the procedure. She climbed up a special wheeled ladder to shoot directly down at the corpse. As she set up each shot, she was careful to include a placard bearing the date and official autopsy case number: March 8, 1986, Case No. 86-626.

When he was finished, Dr. Wetli dictated his autopsy report, translating Stan Cohen's corporeal existence and violent death into sterile scientific prose. "Cause of death: Gunshot Wounds of Head." Regarding the probable time of death, Dr. Wetli could say only that it had occurred between midnight and 6 A.M. on March 7. By the time Wetli was called to the Cohen house, the body had been lying on the floor for at least nine hours, a delay caused by the need to get a search warrant.

Toxicology analysis of samples taken from Stan Cohen's body confirmed that he had consumed no alcohol prior to his death. The drug scan was also negative. The twisted metal fragments Dr. Wetli removed from Stan Cohen's pulpified brain had indeed been fired by the .38-caliber Smith & Wesson revolver found in the Cohens' front yard the day before. It was Stanley Cohen's own gun.

• • •

By midafternoon, the Miami Police investigators and ID technicians had finished processing the crime scene at the Cohen house. Detective Spear called C. J. Levenstein to tell her that the search was completed and she could pick up the Cohens' house keys. The crime scene was officially turned back over to Mrs. Joyce Cohen.

C.J. took her handyman to the Cohens' house with her. She was determined to clean up the master bedroom—wipe up the puddles and spatters of Stan Cohen's blood on the floor and on the mirrored wall, change the sheets, throw out the blood-soaked bedding, remove the gory debris of tragedy. She knew that Joyce, Gary, and Gerri would probably go back to the house soon. She wanted to spare them any grisly reminders, no matter how difficult it was for her.

As she worked, C.J. thought of Stan Cohen and sobbed.

When she finally returned home, C.J. found Anne Sheldon and her sister-in-law, Carol Sheldon, there with Joyce. Joyce told them she was ready to go back to her house. C.J. wasn't sure it was a good idea. But at least, she thought, the master bedroom was reasonably presentable now. The four women walked down the street and up the stone steps to the Cohens' house.

When the others were ready to leave, Carol Sheldon decided to take Mischief home with her. No one knew what else to do with the dog. Joyce refused to leave. She was going to stay there, she insisted, by herself. She wanted to think, to be close to Stan's things. C.J. was dismayed. She thought it was too soon for Joyce to stay alone in the house. But finally her friends left her there as she wished.

C.J., now thoroughly exhausted and emotionally drained, walked back home again. As soon as she stepped off the elevator, Len met her, obviously upset. "C.J., Gary and Gerri are here and want to talk to you," he told his wife. C.J. wondered why.

Gary Cohen had hurried home that day from his vacation in Jamaica. He had spent the afternoon talking with Gerri about the death of their father—and with the detectives who were investigating the case. The cops wanted to talk to Joyce again. When C.J. told Gary and Gerri that Joyce had returned to the house, they said they

were going to take her back to the homicide office for another interview—without her lawyer.

Gary and Gerri drove together to their father's house, determined
to persuade their stepmother to talk to Detective Spear again. And
this time they didn't want her hiding behind her lawyer. They found
Joyce alone in the house, wandering distractedly from room to room.
Whey they told her what they wanted, Joyce sighed and shook her
head.

Gerri held her stepmother by both arms and stared into her eyes.
"If you have nothing to hide," she said, "you'll come with us. If you
won't come, we'll think you were involved in our father's death."

Joyce couldn't believe that Gary and Gerri really thought she had
something to do with Stan's murder. How could they be so cruel? But
in the face of their ultimatum, she reluctantly agreed to go back to
the Miami homicide office. But first she wanted to use her upstairs
bathroom.

Waiting downstairs together, Gary and Gerri were edgy and apprehensive. What if Joyce came running down the stairs with a gun
and shot them both? Or herself? They didn't know what to expect
anymore. They were completely unnerved by the tragedy of their father's murder. But, they told each other, the police had already
searched the house. If there had been any more weapons, surely the
police would have taken them. Wouldn't they?

Finally Joyce walked back downstairs. She seemed calm. There
was no weapon. Together the three of them drove downtown to meet
with Detective Jon Spear. When Alan Ross found out later, he was
furious. More devious police tactics, he thought, trying to get something out of his client when he wasn't there to protect her. But, in
fact, the interview was brief, and Detective Spear learned nothing
new from Joyce Cohen that day.

After the interview, Joyce returned to the Levensteins' home, and
she was furious. Gary and Gerri had practically shoved her into the
car, she fumed to C.J. The trip downtown to see Detective Spear was
definitely against her will. And it was obvious, she said, that Gary
and Gerri thought she had something to do with Stan's death. Joyce
was outraged. After all she had suffered, why were her stepchildren
treating her this way?

But C.J. told Joyce that she had to put those worries aside, at least for the moment. Decisions had to be made about Stan's funeral. It was, of course, Joyce's place to make those decisions, but Stan's family and old friends were there to help. It was all they could do for Stan now.

Rabbi Michael Eisenstat met with Joyce about her husband's funeral, and it was decided that the service would be held at 10:30 the next morning, Sunday, March 9, at Temple Judea, a large concrete-and-stucco synagogue at the edge of the Miami suburb of Coral Gables. Interment would be at Lakeside Memorial Park following the service. Stan Cohen's body was to be prepared at Jimmy Gordon's funeral home. It was a sad duty for Gordon, who was an old friend of Stan's, another Pi Lamb fraternity brother from the University of Florida. In keeping with Jewish tradition, Stan Cohen would have a simple wooden casket adorned only by a wooden Star of David. The casket, of course, would be closed. Viewing the remains is not permitted in the Jewish faith.

There was the question of sitting shiva, the Jewish custom of maintaining a vigil with the family of the deceased. Orthodox Jews follow strict rules. The shiva takes place at the home of the deceased on consecutive nights following burial. The rabbi leads the bereaved family in ritual prayers for the dead each night of shiva. The mourning family symbolically withdraws from ordinary life. They prepare no food; friends bring in food for them and their visitors. They wear special slippers instead of their usual shoes. They may sit only on small hardwood benches, taking no comfort or ease. They may not look at themselves in a mirror—all mirrors in the house are draped with black cloth—and each member of the family wears a torn black ribbon on the left breast, a symbol of rending their clothing in grief.

Gary wanted to sit shiva for his father. It wasn't necessary to follow all the Orthodox rules, he thought. A three-day mourning period would be sufficient. After all, Stan certainly hadn't been a strict observer of religious ritual. But sitting shiva was something Gary knew he had to do.

But where could shiva be held? Not in the house where Stan Cohen had been murdered. That was unthinkable. The Levensteins offered their home, but there were practical problems. Stan's brother, Artie, was in a wheelchair. The elevator up to the Levensteins' penthouse would be a barrier for him, and for Stan's widowed mother, Frances, who was elderly.

Then George Johnnides offered the solution. The shiva could be held at the Johnnideses' home on the Coral Gables waterway. The single-story house was large—all the Cohen family and friends could be accommodated. And it was right down the street from Temple Judea. The family could gather there in the morning to meet the limousines for the funeral. After the service, and every night of the shiva, everyone was welcome at the Johnnideses'. It was a generous offer, which Gary gratefully accepted.

Gary had one more sad task that day. He wanted to choose the clothes his father would wear for eternity. C.J. walked with him to the house and waited while Gary went up alone to his father's bedroom. He came back downstairs carrying a dark suit, white shirt, and tie—formal attire for Stan Cohen's last formal occasion.

That night Joyce stayed in the Levensteins' guest room, while Shawn slept on the sofa in the living room. Sometime that afternoon, Shawn had found time to be alone in the big stone house on South Bayshore Drive. He had grown up in that house, although he hadn't really lived there since his parents sent him off to Rocky Mountain Academy. But the house still echoed with memories of his childhood.

Shawn walked upstairs to the master bedroom his parents had shared. He went into his mother's bathroom, which was behind the sitting room adjacent to the bedroom. He had a destination in mind: the secret cupboard behind the bathroom door.

As a child, Shawn had discovered that the little cupboard was his mother's hiding place for his Christmas and birthday gifts. He never let on, but he had always found his gifts before the holidays, then had to pretend he was surprised.

This time Shawn found a small package in the little secret cupboard. It wasn't a gift for him. But he knew instantly what it was. He removed the package and carefully closed the cupboard door.

# *Eleven*

•

Stan Cohen's funeral was held on Sunday, March 9.

That morning the Levensteins dressed carefully, Len in a somber dark suit and C.J. in a dark dress. Shawn put on the suit someone had bought him the day before. They gathered at the foot of the stairs to wait for Joyce. Finally she came downstairs wearing a simple black dress and a large black hat. C.J. was disapproving. The hat was not right, she told Joyce. Too dramatic. She persuaded her to go back upstairs and remove the hat.

Joyce reappeared, hatless, and started down the stairs again. Then suddenly she tripped, or stumbled, or maybe fainted. Fortunately Len was close enough to catch her as she fell. It was, they all knew, going to be a long, terrible day.

In silence, they drove to the Johnnideses' house, where the family was gathering to meet the limousines that would take them to Temple Judea for the funeral. Joyce walked into the house alone through the back door. Sharon Johnnides was waiting for her. But when she saw Joyce, Sharon was startled by her dazed appearance. She was trembling violently. Her dark stockings were twisted and bagging around her ankles. "I have to do something with my stockings," Joyce muttered. "They're falling down."

Joyce was carrying her jewelry case in her purse. She told Sharon she was afraid to leave her jewelry at the Levensteins' during the funeral. It might be stolen. Well, you can't take your jewelry with you to the funeral, Sharon said. Why don't you leave it in my bedroom? Sharon helped Joyce fix her sagging stockings and pull herself together. She could see that Joyce was going to need a lot of help.

Through the kitchen doorway, Joyce glimpsed Stan's family assembled in the living room. Gerri was sitting on a sofa near the fireplace. Joyce drew back. "You know, Gerri thinks I had something to do with this!" she whispered urgently in Sharon's ear.

Sharon was taken aback. Oh, God, what's going on, she wondered? Gerri hadn't said a word to her about that. It seemed crazy, beyond belief. And Sharon was afraid Gerri might have overheard Joyce's insistent whisper.

"Look, don't worry about that now," Sharon whispered back to Joyce. "Just get through this day."

As she crossed the living room, Joyce halted in front of her stepdaughter. She bent to kiss Gerri's cheek. Wordlessly, Gerri turned her head, averting her face. Joyce kissed empty air.

Finally the somber group boarded limousines for the short ride to Temple Judea. C.J. rode with Joyce, Shawn, and Michael Cohen, the son Stan had adopted during his brief second marriage. Michael had obtained emergency leave from the army to come home for the funeral.

By 10:30 A.M., Temple Judea was packed. Cars jammed the parking lot, and an overflow crowd waited patiently on the sidewalk in the bright spring sunshine. Inside, Stan Cohen's plain wooden casket rested near the pulpit at the front. His family gathered in the small, private alcove nearby. Again, C.J. sat with Joyce, Shawn, and Michael. She noticed that Stan's mother, Frances, also sat near Joyce. Despite her own grief, Frances was solicitous of her daughter-in-law.

Shortly before the service, Frances Cohen had decided that she wanted a eulogy for her beloved son. She asked Len Levenstein to speak for Stan. He was touched by the request, but he wasn't sure he could handle the task. He was still terribly emotional about Stan's death, and he didn't want to embarrass himself or Stan's family by breaking down publicly. But it seemed there was no one else to do it, so he agreed and went off alone to the rabbi's study to gather his thoughts about his friend of thirty years. What could he say about their friendship? How could he sum up Stan Cohen's life?

Later, Len couldn't really remember what he had said in the eulogy. Something about Stan being a wonderful father and family man, he was sure, and a great friend. He had tried to capture Stan's love of life, his vitality, his robust masculinity. He hoped he had done a good job. But at least he hadn't broken down and cried, although he had felt like it. The family seemed pleased, especially Frances Cohen. But it was, Len thought, the most difficult thing he had ever done.

At the conclusion of the service, the mourners filed out the side door and gathered to watch the pallbearers—Len Levenstein, Jay Rossin, Marvin Sheldon, and his brother Arthur—carry Stan's casket to the waiting hearse. Then a long line of cars followed the hearse and the family limousines to the cemetery. There the casket was carried to the graveside and placed upon a lowering device suspended over the open grave. Stan's friends gathered around a small canopy that sheltered chairs for the family. Joyce walked haltingly to her seat, supported by Shawn on one side and Michael on the other. When all were assembled, Rabbi Eisenstat led traditional committal prayers. Then the Cohens' friends formed two lines of condolence through which the family would walk back to the limousines. As she stared down into the open grave, Joyce fainted.

Back at the Johnnideses' house, final preparations were under way. Marvin Sheldon had arranged for a caterer to deliver platters of food—bagels, lox, nova, slices of tomato and onion, cream cheese, chopped liver, pumpernickel and rye breads, cold cuts and sandwich makings, coleslaw, salads, desserts. A generously stocked bar was set up on the patio overlooking the languorous Coral Gables Waterway. Chairs were arranged in the spacious living room, in the dining room, and on the sunny patio.

Soon the large house filled with mourners. Joyce arrived, assisted by Shawn and Michael, one on each side, as before. Her face, without makeup, was red and blotchy, her eyes swollen. She seemed dazed. Friends lowered her to the sofa near the fireplace carefully, as if she were an invalid or an old woman. There she was surrounded by her loyal friends Myra Wenig, Shu Sampson, and the others, except for Ed and Sam Smith, who were skiing in Europe. They sat beside her, patting her, holding her hands, trying to comfort her. But there was little to say.

Joyce herself said nothing at all. Her face was a mask of grief.

Len Levenstein watched the scene with consuming interest. When Gary and Gerri Cohen had told him about the detectives' suspicions of Joyce, Len had rejected it out of hand. He didn't believe that Joyce could possibly be involved in her husband's murder. But he could see that others were not so sure. Even there at the Johnnideses' house, right after the funeral, he saw people beginning to take sides. It was like pregame in football, Len thought. First a lot of general milling around, no pattern to the interaction of players on the field. But then the buzzer sounds and suddenly the amorphous mass forms two teams, two completely separate, opposing forces.

No buzzer sounded that Sunday in the Johnnideses' home, but some inaudible signal was passed. Suddenly there were whispered conversations on the patio, over drinks at the bar, where Stan's mourners were gazing through the open french doors at Joyce, dressed in black, sitting on a sofa in the living room. At the center of the group were Gary and Gerri Cohen.

Meanwhile, the cluster around Joyce was growing smaller—just Myra Wenig, Shu and Skip Sampson, Shawn and Michael Cohen.


After Stan's funeral, Joyce and Shawn moved out of the Levensteins' penthouse. Joyce turned to Skip and Shu Sampson for shelter. Shu was a compassionate woman who had been a staunch friend. Now she offered sympathy, hospitality, and unflagging support, which Joyce gratefully accepted. She was going to need all the friends she had.

Joyce had another meeting with Alan Ross in his office. This time, Shawn came with his mother. He had never met Ross before, but he had already heard that he was a drug lawyer. Why did his mother need a lawyer at all? Shawn wondered. And why would she choose a drug lawyer to represent her? Shawn worried that it made his mother look guilty. He knew she hadn't had anything to do with his stepfather's murder, despite the ugly rumors that had reached his ears.

While Joyce conferred with her attorney, a secretary took Shawn to the law firm's "victory bar," a luxurious leather-paneled lounge with a well-stocked bar and a nice view of Miami. There, she said, Shawn could help himself to cold Coca-Colas in the refrigerator while he waited for his mother to finish her meeting.

When he was alone, Shawn took a Coke out of the refrigerator and poured it into a glass with ice—and then decided to spike it liberally with rum he found in the bar. He soon began to feel strange, lightheaded. Earlier that day, he had swallowed some Valium sneaked out of his mother's purse. As Joyce's conference with Ross wore on, Shawn went back to the bar again and again.

Eventually Joyce came to retrieve her son. They were going out, she told him, in Alan Ross's car. Shawn said nothing, although he was beginning to feel seriously queasy. They climbed into the car, a 1982 Porsche 911 in a color Ross called charcoal black. Shawn squeezed into the tiny back seat, and as the car began to pick up speed, so did his heaving stomach. He desperately tried to get his head out the open window, but it was too late. He sprayed the car— the leather interior, the carpet, the door, the window, even the charcoal black exterior—with vomit.

Through tightly clenched teeth, Ross muttered to his client, "Nice kid."

Ross traded in the charcoal black Porsche 911 for a brand-new white one.

# *Twelve*

•

$E$ver since he saw the first *Miami Herald* article on the day after Stan Cohen's murder, Alan Ross knew his client was facing an uphill battle in the media. News stories that appeared in the next few days echoed the tenor of the first: Joyce Cohen had something to hide, she must be guilty, she must have killed her husband. There were less-than-helpful quotations from the cops. "We're not baffled," Lieutenant Ed Carberry had commented about the investigation. Then there was prosecutor David Waksman's classic: "This is the first time I've been asked to prepare a search warrant because the widow would not allow the police to come into her house to conduct a crime scene search." Ross was determined to clear Joyce of suspicion so that detectives could redirect their efforts and start looking for the person who had really killed Stan Cohen.

Ross decided to ask his client to take a polygraph—a lie detector test. He knew Miami police and prosecutors often used polygraphs during investigations. Sometimes they ruled out possible suspects, sometimes they confirmed leads. His problem, Ross knew, was to choose an examiner the cops would have confidence in, someone they themselves used and trusted. That way, when Joyce Cohen passed the polygraph, as Ross believed she would, the cops would have to drop her as a suspect in her husband's murder. That was his plan.

Ross knew just the right polygraphist. He was a man the Miami homicide detectives and the prosecutors at the Dade State Attorney's Office had relied on for years, a man who had impeccable professional credentials, a solid reputation, and nearly twenty-five years' experience as a polygraph examiner. A former New Jersey state trooper and former United States Marine, that man was George B. Slattery, Sr.

Among Ross's colleagues in the Miami criminal defense bar, George Slattery was sometimes jokingly referred to as "the king of fail" because so few suspects passed his polygraph examinations. Sometimes they actually confessed to Slattery during the test. But Ross had confidence in Joyce Cohen, and he expected her to pass the examination. And if she failed for some reason, Ross might as well know about it now. The only question was whether Joyce was willing to submit to the polygraph.

Ross consulted his client. The test was strictly voluntary and confidential, he told her. Test results were protected from disclosure by the attorney-client relationship. If Joyce passed the test, of course, Ross would advise the detectives, using the favorable test result to exonerate her. If she failed, the cops would never know about the test at all.

Joyce's response was immediate. She would take the polygraph. Ross phoned Slattery's office to make arrangements for a test the following day.

On Tuesday, March 11—just four days after Stan Cohen's murder—Joyce appeared at Slattery's Miami office at 9:30 A.M., accompanied by Alan Ross and his private investigator, Steve Kiraly. Slattery had polygraphed other clients for Ross. He knew Ross understood the procedure and would provide the necessary background information for the test. After he was introduced to Mrs. Cohen, Slattery asked her to wait in his reception area while he met privately with Ross and Kiraly.

In the interview room, Slattery asked Ross for the basic case information. Usually there was an arrest affidavit or police report giving the cops' version of events, but today there was nothing for Slattery to read. Ross quickly described the situation. His client was an unofficial suspect in the murder of her husband, Stanley Cohen, four days ago. She had found him upstairs in the couple's bed, bleeding from fatal head wounds. The police suspected her of the murder because she was the only other person in the house at the time and because she had refused to let them search the house, as the cops put it. There had been a lot of bad publicity for his client, and Ross was anxious to clear her name. He wanted to get the test done as soon as possible.

Ross believed his client was innocent, but he didn't try to persuade Slattery, as some lawyers did. "I just want to know where we stand," Ross told him. In Slattery's experience, that was the way Alan Ross and his partners, Jeff Weiner and Bill Tunkey, approached their polygraphs. They were straight lawyers, and he respected that.

But also based on his long years of experience, Slattery figured that Joyce Cohen was a legitimate suspect in her husband's murder. Most suspects were chosen for a reason. The cops didn't just drag random characters off the street. So Slattery wasn't surprised that most suspects failed his polygraphs. Yes, he thought to himself, Joyce Cohen probably did it, and he expected her to fail the polygraph. But he said nothing to Alan Ross.

"What do you want me to cover?" Slattery asked him instead.

"Everything," Ross replied. "I want to know did she do it, was she involved, does she know who did it."

As he listened to Ross, Slattery began to plan the specific questions he would ask Joyce Cohen during her polygraph test. He used a polygraph examination method called the Backster Zone Comparison Technique, which he believed to be the most reliable. In the Backster method, the subject's psychophysiological reactions—blood pressure, pulse, respiration, and galvanic skin reflex—are measured in response to two types of questions: "control questions," which are about issues other than the matter at hand; and "relevant questions," which are specifically about the matter at hand. The subject's psychophysiological reactions are recorded on a graph called a chart or polygram. The polygraphist then compares the subject's reactions to control questions and relevant questions.

The theory is simple. The fear of detection in an important lie causes the subject to react to relevant questions. But in practice, lie detection is not so simple. It requires carefully controlled conditions, a subject capable of taking the test, and, most important, a skilled examiner.

Slattery began his private interview with Joyce Cohen by recording personal information—her name, birth date, address, and so on. Immediately he observed that Mrs. Cohen seemed very upset, and he was concerned about whether she was physically capable of taking a valid polygraph test that day. She had recently suffered severe trauma, he knew, and if she was still very disturbed, her test charts might be inconclusive.

She felt "okay" to take the test, Joyce told him, but she had had very little sleep since the night her husband was killed. She had slept only about four hours the night before, despite having taken a 10 P.M. dose of Halcion, a powerful sleep medication prescribed for her. She had had her usual breakfast that morning, she reported—half a banana and a cup of coffee.

Slattery thought Joyce was very stressed. Although he doubted a valid test could be conducted that day, both Joyce and Alan Ross were anxious to make the attempt. Slattery decided to try it. He asked Joyce for her version of her husband's murder, and she told him just what she had told Alan Ross, Detective Jon Spear, and all the others. She believed her husband was killed by the intruders she saw in her home on the morning of March 7. She did not kill her husband, she said, and she had no knowledge of who did. She didn't have him killed, and she didn't know beforehand that he would be killed. She insisted she had absolutely no knowledge of or participation in her husband's murder.

Slattery tried to make Joyce comfortable as he carefully explained the polygraph test procedure. She would answer only yes or no during the test. No other talking was permitted. He would go over with her every word of every question which he would ask her during the examination. There were no trick questions, no surprises, he assured her.

Since Ross wanted to cover "everything" in Joyce Cohen's polygraph, Slattery used a method called the S-K-Y technique, which probes a subject's knowledge about an event in addition to any degree of participation. He drafted these relevant questions to ask Joyce Cohen:

"Regarding the shooting death of Stanley Cohen, do you know for sure who shot and killed him?"

"Regarding the shooting death of Stanley Cohen, did you shoot and kill him?"

"Regarding the shooting death of Stanley Cohen, did you know that someone was going to kill him before it happened?"

He went over each question with Joyce. These were the exact questions he would ask her about the murder. The questions would be asked three separate times, in varying order, on three different charts.

Then Joyce sat in the examination chair, and Slattery attached her to the polygraph instrument he would use for the test. Two convoluted rubber tubes were fastened around her waist and chest to record her breathing patterns. As she inhaled or exhaled, the tubes stretched or contracted, and the result was recorded by a pen on the moving chart paper. Electrodes were attached to her fingers. The imperceptible electric current flowing through the electrodes would reflect changes in her skin's resistance to electricity, which would be recorded on the chart. Finally, a blood pressure cuff was placed on her right arm and inflated with air. Her pulse rate and blood pressure changes would be recorded by the rise and fall of the pen on the moving chart paper.

Slattery was now ready to administer Joyce's polygraph. But as he began with questions on Chart I, he immediately noted that Joyce was having difficulty. There were frequent distortions in her breathing. The pen moved erratically on the chart. Several times he marked "DB" on the paper, meaning "deep breath"—or maybe it was a sob. She seemed to be having trouble concentrating on the questions. The reactions and distortions on the chart showed no pattern in relation to the questions asked. Sometimes there were distortions when he hadn't yet asked a question.

Slattery decided to do a verification test to see whether Joyce was able to focus her attention and respond to questions reliably. He placed three small pieces of paper on the table. Each had a number on one side: a 2, a 4, and a 6. He turned the papers face down, shuffled them, and asked her to take one and look at the number without showing him or telling him what it was. She did.

Now, Slattery said, I'm going to ask you whether the number you have is a 1, 2, 3, 4, 5, or 6. I want you to answer no to each number. Since he knew Joyce had only one of three numbers—the 2, the 4, or the 6—when she answered no to each of his questions, she would be lying one time and telling the truth five times. Is it the 1? he asked her. No, she replied, and so on with each number. He watched her responses recorded on the moving chart paper. Next he asked, did you pick the 6? No. The 4? No. The 2? No. Again he noted her responses.

Now, Slattery said, I'm going to ask you again and this time I want you to answer *truthfully*. Is it the 2? No. Is it the 4? No. Is it the 6? No. But Slattery knew she had to have one of those numbers. She wasn't following his instructions. He checked her chart again. It showed a reaction each time she denied having the number 6. That must be the lie, he thought. Which number did she have? Slattery asked her.

Joyce turned over her paper. On it was a 6.

Although Joyce's charts showed reliable reactions on the verification test, she hadn't followed the simple directions Slattery had given her. Maybe she was just too tired to concentrate, he thought. Still, he decided to try again.

Slattery moved on to Chart II. There were more distortions. Joyce moved her arm, and her blood pressure suddenly increased, then dropped. A noise outside the room caused a reaction, which Slattery marked on the chart as "OSN," for "outside noise."

"Regarding the shooting death of Stanley Cohen," he asked Joyce, "do you intend to answer truthfully each question about that?"

"Yes, I do," she replied. Again she wasn't following instructions. Only a yes or no response was permitted. Talking threw off reactions.

"Regarding the shooting death of Stanley Cohen, did you shoot and kill him?"

"No, I did not."

Slattery discontinued Chart II. Please answer only yes or no, he reminded her. And please try not to move. He started again. Joyce fidgeted, moving her left hand, her right arm. He stopped again.

On Chart III, there were more distortions, no consistency of reactions, no focus. There simply was not enough for a clear-cut opinion. They were just wasting time. Slattery stopped the test and marked it "inconclusive"—the charts did not conclusively indicate either truth or deception on the relevant questions. It was 2:01 P.M. Joyce had been in George Slattery's office for four and a half hours.

"The results are not clear enough for an opinion," he explained to Joyce and her lawyer. Ross knew what "inconclusive" meant. Then Slattery suggested that they attempt to remedy Mrs. Cohen's problem, whatever it was. "If it is lack of sleep, get her someplace where she can rest. Let her eat, let her get herself in shape to take a test."

Slattery also recommended that they talk to Joyce's physician to see if he could prescribe some milder sleep medication for her (or, preferably, none at all), so that she would have no medication in her system when she came in for another test. But he wasn't too worried about the effects of medication on test results. In his experience, there was no medication that could selectively suppress psychophysiological responses—that is, block out reactions only to relevant questions, leaving the subject otherwise functioning normally. And if a person was overmedicated, he simply showed flat charts, no reaction to anything, an inconclusive test result.

The following morning, Wednesday, March 12, Joyce Cohen and Alan Ross returned to George Slattery's office for another polygraph. This time, Joyce assured Slattery, she was rested and ready.

Slattery repeated the polygraph with Joyce, using the same procedure and the same relevant questions he had used the day before. Joyce responded no to each relevant question, and this time the test results were conclusive on all three charts: "No significant or consistent psychophysiological reactions indicative of deception" to the relevant questions. Joyce had passed the polygraph.

Alan Ross was elated. Now he had something concrete to give the Miami homicide detectives. Now they would have a reason to redirect the murder investigation—away from Joyce Cohen. Ross wanted to call a press conference, he told Slattery, to announce the results of the polygraph. Joyce had already endured so much bad publicity, maybe a public announcement that she had passed the polygraph would give her a fair shot in the investigation. Would Slattery agree to participate in the press conference?

Slattery hesitated. He had avoided press conferences throughout his professional career. Confidentiality was his job, not publicity. Even when a test subject and his attorney specifically asked him to make results public, he feared that publicity undermined the public perception of confidentiality—and of Slattery's professional integrity. Someone who saw him on television might think, "Here is a guy who might test me and then go talk about it on TV."

But Ross was persuasive. It was important, he said, to counteract all the terrible publicity his client had already had. Reluctantly, Slattery agreed to participate in a press conference with Alan Ross and Joyce Cohen. Ross would make the arrangements and call Slattery's office. And as he headed back to his own office, Ross was delighted at the prospect of the press conference.


Unknown to Alan Ross or George Slattery, at that very moment Jon Spear, Ed Carberry, and Steve Vinson were in Ross's office requesting a meeting with him. They wanted him to agree to a polygraph of Joyce Cohen. The detectives left their message with Ross's staff and departed. They would be in touch.

When he returned to his office, Ross was told that the detectives wanted to polygraph his client. The opportunity was simply irresistible, and he decided to have some fun.

First Ross called Carberry at the homicide department, and their conversation quickly turned to the detectives' request for a polygraph of Mrs. Cohen. Ross played along. He might agree to a test, he said, but it would have to be given by an independent polygraph examiner, not one of the homicide detectives who gave polygraphs for the police department. Carberry was agreeable. And whom would Carberry suggest as an independent examiner? Ross asked. George Slattery's name came up.

"All right, Ed," Ross responded amiably. He was, of course, secretly delighted. "As long as we're in agreement, let's go over some proposed questions to make sure this is what you want her to be asked." Ross then read off the relevant questions on the test which Slattery had already given Joyce Cohen—and which he had already said she passed.

Fine, Carberry agreed.

"Let's meet at my office this afternoon to set up the polygraph. Make it 4 P.M.," Ross suggested.

So it was agreed, and Ross was gleeful. Now he was ready to spring the trap. He quickly arranged for a press conference in his office at 3 P.M. The word was passed to Slattery, who agreed to attend. But no one told Slattery about the byplay with the homicide detectives. And no one told the cops about the press conference at three o'clock, an hour before they planned to meet with Ross to arrange his client's polygraph.

At three o'clock that afternoon, television and newspaper reporters jammed the law library of Weiner Robbins for the press conference. Against the staid backdrop of legal volumes on custom-built wooden shelves, Alan Ross sat at the head of a long polished wood conference table. To his right sat his client, Joyce Cohen, wearing a tailored black blazer and black pants. A torn black ribbon, the traditional Jewish symbol of mourning, was pinned to her striped blouse. Joyce's shiny black hair was perfectly coiffed in her usual french bob style. Just visible beneath her hair were large diamond stud earrings. Her eyes were puffy, heavy-lidded, her pale cheeks highlighted with pink blush that matched her lipstick. She sat motionless, lips compressed, eyes downcast, no expression crossing her face. She looked exhausted.

George Slattery was there, dressed in a somber dark suit, white shirt, and tie. He brought his twelve-page professional résumé with him and his six-page "Report of Polygraph Examination of Joyce Lemay Cohen re Murder of Stanley Cohen."

As the television cameras focused in tight, Ross opened the press conference by reading a prepared statement: "Unfortunately, and without foundation, the City of Miami Police Department cast a cloud of suspicion over Joyce Cohen, at a time when she should have been permitted to grieve in private. Equally unfortunate and disheartening is the fact that the media reported this investigation with little regard for Mrs. Cohen's presumed innocence."

In light of accusations by the police, Ross continued, Mrs. Cohen was compelled to take a polygraph examination. He introduced George Slattery as the examiner chosen by the Miami Police Department, who had tested Mrs. Cohen using questions approved by the police. Joyce Cohen passed that polygraph, Ross announced. "There is no doubt that she is innocent of any involvement at all in the murder of Stanley Cohen."

Next George Slattery read the relevant questions and Joyce Cohen's responses denying that she had any knowledge of or participation in her husband's murder. He confirmed that she had passed the polygraph and said, "It's my very firm opinion that Mrs. Cohen truthfully answered those questions."

Ross concluded the press conference by announcing that obviously Joyce Cohen was no longer a suspect in her husband's murder. With his deep, resonant voice and dramatic presence, he looked and sounded like a Hollywood actor playing a criminal defense attorney. He handled the event masterfully. The media loved it.

As Slattery started to leave the library, Ross called him aside. "Come on in here," he said, "I want you to hear this." They walked into an empty office, and Ross placed a call to the Miami homicide department. He put the call on the speakerphone so Slattery could hear it. Slattery wasn't sure who was on the other end of the line.

"You want her tested?" Ross said into the speakerphone. "Who do you want to use?"

"Slattery" was the response.

"Okay," said Ross, laughing, "Well, guess what, folks? We already did. Watch the Channel 4 news at 6 P.M." The speakerphone was disconnected. Ross laughed uproariously.

Slattery was dumbfounded. Ross's reference at the press conference to "the examiner chosen by the Miami Police" had been ambiguous. Now Slattery realized that the Miami homicide detectives had wanted to use him for a polygraph of Joyce Cohen. And he recognized exactly what had happened. Ross had sandbagged the detectives—and made it look as if he was part of the plot.

Without a word to Ross, Slattery turned on his heel and strode out of the office. He knew he had to get out of there before he said something to Ross that he might regret. He was seething, absolutely furious. This might have been a big joke to Ross, but for Slattery it was devastating. He knew he would be unfairly tagged as part of Ross's scheme, and he knew the professional repercussions would be severe. The cops and prosecutors—law enforcement professionals he had worked with for years and who had trusted him—would feel tricked, betrayed. He could hardly blame them for what they would think. And he had absolutely no way to defend himself.

Ross's press conference had the desired effect. Reporters dashed to Miami police headquarters for comment, and caught by surprise, a police spokesperson could only stammer that the polygraph was not given under Police Department supervision. The investigators offered to arrange another polygraph for Joyce Cohen, this time under their supervision. But Ross quickly declined. His client had been harassed enough, he complained.

Privately, the Miami detectives were seething. George Slattery was right. More battle lines had been drawn. Joyce Cohen remained the cops' number one suspect, regardless of her polygraph. And Slattery was now firmly in the enemy camp, as far as detectives were concerned. The word spread quickly in Miami's law enforcement community: Don't use Slattery. He must be up to something with Alan Ross. His test on Joyce Cohen was suspicious. It would be years before Miami police or prosecutors called George Slattery for polygraphs. He had just lost hundreds of thousands of dollars in fees, he calculated. Worse, he wondered whether his professional reputation would ever really recover.

All the local television stations ran tape on Ross's press conference and the follow-up interview with the Miami police spokesperson. Ross and his law firm colleagues gathered to watch the six o'clock news on an office television set, hooting with laughter at excerpts from the press conference and the cops' befuddled response. They finished the afternoon with an impromptu celebration at the victory bar in their office.

Ross was jubilant. His strategy had worked, and Joyce Cohen was no longer a suspect in her husband's murder. He advised her to try to recover from her ordeal and put this tragedy behind her. Then he turned his attention to the legal problems of his numerous other clients. And he took time out for a little fishing on the *Knot Guilty*.

But the very day of Alan Ross's triumphant press conference, March 12, 1986, Gary and Gerri Cohen took legal action against their stepmother. Their lawyers filed a petition for the administration of Stan Cohen's estate. The thrust of the dry legal language was clear. They wanted to cut Joyce Cohen off from their father's estate.

# *Thirteen*

•

*I*f Joyce had, in fact, been in any way involved in their father's murder, Gary and Gerri knew there could be only one motive: money. And to find out how much money there was, they turned first to Jay Rossin, who had been Stan Cohen's accountant and trusted business adviser for more than twenty years. He was also the executor, or personal representative, as it is called in Florida, of Stan's estate. The two men had been friends since their days at Miami High School and fraternity brothers at the University of Florida. Stan's death was a real blow to Rossin. But as CPA for SAC Construction Company and for Stan personally, he knew all about his complicated financial affairs, his personal projects and investments, his assets—and his debts.

Rossin sighed as he handed Gary and Gerri Cohen a copy of their father's will and sat back to discuss it with them. The will, which Stan had executed in July 1984, left $200,000 each to Gary and Gerri; $50,000 to Stan's adopted son, Michael Cohen; and a trust to be funded by $100,000 for the benefit of Stan's brother, Artie, and their mother, Frances. Everything else—houses, condos, furniture, real estate, investments, jet plane, stock in SAC Construction Company, proceeds of several life insurance policies—was left to Joyce Cohen, "to be hers absolutely."

Gary recalled a brief conversation with Joyce years before, when the subject of revisions to his father's will came up. Stan wanted to establish a trust for her, she had told Gary, but she preferred that everything be left to her outright. Gary hadn't paid much attention at the time. His father's death was simply inconceivable.

As to the value of Stan Cohen's estate, a preliminary review showed assets totaling approximately $13 million. But, as Rossin carefully explained to Gary and Gerri, this figure had almost nothing to do with the estate's net value. In the first place, there was very little cash, certainly not enough to fund the specific bequests of $200,000 Stan had left to each of them. Most of the estate's assets were real estate in Florida and Colorado, and the market was falling in both states. The value of those assets would be whatever each property could be sold for, minus debts owed on the property, of course. The outlook was not good.

In addition, the estate's liabilities were enormous. Stan Cohen, as his business associates knew, was a master of leverage in a decade when leverage was an art form. He was a financial plate spinner, like a juggler who kept several plates whirling in the air on long, flexible sticks, giving each stick just enough flick of the wrist to keep them from crashing down. As long as the juggler was around to tend the sticks, the plates spun merrily overhead.

To finance his lifestyle and his high-visibility projects, to keep all those pretty plates spinning overhead, Stan had borrowed heavily. He had borrowed $450,000 from SAC Construction Company and pledged his SAC stock, valued at $500,000, as collateral. He had borrowed $400,000 against his pension. He had borrowed against his life insurance policies. And this was all in addition to the money borrowed against his various real estate projects. There were notes and mortgages on all of them, as well as tax liabilities.

In short, Rossin estimated that after all the debts, nearly $11 million in total, were repaid, the net value of the estate might be $2 million before taxes—if the estate could meet payments on its current obligations so that property could be sold in an orderly manner and if he could get good sale prices for the properties. "It is," he said, "a troubled estate."

But Gary and Gerri had a more pressing concern. Whatever the value of their father's estate, they were determined to keep their step-mother from getting any of it. Investigators had told them they were nowhere near an arrest in the case. In the meantime, unless some-thing happened soon, Joyce would take over their father's homes—the house on South Bayshore Drive, the penthouse condo across the street at Port By-Water, and Wolf Run Ranch in Steamboat Springs. She would collect on all his life insurance policies, which totaled $565,000, and everything else she was entitled to under the terms of their father's will. And then she might just disappear.

Gary and Gerri knew they would have to move fast. Gary con-sulted his colleagues at Fine Jacobson, and they quickly developed a plan. But it was going to be expensive, very expensive. And the Cohens would have to pay their lawyers just like the firm's other clients.

The plan began to take public form when Gary and Gerri peti-tioned the Dade County Probate Court to freeze all the assets in their father's estate pending the investigation into his murder. Next, the in-surance companies from which Stan had bought policies on his life were warned not to pay the proceeds of those policies to his widow—a suspect in her husband's murder, they said. Finally, Stan's children moved to cut Joyce off from using any of the couple's property—houses, condos, leased cars—until the criminal investigation was completed.

The abrupt legal maneuvers caught Joyce and Alan Ross by sur-prise. Gary and Gerri's actions were simply incomprehensible to Joyce, another terrible blow. Would this nightmare never end? Why were they making her suffer so? She had loved Stan, and she had never said an unkind word about Gary and Gerri. What was she go-ing to do now? A battle was looming in probate court, Ross ex-plained, and she would need another lawyer to protect her rights there. He was a specialist in criminal law, not probate law. Joyce hired Robert Rosenblatt, a well-known Miami civil lawyer, to block her stepchildren's plan to tie up Stan's estate.

But despite Rosenblatt's strenuous efforts, Gary and Gerri won the first round. Their lawyers succeeded in cutting Joyce off—at least temporarily. She got only $6,000 in cash, Florida's statutory "widow's allowance." And there would be no further distribution of the estate's assets pending the investigation into Stan Cohen's murder, the probate court ordered.

There was more. Unless Joyce agreed to pay rent to Stan's estate, she couldn't live in any of the houses she had shared with her husband in Florida and Colorado. And since her white Jaguar and Stan's tan Bronco were leased by SAC Construction Company, she had to take over lease payments herself if she wanted to continue driving. Or she could buy herself a car, but as everyone knew, Joyce had no income of her own. Her fledgling interior decorating business was hardly more than a hobby. And without money, she couldn't afford to pay rent to Stan's estate or lease a car. That $6,000 wouldn't last her very long. Then she might be literally out on the street.

Joyce's friends were stunned. They didn't believe that nonsense about her being a suspect in Stan's murder. They knew Joyce simply didn't have it in her to do something like that. And she had passed the polygraph test. If she had been unhappy with Stan, she could have gotten a divorce—and a big settlement from her rich husband of eleven years.

It must be simple greed, Joyce's friends concluded, that motivated Stan's children to suspect their stepmother of murder. They wanted Stan's money, and a nickname was coined for Gary and Gerri Cohen: the vultures. No one ever repeated it in their hearing, but it was obvious they were pressuring the police for action against Joyce, her friends said. And apparently they had the clout to do it. After all, Gary was a lawyer with a powerful Miami law firm, and Gerri was a local television news personality who was about to marry into one of Miami's influential families. Joyce had always seemed to have a close, affectionate relationship with her stepson, Gary. But everyone knew there was friction between Joyce and Gerri. It must be Gerri Cohen, Joyce's friends decided, who was the instigator.

In fact, there had been bad blood between Gerri and her stepmother almost since the day they met. Gerri had always thought of herself as her father's favorite. Everyone said she was her father's daughter—spunky, outspoken, determined to a fault. Gerri was proud of the comparison. She adored her dad. And her stepmother was a natural rival for his attention.

Stan and Gerri had been especially close when she was a young teenager whose two loves were her father and her show horse. Stan bought Gerri the horse, named Carolina Brass, and a trailer with the horse's name on it. Gerri was the only one of Stan's children who shared his love of riding. Gerri competed in a horse show every Sunday. She was a good rider. She won many ribbons and more than one hundred trophies, which she kept at her dad's bachelor house in the Grove. Stan was proud of Gerri's riding prowess. He often brought his girlfriends, some just a few years older than Gerri, to the Sunday horse shows to watch his daughter compete. The girlfriends were quick to recognize that Gerri was her dad's darling.

Then Stan started dating Joyce McDillon, someone he met at work, he said. At first, Gerri had paid little attention to her father's new girlfriend. But then the worst happened. Stan announced he was going to marry Joyce, and soon after the wedding, Gerri began to feel left out of her father's life. It seemed to her that Joyce found ways to exclude her from the new family group. By then, Gerri had left her horse show days behind in favor of an after-school job, school activities, and boys. But there was nothing to take the place of those special Sundays with her father at the horse shows. One day Gerri realized that her ribbons and riding trophies had simply disappeared from her father's house.

One summer Stan had loaded Joyce and all the children into a Winnebago motor home for a trip out west. Somewhere in New Mexico, they stopped at a roadside souvenir shop. While Stan was outside with the motor home, Joyce and seventeen-year-old Gerri browsed at a jewelry counter inside the shop. Gerri picked out a silver-and-turquoise bracelet and told Joyce how much she liked it.

Just then Stan came into the shop. Before Gerri could say a word, Joyce showed him the same bracelet and asked him to buy it—for her, not Gerri. "Sure," Stan replied casually.

Gerri was stunned, then furious. "You bitch!" she whispered under her breath. Undeterred, Gerri asked her father to buy a bracelet for her, too, and chose one that cost $90, about the same as the bracelet he had just bought for Joyce. Stan was irritated. He agreed to buy the bracelet for Gerri on one condition. She must pay him back. Gerri agreed—she couldn't back down then—but inside she seethed with anger.

After that there were other slights, and Gerri could recall each one. There was the time when Stan took Joyce and all the children on a family ski trip to Colorado, and she outfitted herself and Shawn in new parkas, pants, sweaters, and boots. Gerri, who had no ski clothes of her own, was given an old parka and pants of Joyce's to wear. On the ski slope, Joyce bought lift tickets for herself and Shawn, as Gerri waited beside her. Then she turned away and left Gerri without a ticket. When she protested, Joyce grudgingly bought her a ticket, but Gerri was humiliated and angry.

As time went on, Gerri felt increasingly unwelcome in her father's life and avoided family gatherings. A rift developed between father and daughter, all the more painful because they were so much alike. And Gerri still adored her father and blamed Joyce for their estrangement.

Gary's relationship with his father was easier. Gary himself was more amiable, less assertive than his sister. One day at the University of Florida, where he had joined his father's fraternity, Pi Lambda Phi, Gary returned to the fraternity house for lunch and discovered a large funeral wreath addressed to him.

"What happened? Did someone in your family die?" Fraternity brothers crowded around.

"Gee, I don't think so," he replied uncertainly.

Gary read the card aloud: "For my son Gary, who must have died because I haven't heard from him in two weeks. Stan Cohen."

Gary worked to maintain an amicable relationship with his stepmother, and he became the self-appointed family peacemaker. But still he couldn't heal the breach in his family. Finally, while Gerri was in college at Florida State University in Tallahassee, she wrote her father a twenty-page letter explaining why she blamed Joyce for coming between them. Her chronicle began with the bracelet incident in New Mexico.

Shortly after Gerri sent him the letter, Stan suffered a mild heart attack. Three days later, Gerri was at his bedside in Miami, where Stan would undergo heart bypass surgery. He clutched his daughter's hand and tearfully begged her to reconcile with Joyce. Gerri agreed for her father's sake, but in her heart she knew nothing would change between her and her stepmother.

And now her father was dead.

• • •

One evening after the funeral Gerri discussed her suspicions about Joyce with an acquaintance. "The very night my father was murdered, the police told me that Joyce might be involved," she confided. Gerri bitterly resented her stepmother's pose as the grieving widow. Joyce told her she had helped the police all she could, and now she simply wanted to be let alone to grieve in private. "I've been down to the police station every day," Gerri fumed. "I'd take a hundred lie detector tests or whatever they wanted me to do to help. Why isn't *she* cooperating? To say she wants to grieve in private isn't right when the police need her help."

Gerri was chagrined to see her comments repeated in a *Miami Herald* article the following day, complete with a photograph of her. After establishing a career as a professional in the news industry, she suddenly found herself a subject of the news—grisly, sensational news at that. Ironically, her colleagues now sought interviews with her about the case. To protect her professional status and try to salvage some of her privacy, Gerri chose a prudent course. Although she was "on" the news, she would not be "in" the news—at least not voluntarily. She would not give interviews nor comment on any aspect of the case. And she would be very cautious about confiding in friends and acquaintances.

Gary and Gerri talked with the Miami homicide detectives every day. They brought up any incident, no matter how trivial, that they thought might help the investigation. It was hard to think of Joyce Cohen as a violent person, capable of murder. Yet she had shown occasional flashes of rage, like the time she set Gary's shirt on fire. The shirt had been a birthday gift to him from Joyce, during a time when Gary was staying with Joyce and Stan. Gary liked the shirt but left it lying on a table in the box for several days after his birthday. Then he came home and found the shirt literally in flames. Joyce had set it on fire in a fit of pique at Gary's unintended slight in leaving the shirt in the box.

Detective Spear listened patiently to Stan Cohen's children. He was suspicious of Joyce, too, but there wasn't much to go on. What would her motive for murder be, he wondered. A boyfriend? Money? And in whom, Spear wanted to know, would their stepmother confide? Most people tell someone when they commit murder—a boyfriend, a girlfriend, a relative. Who were Joyce's friends? To whom would she turn?

Gerri and Gary pondered the question. They knew who some of their stepmother's friends were: C. J. Levenstein, Sharon Johnnides, Shu Sampson, Sam Smith, Myra Wenig. C.J. and Sharon were not possibilities—they hadn't been very close to Joyce in recent years. And Shu seemed like such a straitlaced God-fearing Christian, it was hard to imagine Joyce confiding murder plans to her.

But Myra Wenig—she and Joyce were very close, almost like sisters. At Joyce's invitation, Myra had lived with the Cohens in the house on South Bayshore Drive for several months after she broke up with a difficult boyfriend. If Joyce had a confidante, it was probably Myra Wenig, they concluded.

Gary called Myra, and they agreed to meet for lunch. You know we are trying to help the police solve my father's murder, Gary began when they met, and we need your help. Of course, Myra replied. What can I do? Then came the touchy part. Well, Gary said, the police think Joyce may have been involved in it somehow. Do you know anything about it? Did she tell you anything? Can you help us?

Myra was incensed. It was impossible that Joyce had anything to do with Stan's murder, she said. She knew both Stan and Joyce well, had known them for years and loved them both. It was simply unthinkable. Poor Joyce had already been through so much, and now this. Myra couldn't believe that Gary would have the nerve to ask her these things. She angrily refused to talk to him anymore. There was nothing to talk about.

If you change your mind, or you think of something, please call me, Gary said. He paid the bill and left. Another dead end.


In the aftermath of her father's murder, Gerri Cohen faced a serious dilemma: what to do about her forthcoming wedding to Steve Helfman. The date had long been set—March 29—and invitations for 125 guests had gone out. In January, Stan had put down a deposit with the Grand Bay Hotel, reserving the Continental Ballroom, the Crystal Room, outdoor terraces, and the hotel foyer for the five-hour event. But then, just three short weeks before the planned wedding, Stan had been murdered.

Gerri's life was in chaos. She didn't really have the heart to go through with her plans in the wake of her father's murder, but she wasn't sure what to do. She ordered announcements for herself and Steve stating that the death of Mr. Stanley Cohen obliged them to re-call their wedding invitation. But, still undecided, she hesitated to send them out.

Then Gerri received a phone call from a Miami travel agent, who said that Stan Cohen had ordered a honeymoon travel voucher for several thousand dollars as a surprise wedding gift for his daughter and her fiancé. When she read of Stan Cohen's death, the travel agent had called Joyce to ask her preference: should the travel voucher be delivered directly to Gerri Cohen and Steve Helfman, or would Mrs. Cohen rather present the gift to them herself? Joyce's response star-tled the travel agent: Cancel the travel voucher and credit the amount to my account.

Gerri was surprised and deeply touched by her father's gesture in planning the unexpected wedding gift. And she was furious that her stepmother had canceled it. My father's *dead*, she thought bitterly, and Joyce is still trying to come between us. Finally Gerri made up her mind. She would have her wedding on March 29 as planned. She did, however, send out two of the cancellation announcements. One went to her stepmother, the other to Myra Wenig.

Gerri and Steve then turned to the details of their wedding and de-cided to curtail their plans somewhat. A less elaborate celebration was appropriate, they thought, in view of the recent family tragedy. Rabbi Bernat Haskell would marry them in the ballroom of the Grand Bay Hotel, but the reception would be champagne and hors d'oeuvres on the outdoor terrace rather than a sit-down dinner. There would be no dancing.

And they would have to make certain financial arrangements, even with the reduced plans. Stan had already put down deposits, but there were still substantial balances due to the hotel, the caterer, and others, expenses that he had planned to pay for his daughter. With her father gone, those expenses were a problem for Gerri. She turned to Marvin Sheldon, her father's friend and partner. She needed money, she said, to take care of wedding expenses. She would repay Sheldon out of her inheritance, but she wasn't sure when the funds would be available. Marvin, who was very fond of Stan's children, was anxious to help out. He gave Gerri about $17,000 and told her not to worry about when she could repay it. But Gerri insisted. Several months later, she paid back every cent.


Shawn had gone back to school, and Joyce had moved again, this time to stay with Ed and Sam Smith. But no matter where she went, she seemed completely obsessed with Stan's murder. She hardly slept. She couldn't drive. If she had to go out, Sam drove her. Joyce and Sam spent most days sitting on the patio of the Smiths' Coral Gables house. Joyce sometimes wore Stan's sport coat, and she carried his picture constantly. She sobbed uncontrollably. "Why did this happen to me?" she cried. "What am I going to do without Stan?"

She talked incessantly about the murder, reliving her horror over and over again. "I had Stan's head in my lap," she told Sam and Ed as she sat on the floor, rocking and sobbing hysterically. "And he was bleeding all over me! And I took a towel and I was trying to stop the blood from coming out! And I didn't know what to do! And I couldn't stop the blood from coming out!"

Finally Ed couldn't stand any more. He told Sam that Joyce would have to leave. She was disrupting their lives, he said. Sam was spending all her time trying to take care of Joyce.

Joyce seemed to have no alternative but to leave Miami for Steamboat Springs. She said she wanted to distance herself from the tragedy, and even though it seemed so unfair, she agreed to pay $500 per month rent to Stan's estate for Wolf Run Ranch. It was her house, too, and she had decorated it with such care just a few years ago. And since Stan's tan Bronco would be more practical in Colorado than her white Jag, she bought the Bronco from SAC Construction for $9,000. She signed promissory notes for the car and for another $4,990 that she borrowed from SAC.

Prosecutor David Waksman and Detective Jon Spear did not object to Joyce's plans to move to Colorado. They knew where to find her there. And they expected she wouldn't just disappear as long as Stan Cohen's estate hung in the balance. They still considered her their prime suspect in her husband's murder. But, as they patiently explained to Gary and Gerri over and over again, they just didn't have probable cause to arrest her. The investigation would have to proceed at its own pace. And it was certainly possible that Joyce was entirely innocent of any crime.

Just three weeks after Stan Cohen's murder, on March 29, 1986, the invited guests attended the wedding of his daughter, Gerri, and Steve Helfman. The guests did not include Joyce Cohen and Myra Wenig. Gary witnessed the marriage for his sister. All the old Cohen family friends were there—the Sheldons, the Rossins, the Levensteins, and others—a group that extended back in time to the Gainesville days, when they were young and their lives lay ahead like a bright promise. The Helfmans and their friends were there, and there were colleagues from the law firm of Fine Jacobson, where both Gary and Steve practiced law. Some well-known local television personalities were also there, friends of the bride.

The wedding in the hotel ballroom was beautiful but subdued, restrained, shadowed by the tragedy of Stan Cohen's murder. The bride was lovely, thinner than ever, striking in her long, lacy designer gown. But guests noticed that her eyes sparkled with unshed tears as she walked down the aisle alone. They knew what was in her heart—her father should have been beside her on that day. It was a poignant moment for all those gathered to witness the marriage of Stan Cohen's only daughter. He was in their thoughts as surely as if he stood next to them, laughing, proposing a toast, joking with his pals.

Myra Wenig was furious at being disinvited to the wedding. And she was deeply offended that Gary had tried to enlist her support in drumming up evidence against Joyce. On March 29, the evening of Gerri Cohen's wedding, Myra took herself to dinner at Buccione's, the restaurant where she had spent so many happy evenings with Joyce and Stan. She intended to spend on herself exactly what she had planned to give Gerri Cohen as a wedding gift: $60.00.

Myra ordered herself dinner and a good bottle of wine. Then she offered a bitter wedding toast: "To Gerri Cohen. May she rot in hell!"

# III

·

## Reasonable
## Doubt

# *Fourteen*

*T*he dreams began right after the funeral. Ben Abernathy, Stan Cohen's young protégé at SAC Construction Company, dreamed about Stan nearly every night for a year. Sometimes he dreamed of frightening death scenes. Sometimes Stan wasn't really dead after all. He had faked his death, trying to get away from somebody who was after him.

In one dream, Ben would walk into the office to see Stan sitting at his old desk. "Come on in, guys," he would yell down the hall. "Business as usual!"

"Stan! I'm glad you're back!" Ben would call out weakly. Then, in his dream, he would huddle with Jack Jamme, his associate at SAC. "What are we going to do?" he would whisper frantically. "Here we've remodeled his office and he's come back!"

Sometimes, when he first woke up in the morning, Ben wasn't sure Stan was really gone. Jack Jamme had dreams about his murdered boss, too. Stan Cohen was just too big to die.

Ben was haunted by one conversation he had had with Stan. They had gone out to look at a condominium on Grove Isle, and on the way back, Stan told him that the condo's owner was once a suspect in a big Miami murder case in the 1960s—the Mossler murder. A wealthy older man, Jacques Mossler, was found dead in his Key Bis-

cayne apartment by his beautiful young wife, Candace. A suspect
was apprehended running across the causeway from Key Biscayne to
Miami but was never charged in the case. Candace Mossler and her
handsome young nephew, who was also her lover, were arrested and
tried for the murder. Both were acquitted, and nearly twenty years
later, an aura of mystery still clung to the case.

"A big trial, a Hollywood-type murder case," Stan had told Ben
that day. "You'd never believe it was a local thing." It reminded Stan
of another famous murder, out in Aspen, Colorado, where singer
Andy Williams's wife, Claudine Longet, shot and killed her lover,
Spider Sabich. "Same type of case," Stan said excitedly. "A perfect
made-for-TV movie."

But Stan had been particularly fascinated by the details of the
Mossler murder. He couldn't stop talking about it that day—the
beautiful young widow, the vicious stab wounds on the corpse,
the bloody palm print found at the scene, the sensational trial.
The widow, Stan had assured Ben, got away with murder.


Gary and Gerri came to the SAC Construction Company office to
collect Stan's things. There were childhood pictures, family photographs, little mementos. But they didn't want the gilt-framed portrait of Joyce as a bride that Stan had hung so proudly in his office.
Joyce never came to claim it. Finally Ben Abernathy took it off the
wall and stuck it in a closet in Stan's gym. He turned her face with
its enigmatic smile to the wall.


Within a week of Stanley Cohen's murder, Detective Jon Spear hit
the road in search of some clue that would shed more light on the
case. What he learned on his travels didn't surprise him. The Cohens'
marriage had been no bed of roses.

Spear flew to Nashville, Tennessee, to interview the woman Joyce
Cohen had boasted was a friend, the blond country music singer
Tanya Tucker. The singer showed up for the interview wearing tight
jeans and a plaid shirt. Without makeup, she was pretty in a fresh-
scrubbed, down-home way. Tucker was reluctant to discuss her partying with Joyce, but finally, under Spear's persistent questioning,

she recounted her overnight visit at Wolf Run Ranch shortly before Stan's murder.

The two women drank champagne, tooted a little coke, and got to know each other, Tucker told the detective. Joyce had been in a talkative mood that night. Fueled by cocaine and the excitement of her new celebrity friendship, she had talked at length about her "miserable" marriage. Her husband was unfaithful. He had even gotten a girlfriend pregnant once, or so she had claimed. "Bottom line," Tucker told Detective Spear with a sigh, "she was extremely unhappy. Not just sad—it didn't seem like it was something that was going to go away."

She wanted out of her marriage, Joyce had told her new friend, but not without the money. "She liked the money," Tucker said. "That's the only thing she liked as far as, you know, what I read from her. That was the only thing that was getting her along."

Did Joyce ever mention anything about killing her husband, Spear wanted to know. "No," Tucker replied, "I don't recall her saying that to me."

The interview with Tanya Tucker confirmed rumors that Detective Spear had already heard, but added no solid evidence to the case. He still had nothing concrete to link Joyce to her husband's murder. But he did get an autographed album from Tucker—and he had his picture taken kissing her on the cheek. A very pretty lady, he thought. He kept that picture in his desk for years.

Next Spear went looking for Frank Wheatley, former manager of Stan's Colorado construction projects. Spear had heard rumors about Joyce's frenetic partying in Steamboat Springs—drugs, drunk driving tickets, and car crashes. There were stories about affairs, about nude sunbathing and wet T-shirt contests. The rumors had filtered back to the SAC Construction Company office while Joyce was alone in Steamboat—and Wheatley was there managing SAC Construction projects. He should know what had gone on, Spear figured.

Wheatley was not anxious to be found, but Spear finally tracked him down in Atlanta. He was a tall man with neatly trimmed dark hair and dark-rimmed glasses. There was a conservative, almost studious air about him. Speaking in a soft voice smoothed by a noticeable southern accent, he wouldn't have looked out of place in a roomful of Georgia insurance salesmen—until he began to talk about his life in Steamboat Springs with the Cohens.

Wheatley spoke slowly, reluctantly. He had moved his family out of Steamboat Springs in January 1985, he told Spear, because he thought the cocaine-and-party scene was getting out of hand. Wheatley had gone to Steamboat Springs in 1981 to supervise SAC Construction projects there. The social atmosphere, he found, was very laid-back. There were lots of parties. And coke was a popular party drug.

At least some of the rumors about the Cohens were true, Wheatley admitted. Both Stan and Joyce snorted cocaine when they partied, but Joyce was really into it. Wheatley had gotten to know Joyce better when she stayed on in Steamboat after Stan returned to Miami. They began to party together, just a few drinks and a little coke. Eventually Joyce began to confide in Wheatley. There were problems in her marriage, she said. Stan was slowing down, didn't want to party much anymore. She said she wanted out of the marriage, but she didn't want to give up the money. She had even asked Stan for a divorce, she had told Wheatley one night over a few lines of coke. Her price: $1 million. But Stan had just laughed. "You'll go out of this marriage the same way you came in," he'd jeered. "With nothing!"

What Wheatley said next made Spear's blood race. Once Joyce told him that she wished she could find someone to kill her husband—or have the nerve to do it herself. But he thought she was only joking—and she probably was. Soon afterward, she had asked him playfully, "Did you find me someone yet?" She laughed. He laughed. The moment passed.

"It was just a bullshit conversation," Wheatley had concluded. But now he wasn't so sure.

Other Miami detectives traveled to Steamboat Springs to interview the Cohens' friends and associates. They talked to Scott Flower, resident manager of Wolf Run Ranch, who was not impressed with the real-life Miami Vice investigators. He thought they threw their weight around, for one thing. And they looked ridiculous for another. "They arrived in the middle of mud season in their Gucci loafers," Flower told *Miami Herald* reporter Edna Buchanan. "You couldn't miss them. They talked to everybody up here and made a lot of accusations. People finally got fed up and told them to come when they had facts." Flower couldn't believe Joyce Cohen had anything to do with her husband's murder. And he never would.

When he returned to Miami, Spear called Sharon Johnnides, who agreed to come in for an interview. She had known Stan and Joyce for several years, she told him. And yes, she was aware that Joyce had a problem with cocaine. Sharon vividly remembered the time she had tried to talk to Joyce about it. One Saturday she had run into Joyce in the Grove, and Joyce suggested lunch at Grove Isle. Sharon hadn't seen Joyce for a while, but she had heard rumors about her using coke. She was troubled. Lunch would be a good opportunity to speak to Joyce about it.

"I think you have a problem," Sharon began haltingly over lunch.

"Like what?" Joyce asked as she picked at her salad.

"Well, maybe you're using too many drugs, or maybe things are a little out of control."

"No." Joyce was emphatic. "But maybe I'm drinking a little more than I should."

Sharon was mystified. Joyce was never a drinker, she thought. Just a glass or two of wine, and that would be it.

"I'm okay, but I'm worried about Stan," Joyce continued.

"*You* are worried about *him*?"

"Yes. I can hear him sometimes in the morning when he gets up. In the bathroom. I can hear him snorting in there."

Sharon didn't believe it. Well, she thought, that's it. She shrugged her shoulders and told herself, I've said my piece.

Joyce had changed the subject. "I was hostessing at the restaurant," she said excitedly, her face lighting up. "And this guy came in. He was attractive and he was like looking at me, and finally he spoke to me. He said, 'I think you're very attractive. I'd like to meet you for lunch or dinner.' And I said to him, 'Well, you know, my husband owns this restaurant.' And he said, 'That's no problem. I'd just like to meet you and have lunch with you.'"

"What are you going to do?" Sharon asked.

"I don't know. I'm just thinking about it," Joyce replied with a smile. She never mentioned a name. Sharon had no idea whom Joyce had been talking about.

But Spear had a hunch: Lynn Barkley. He had already heard about

Barkley. He worked occasionally as a professional photographer, he said, and had lived off and on with various friends in the Grove. He claimed to have worked at Studio 54 in New York and said he once managed a rock band.

On the morning of the murder, Barkley had stopped by the Cohen home to see what was going on. A police officer recalled a strange question from Barkley that morning: "Did she do it? Did she finally shoot him?" Barkley denied saying that when Spear contacted him, but he agreed to come to the homicide office for a talk. The interview lasted several hours.

"I'll talk to you," Barkley sighed as he settled into a chair. "I'll tell you the truth." This is it, Spear thought. Barkley had a smug, almost snide way of speaking that raised Spear's hackles. But he seemed very hip, very cool. And with his rangy build and shaggy blond hair, he was probably attractive to women. Just the type Joyce Cohen might go for, Spear thought. If Joyce was having an affair, this might be the guy. She could have killed her husband to run away with him.

Spear watched Barkley speculatively. But once Barkley started talking, he actually said very little. He admitted having a brief affair with Joyce—just one sexual encounter in 1984, he claimed. It was after a cozy dinner at the Cohens' while Stan was conveniently away. They drank some wine, tooted a little coke. One thing had led to another. But since that night they had just been friends, Barkley insisted. He knew Joyce had a problem with cocaine. Yes, she was unhappy in her marriage. She talked about divorce. No, she never discussed murdering her husband. Absolutely not.

This guy's flaky, Spear thought. At first Barkley acted as though he was going to give them some information, then he denied knowing anything about the murder. Spear called in prosecutor David Waksman, and they decided to ask Barkley to take a polygraph with Detective Ron Ilhart, a Miami homicide investigator trained in polygraph administration. But Waksman was concerned that if Barkley failed the polygraph, he would claim he had been coerced during the long hours of intensive interviews that day. He needed something to counter that argument. He handed Barkley a piece of paper. On it was written: "5 P.M. Leave, get out of here. David Waksman."

"Now, get out of here," Waksman told Barkley. "You've been lying to us all day."

"No, no, no. I want to talk to you. I want to take a polygraph," Barkley insisted.

Waksman was satisfied, and Detective Ilhart began to hook Barkley up to the polygraph machine. He handed Barkley the standard Miranda rights form to sign. When Barkley saw the form, he changed his mind. "That's it, I'm not talking," he said. "I'm leaving." Barkley bolted out the door.

Very suspicious, the detectives thought. We must be onto something. Barkley's name had also come up during an interview with Robert Bramerel, who, Spear was told, might have sold cocaine to Joyce. Bramerel denied that, and Spear believed him, but he did say he knew Joyce Cohen—and he didn't like her. He remembered meeting her in the fall of 1985 when Barkley was staying with him. "Meet Joyce Cohen," Barkley had said by way of introduction. Bramerel saw the white Jaguar in his drive. He knew who Stan Cohen was. And he didn't want Stan's wife in his house.

Bramerel told Spear that he saw Joyce again on March 6, 1986, just hours before her husband was murdered. At 4:30 that Thursday afternoon, the door had burst open in his bedroom as he sat chatting with a friend. Bramerel was startled, but he immediately recognized the intruder as Joyce Cohen.

Where is Lynn? Joyce had demanded.

"Lynn Barkley is not here," Bramerel replied. "Why don't you go check at the Matilda address?" It was Barkley's current address.

"Well, you know where he is. He's not there," Joyce said. She looked anxious, upset.

"Well, I don't." Bramerel was aggravated. "And excuse me, you're in my private bedroom here on the porch, and please leave."

But Joyce stood her ground. "I'm not leaving until you tell me where he is," she insisted.

"Please. You're leaving. You're out." Bramerel grabbed Joyce by the arm and shoved her out the door with his foot.

"You can't treat me this way!" Joyce yelled. "I'm going to call the police on you!"

She retreated to the white Jaguar and drove off, speeding a few blocks down the street to a market with a pay phone outside. Joyce parked at the curb, intent on calling the police to arrest Bramerel for assault and battery.

By coincidence, Lynn Barkley saw Joyce and the white Jaguar as he was driving by. He honked and waved, then pulled over to meet her. Angrily, she told him about her encounter with Bob Bramerel, but when she calmed down, she decided to forget the call to the police and agreed to go have a drink with Barkley at the outdoor bar at Monty's Bayside Restaurant. They dropped Barkley's car off at his new address and went to the restaurant in Joyce's Jag.

A few minutes later, Barkley had called Bob Bramerel. "You know, Joyce Cohen was going to press charges against you for assault and battery," he informed Bramerel, "but I talked her out of it." Bramerel hadn't seen Joyce Cohen since that day, he told the detectives. He knew nothing about the murder of her husband.

Bramerel's story rekindled the investigators' interest in Lynn Barkley. Why had Joyce been so anxious to find him that afternoon? Was their meeting really coincidental? What had they talked about at the restaurant? Was there some connection between Barkley and the intruders who had murdered Stan? Was he one of them? Or maybe Barkley and Joyce had conspired to kill Stan.

Confronted by these new suspicions, Barkley hired an attorney and arranged to take a polygraph with examiner Warren Holmes in April. He passed the test. Holmes concluded that Barkley was telling the truth when he denied having any knowledge whatsoever about Stanley Cohen's death. He was convinced that Barkley "was not criminally involved in any way." Another dead end.


The police still had no solid evidence to connect Joyce with her husband's murder. But she remained the target—the sole target—of the investigation. It was the only scenario that made any sense. The intruders in the Cohens' house that night were not burglars. Nothing was stolen or even disturbed. Nor had they come just to have a chat with Stan. They had come to kill him, and they knew exactly where to find him. They broke into the kitchen, made a beeline for the master bedroom upstairs, shot Stan in the head while he was lying face down on the bed, probably sound asleep, and then got the hell out. The crime had all the earmarks of a hit: the alarm system conveniently turned off, Joyce and the dog conveniently in another part of the house. Spear had so far been able to find no one else who might have wanted Stan Cohen dead. It *had* to be Joyce.

Of course, it was also possible that Joyce's story about intruders was a fabrication. There was the unexplained mystery about the apparent lapse of time between the calls from Colorado, when Joyce claimed she saw the intruders and discovered Stan's body, and her hysterical call to the police. Phone records showed calls from Colorado at 5:18 and 5:20 A.M., but Joyce's call to 911 didn't come in until 5:25. What was she doing for five full minutes before she finally called for help? She could have killed her husband with his own gun, then dropped it in the underbrush in front of the house for the police to find. Either way, Joyce was somehow implicated in this case. And there had to be a way to prove it. Spear wasn't about to give up. He knew it was just a matter of time. And he had all the time in the world.

The Miami detectives got in touch with Joyce's friend Myra Wenig. Myra had known the Cohens for ten years, she told them. She, too, had heard that Joyce was using cocaine, but she had never seen her do it. The Cohens argued occasionally, like most couples, but she insisted there were no serious marital problems.

Myra Wenig could have said much more.

Early one morning a year or two earlier, Joyce had called Myra with an urgent request: "Meet me at the Burger King on Twenty-seventh Avenue."

When Myra arrived, Joyce was agitated. Stan was in Steamboat Springs on business, she told Myra, and so was Julie Belcher. Joyce suspected that Stan was having an affair with Julie, the rich young oil heiress who had invested in Stan's residential development project in Steamboat. Julie and Stan were out there together. A project meeting, Stan had said.

"When he comes home, I'm going to ask him," Joyce said. "I already think something happened, I just do. If he lies to me, I'll know it. And I can promise you this. Whatever the outcome, I'll stay with him. But I want you to know that it'll be only for one reason—my son!"

Myra tried to calm her friend. Then a few days later she called Joyce. "What's up?" she asked.

"He denied it, of course." Joyce replied. "He said they had a few beers, they got a little dizzy, they talked all night, that's it."

Both Stan and Julie flatly denied there was anything between them. Joyce didn't believe them.

Then there was the Abby Perlmutter episode. Joyce had always been jealous of Abby, an attractive, statuesque brunette who worked for a while at SAC Construction Company, leasing office space. Finally she confronted Abby at a party one night, accusing her of having an affair with Stan. Abby denied it and there was an ugly scene. Joyce never found any proof of an affair, but she refused to let it drop.

But the woman Joyce had been most upset about in February 1986 was Carol Hughes, an art teacher and well-known Grove artist. Stan had been engaged to Carol Hughes when he met Joyce back in 1974. Abruptly he broke off the engagement and married Joyce instead. But Carol was still in love with Stan. And Joyce had heard that Stan was seeing her again.

The detectives called Carol Hughes for an interview. She was a tall, dark-haired woman in her forties, obviously intelligent, pleasant-looking rather than pretty. She was thoughtful and composed as she answered the detectives' questions. But it was obvious she had cared deeply for Stan Cohen.

She had run into Stan in the Grove one Friday evening in February 1986, Carol recounted. Stan had been alone—and lonely. Joyce was still in Steamboat Springs, partying and skiing. Stan had wandered into a favorite old haunt from his bachelor days, the Taurus Restaurant. By coincidence, Carol dropped by the restaurant that night after a gallery opening nearby. The former lovers greeted each other affectionately.

Stan was anxious to talk to her, Carol recalled. As the noise at the Taurus grew louder, they left for a quiet bar where they could talk. They stayed until 2 A.M. Stan was troubled, he confided. But he didn't elaborate. That night he took Carol home, just to be sure she was safe. He went home alone.

The following Friday night, there was a knock at Carol's front door. It was Stan.

"What are you doing here?" Carol asked.

"I need to talk to you. I want to talk to you," he replied. "Will you have dinner with me tonight?"

Carol agreed. "Where are we going?"

"Well, I don't know. Let's go to the Taurus."

"The Taurus? You're going to take me to the Taurus?" Carol knew he would never take her there unless he didn't care who saw them together. Something must be wrong with his marriage. "I don't want to go to the Taurus," Carol said. "I want to go to Key Biscayne." She wasn't sure what was going on with Stan, but she preferred discretion.

They sat at the Sand Bar on Key Biscayne, a waterfront place from their past, until nearly ten o'clock that night. Then they moved on to Horatio's on the Rickenbacker Causeway. It was a cozy, romantic place where they could watch the play of Miami's lights on the water.

Over dinner and a glass or two of wine, Stan talked to Carol. His marriage, he admitted, was in trouble. Joyce was abusing cocaine. He had tried to get her help, but it didn't seem to be working. Now she was refusing to come back from Colorado. He was going to have to go get her, he said. "I should have married you," he told Carol sadly.

Stan talked about the future. He was thinking of retiring in a year, he said. He wanted to live in Colorado. Would Carol be able to retire from her job? Yes, she said, she had just completed the required twenty years' teaching. Would she mind selling her home and moving? Carol understood that Stan was asking her if she would go to Colorado with him. That night, when he took her home, he stayed. They made love.

The next time Carol saw Stan was Sunday, March 2. That afternoon she had walked three blocks from her home in the Grove to Monty's Bayside Restaurant, where she decided to get something to eat, maybe have a drink. She sat alone at a table on the outdoor deck overlooking the bay. Glancing along the waterfront, she recognized a familiar figure striding down the dock. It was Stan, walking alone. The look on his face was pensive, troubled. He didn't notice her.

Carol yelled hello, called his name, and waved. Stan looked up. He waved back but kept walking. Too late, Carol saw the white

Jaguar—Joyce's Jaguar—parked at the curb. Joyce was sitting in the passenger seat. Stan hopped in and they drove away.

But Stan was gone only five or ten minutes—just time enough to drop off his wife. Then he came back alone to meet Carol. They talked for an hour. He was still having problems, he said cryptically. He had to get these problems solved, and when he did, he would get back to Carol.

"Well, I'll call you soon," he said as he left. It was the last thing Stan ever said to her, Carol Hughes recounted sadly.


Detective Spear stopped by Buccione's, the restaurant Stan Cohen had owned, to talk to the manager and staff. He wasn't surprised to find out that they knew about Joyce's coke problem. They told him that she would come into the restaurant in the evening, gulp some champagne, hit the ladies' room a few times, then head off to Ensign Bitters or Biscayne Baby. Sometimes the waiters overheard Stan telling Joyce he didn't want to go with her. It was obvious they weren't getting along. Occasionally Stan would leave with his wife around 11 P.M., then be back to check on things at the restaurant about 12:30 before heading home alone to get some sleep. Joyce often partied until three or four in the morning, they heard.

When Stan wasn't around, Joyce usually perched at Buccione's tiny bar, drinking champagne and chatting with the bartender. The waiters noticed that her sorties to the ladies' room became more frequent, and they wondered how Joyce could be so brazen about snorting coke in there. Anyone might walk in. Even Dade State Attorney Janet Reno occasionally dined at Buccione's. But Joyce never seemed concerned. On occasion she even asked someone at Buccione's to get her coke. A phone call would be made, and there would be a discreet delivery right at the restaurant. Someone would come in to the bar, a head would nod in Joyce's direction, and a package might be slipped into her open purse lying on the bar as she casually looked the other way.

If Joyce started on the champagne-and-coke routine around nine, by 10:30 she would be a different person—chatty, bubbly, holding a champagne flute aloft as she strolled about the dining room, smiling and helloing.

"Do I look funny walking around the dining room?" she asked a waiter one night when Stan wasn't there.

"No, you don't look funny," the waiter replied. "Why?"

"Well, Stan says I shouldn't be here."

Another waiter had told Stan that Joyce was causing scenes in the dining room. When she walked around with her champagne flute, customers would ask her if they could buy her a drink. She would decline but then later come up and say, "Thanks for the drink!" The waiter had complained to Stan that she was so bombed she didn't know what was going on. It was embarrassing.

One evening Joyce hosted a party at Buccione's for some friends—Toni Pollack, her partner at SAC Interiors, Geri Carroll, Myra Wenig, Sam Smith, and a few others. She looked especially good that night in a burgundy outfit with high black leather boots. She arrived early to be sure everything was perfect for her guests at table three, the big round table at the front of the restaurant. But as soon as she walked in, Joyce started with a couple of glasses of champagne, then a trip to the ladies' room. When her friends arrived, wine was poured and salads served.

Suddenly, just as she started on her salad, Joyce slumped over her plate. The waiters were alarmed. They thought she must have taken a Quaalude or something—she came down so hard and fast. With a friend taking each arm, Joyce was helped out of the restaurant and into her car. After they drove her home, they returned to finish their dinner.

The next day, a waiter told Stan what had happened. He was furious. "Don't worry," he fumed to the waiter. "She'll never be in here again."

In fact, Joyce spent no more evenings in the restaurant. But she did stop by once more, to apologize to a waiter for the scene she had created that night. She was so embarrassed, she said. She had been taking prescription medication, and the combination of that and the champagne just hit her.

"Don't worry," the waiter said kindly. "We all have times like that." He felt sorry for her.

A few months later, Stan sold Buccione's. It was the end of an era, the waiters told Spear sadly.

• • •

Alan Ross was growing uneasy. Despite Joyce Cohen's exculpatory polygraph with George Slattery, he had heard that the Miami detectives were still pursuing her. He just couldn't understand it. But he knew he had to keep tabs on the investigation. So he put his private investigator, Steve Kiraly, on the trail. Kiraly's technique was simple. He interviewed witnesses right after the detectives did and bluntly asked them to repeat what they had told the police.

What Kiraly learned alarmed Ross. Witnesses were lining up to tattle about Joyce's marital problems—and her cocaine habit. Although tooting coke doesn't make you a murderer, it's a brush that paints broadly, especially in Miami, where drugs and death so often collide. And there were rumors that the Slattery polygraph had been rigged somehow—maybe Joyce Cohen had taken some kind of drug to help her pass.

Reluctantly, Ross called his client in Steamboat Springs and suggested that she return to Miami for another polygraph test. This time, he told her, they would do a simultaneous drug screening. They had to show the cops that Joyce wasn't doing any drugs.

But which examiner to use this time? Ross was still hoping to get a test the prosecutors and investigators would rely upon, without, of course, actually permitting them to participate in the process. He called an old friend in the Miami criminal defense bar and asked a favor. Please call George Yoss at the Dade State Attorney's Office and tell him you need a polygraph. Ask him which polygraphist his office would choose. Tell him George Slattery can't do it because he has a conflict.

Ross's friend called back shortly with the answer: Yoss had named Dudley H. Dickson of Dickson Polygraph Laboratories in Tampa. Ross recognized the name. Dickson was a pilot as well as a polygraphist, and he flew his own plane around the state to conduct examinations. His credentials were excellent, his reputation impeccable. Ross set up the polygraph for April 18, 1986, about five weeks after George Slattery's test.

Joyce flew back to Miami, accompanied by her friend from Steamboat Springs, Kathy Dickett. On the appointed day, Joyce and Alan Ross met with Dudley Dickson in Ross's third-floor conference room for the pretest interview. Ross summarized the facts of the case for Dickson, as well as the allegations against his client. Then he handed Dickson a copy of George Slattery's polygraph report and conclusions.

"What do you think you're doing?" Dickson exploded. "Are you trying to tell me it's a foregone conclusion? That I'm supposed to find the same thing Slattery did?"

"Hey, look, I am not trying to influence—" Ross began.

"No, you look. If she committed this murder, I'm going to know it!"

Ross left the room, and Dickson prepared his own relevant questions for Joyce Cohen.

"Did you shoot Stanley Cohen?"

"Did you encourage or have anyone shoot Stanley Cohen?"

"Do you have any actual knowledge as to who shot Stanley Cohen?"

"Do you know the identity of any person, other than you and your husband, being in your house between 6 P.M. on March 6, 1986, and the time the police arrived?"

During the polygraph test Joyce Cohen answered no to each of those questions. Then Dickson asked, "Did you observe someone leaving the front door of your house a few seconds before you went upstairs and discovered your husband had been shot?"

"Yes," she replied.

When Dickson had finished with Joyce, he told Ross, "She had nothing to do with the murder." He put it all in his report and concluded: "Based on the subject's polygraph responses and comments, it is the examiner's opinion she was truthful as indicated above and did not personally shoot her husband or have anyone do so. There was no indication she had actual knowledge as to who had shot Stanley Cohen."

Joyce also passed the drug screening—no drugs, no alcohol, no nothing. She was clean.

As far as Ross was concerned, the case against his client was now truly over. A second examiner, selected by the prosecutor's office, had unequivocally passed her—using a different set of questions and an entirely different polygraph format. And the drug screening was completely negative. What more could the cops possibly want?

Ross handed his client's polygraph results to prosecutor David

Waksman, along with a suggestion. Look into Stan Cohen's contacts with fugitive Miami attorney Frankie Diaz. Diaz had sneaked back to Miami and made a clandestine late-night visit to Stan Cohen at his home just five days before his murder, Ross told them. It was rumored that Cohen was holding money for Diaz—money that came from drug trafficking. Others said Diaz had come to negotiate for Cohen's Sabreliner. The plane had been placed on the DEA's "Watch List," suspected of transporting drug money to Panama. Even so, Waksman and Spear never really considered Frankie Diaz a suspect in the case. They were pretty sure they knew who killed Stan Cohen. But they couldn't prove it—yet.

While she was in Miami with Joyce, Kathy Dickett turned up in David Waksman's office, accompanied by a Miami criminal lawyer, Glenn Kritzer. Waksman was surprised to see her. He had sent Dickett a subpoena in Steamboat Springs, but he never expected her to just show up in Miami. She was youngish, maybe in her twenties, Waksman thought, thin, athletic-looking, medium-length blondish hair. Definitely an attractive woman. He pegged her as Joyce's bar buddy out in Steamboat Springs.

Waksman decided to take a sworn statement from Kathy Dickett while she was there. But the picture she painted of Joyce's life in Steamboat contrasted sharply with what the investigators had heard from others. Kathy had known Joyce less than a year, she said. They had met at Cafe Blue Bayou, the Steamboat Springs restaurant that Kathy owned with a partner. Joyce came into the restaurant frequently, and the two women became friends.

"How was the Cohens' marriage?" Waksman asked.

"The feeling I got, the marriage was fine, they got along fine. They had a good marriage," Kathy replied.

Waksman eyed her speculatively. "Okay, did you ever see her doing cocaine?" he asked.

"No, I didn't."

"You understand you are under oath now?"

"Yes, I do."

"I'm telling you that this is important to our investigation, do you

Millionaire Miami contractor Stanley Cohen (far right) celebrates his winnings in Las Vegas with friends in 1974. A few months later, in a lavish Vegas ceremony, he married his fourth wife, Joyce McDillon, a shy young divorcée who worked in a construction office.

Adored and indulged by her husband, Joyce Cohen blossomed into an exotic beauty with a taste for expensive jewelry, high-fashion clothes, and Miami nightlife.

Posing for the camera, Joyce displays her sense of flair and style.

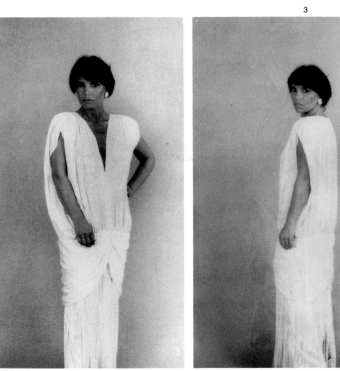

4

The landmark residence at 1665 South Bayshore Drive that Stan bought for Joyce in the exclusive Miami suburb of Coconut Grove.

Both avid skiers, Stan and Joyce spent their winter vacations at Wolf Run Ranch, the spacious house Stan built on 650 acres in Steamboat Springs, Colorado.

5

6

7

Stan was part owner of *Bull III*, a 43-foot Egg Harbor, fully equipped for fishing expeditions or leisurely cruises with friends.

"The Jews," Stan's spear-fishing team, which had rowdy annual competitions with another team dubbed "The Christians."

8

9

A Sabreliner was another of Stan's "toys," used for business, vacation trips to Colorado, and impetuous junkets to the Keys and the Caribbean.

The Miami Ski Club's annual fashion show, a highlight of the winter social season. Joyce is third from left, top row.

10

11

The Cohens, with Joyce's close friend Myra Wenig (left), depart for a costume party in Joyce's white Jag.

13

A proud Stan and a glamorous Joyce at the Good Friends' Christmas party at the fashionable Grove Isle Club in 1985. Friends said they never looked happier.

12 Gerri Cohen, Stan's daughter by his first marriage, on a rare visit to Wolf Run Ranch in 1984. She adored her father but thought Joyce was both too extravagant and too possessive.

Stan, Joyce, and Shawn, Joyce's son by her first marriage whom Stan adopted, pose before the giant tree at Wolf Run Ranch, Christmas 1985. Joyce was wearing a magnificent diamond ring, Stan's present for their eleventh anniversary.

The bridal shower for Gerri Cohen and Stephen Helfman at the Grove Isle Club in February 1986. From left: Mrs. Sue Helfman, Steve, Gerri, Stan, Joyce, and Dr. Richard Helfman. Less than two weeks later, tragedy shattered both families.

16

Joyce discovered her husband's body and, in hysterics, told detectives that intruders had smashed through the kitchen door while she was in another part of the house.

The king-size brass bed where a sleeping Stan Cohen was shot four times in the back of the head.

17

The murder weapon, Stan's own .38 Smith & Wesson, wiped clean of fingerprints and tossed in the foliage outside the Cohen house.

18

Detective Jon Spear of the Miami Police Department investigated the brutal murder that was sending shock waves through Miami society.

19

Prosecutor David Waksman, assistant state attorney for the Dade County State Attorney's Office, was baffled by the crime. Who had a motive to murder Stan Cohen?

20

21

A distraught Joyce at a press conference five days after Stan's murder. A polygraph test she had taken completely exonerated her as a suspect.

22

Shocking new evidence in the case came with the arrest of Frank Zuccarello (above) a home invasion robber who accused fellow gang members Anthony Caracciolo (below left) and Tommy Lamberti (below right) of killing Stan Cohen.

23

24

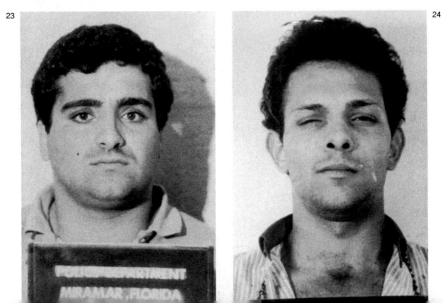

25

Attorneys Robert Amsel (left) and Alan Ross relax in Ross's office. A top Miami drug lawyer, the flamboyant Ross was convinced that the charges against Joyce, his client in the Cohen case, were totally groundless.

26

Lynn Barkley, a photographer and Miami man-about-town, testifying at the trial.

Stan's son Gary, who had been devastated by his father's murder, listening intently to testimony during the trial.

27

Passions were running high when Steve Helfman, Gerri's husband, had to be restrained in a confrontation with Ed Smith, an old friend of Joyce and Stan's.

28

29

The courtroom was hushed during the poignant testimony of Joyce's aunt, Bea Wojtanek (shown here with her husband Ed and Joyce at a family wedding in 1982).

30

Joyce sobs as she listens to the final arguments in court.

Gerri and Steve Helfman embrace when they hear the jury's verdict. For both Gerri and her brother Gary, it was the end of a long ordeal.

The prosecution team celebrates victory. John Kastrenakes (left) and Kevin DiGregory (right) had worked on the Cohen case for nearly three years and gave themselves only a 50-50 shot at conviction.

understand that?" Waksman's frustration was building.

"I understand."

"You have never seen her doing cocaine?"

"No," Kathy replied doggedly.

"Have you ever seen any white powder near her nose?" Waksman persisted.

"No, I haven't."

"I don't want to sandbag you into anything," Waksman continued. "You're not the first person we have spoken to, and we have certain information as to who was doing drugs in Steamboat while Joyce was there. This is not a drug investigation. We are not looking to charge anybody with drugs. This is a homicide investigation. I want you to know you are under oath and this is important information. I'll ask you again, did you ever see Joyce do any drugs in your presence?"

"No, I haven't." Kathy was adamant.

Waksman was suspicious, but he decided to drop the topic for the moment. He wanted to get Kathy's account of the morning of the murder and those strange phone calls from Steamboat Springs to Miami.

Kathy told Waksman that she had been drinking with Geri Carroll and her daughter, Kimberly, at the Carrolls' condo in Steamboat Springs. Calling Joyce at nearly 3:30 A.M. had been her idea, she confirmed. When Joyce answered the phone, she sounded fine. "Good to hear you," she told Kathy. Then Joyce had said, "Call you back in two minutes. I'm going to the other phone." Kimberly Carroll had called Joyce again, and when she answered, Joyce said something like "Kathy, Kathy, Stan's been shot."

Then there was a flurry of phone calls to Miami—to the Metro-Dade police, to the Miami police, to Geri Carroll's attorney husband, P.J., who lived near the Cohens. Finally Kathy called Joyce again, but a policewoman answered and said that she was "unavailable." That's when Kathy decided Joyce needed a lawyer, she told Waksman.

"Could you tell us why?" Waksman was curious.

"After the experience I have had with police officers, you need to be protected or have someone at least to stand by for you, that you will get run over if you don't," Kathy replied knowingly.

Waksman returned to the subject of cocaine. The detectives had a sworn statement from another friend of Joyce Cohen's that she, Joyce, and Kathy Dickett had done cocaine together, he told Kathy. But Kathy flatly denied it.

"Okay, but I'll ask you again, you and Joyce and [her friend], all together, have never done cocaine?"

"No." Kathy shook her head.

"Have you ever seen Joyce do any other drugs?"

"Could I interrupt for a second to discuss with my client?" Kathy's attorney, Glenn Kritzer, asked nervously.

"I think you should," Waksman replied.

Kathy left the room to confer with her lawyer. When they returned, she said, "Have Joyce and I ever done cocaine? I don't know what Joyce has done. I have done cocaine."

"She's never told you she has done cocaine?" Waksman persisted.

"No, I have never asked her. You asked if I've seen her do another drug. I don't think— I might have seen her take an aspirin, never cocaine or take another drug, to be honest."

Waksman concluded the interview. He suspected that Kathy was trying to protect Joyce Cohen. But why?

Kathy told Waksman something else that day. She and Joyce had gone to the Cohens' empty house on South Bayshore Drive the day before and discovered there had been a break-in. The alarm system had been rigged, and something was missing: the brass bed where Stanley Cohen had been murdered.

The possibilities intrigued the detectives. Was it really a break-in? Or had Joyce faked the theft to remove some type of evidence on the bed? Or evidence hidden inside the hollow brass frame? Or had she merely sold the brass to get some quick cash? They couldn't get a lead on the missing brass bed.

Then Detective Spear got a curious call. A home invasion robber arrested in nearby Broward County claimed to know something about an unsolved homicide in Dade County. He had seen the victim's name on the jailhouse television: Stanley Cohen.

# *Fifteen*

•

A s he drove north to Broward County to interview the
would-be informant, Spear pondered what he had learned about the
guy. His name was Frank Angelo Zuccarello, and he claimed to have
connections to the Gambino organized crime family. He had been
arrested on March 11 for a home invasion robbery committed the
day before in Broward County. Zuccarello was already well known
to cops in Broward. He was a member of the Richitelli gang.

The Richitelli brothers—Scott and Jay—had come to Florida from
a rough neighborhood called the Cove in New Haven, Connecticut.
One night they were drinking beer and watching television in their
Fort Lauderdale apartment when they saw something inspiring. It
was a Chuck Norris movie about criminals who vicitimized other
criminals by breaking into their homes and robbing them of drugs,
money, and jewelry. Criminals were perfect victims—they had liquid
assets and wouldn't run to the police for help.

South Florida, the Richitelli brothers knew, was awash in drugs,
drug dealers, and their booty. Nearly every week, it seemed, television news cameras roamed the treasure troves of busted dealers. It
looked like easy pickings. Thus inspired, the Richitelli brothers
formed a loose-knit gang of transplants from their old New Haven
neighborhood to imitate the art they had seen on the small screen.

Their method was simple. Locate the homes of reputed drug dealers through paid informants (usually home improvement workmen), get in through some ruse, and then grab the goods.

They developed effective disguises to get in the door. Sometimes one gang member impersonated a mailman with a special-delivery letter for the occupant. Sometimes they posed as cops, wearing private security company uniforms and carrying badges and police radios they had stolen. To disguise their cultural identities as Italians, they used Spanish aliases—Jay Richitelli's was Hector—and spoke with fake Spanish accents during robberies. That way, if any victims were interviewed by the cops, they would say they had been hit by Cubans or Colombians. And the gang always brought lots of firepower to back them up, once they got in the door. The Richitellis' method inspired the term "home invasion robbery," dreamed up by a *Miami Herald* reporter.

The Richitelli brothers' gang had some hits and some misses. Once they raided the wrong house by mistake, terrorizing a hapless family who had the misfortune to live right next door to a man the gang suspected was a rich bookie. That caper earned them the nickname The Gang That Couldn't Shoot Straight in the press. But some of their robberies were extremely violent. They tied up victims or immobilized them with duct tape, pistol-whipped them, threatened to kill them. During the March 10 home invasion for which Zuccarello had been arrested, they shoved a loaded pistol up a victim's rectum and threatened to fire.

When Detective Spear finally got a look at Frank Zuccarello, he was surprised. Zuccarello had a slender build and a small head capped by curly dark hair that trailed over his collar in the back. His facial features were fine, almost handsome, with limpid dark eyes and thin lips. Although he tried to appear composed and confident, the slight tremor of his hands gave him away. Zuccarello was twenty-one years old, and he was very scared.

Spear wasn't the only cop who wanted to talk to Zuccarello. As soon as he put out the word that he was willing to talk, Zuccarello became the focus of cops from all over South Florida who were eager to clear unsolved home invasion robberies in their jurisdictions. He had already identified more than thirty home invasion robberies in which he or other Richitelli gang members had taken part. But he didn't want to tell all he knew until he saw what kind of deal he could cut for himself with prosecutors. Zuccarello was already a sophisticated player of the plea-bargaining game. He understood the golden rule of the game: The first to "flip," or turn state's evidence, always gets the best deal for himself.

When Zuccarello started to talk about the Cohen homicide, he didn't give Spear much at first—just enough to bait the hook. He knew about the murder, he claimed, because he had overheard gang members planning it—Anthony Caracciolo, the burly leader on that job, and Tommy Joslin, a/k/a Tommy Lamberti. Lamberti, he said, was the son of Louis "Donald Duck" Lamberti, a reputed mobster also connected to the Gambinos. Lamberti sported a large, full-color tattoo of Donald Duck on his right forearm, in honor of his father's nickname.

Zuccarello told Spear that Caracciolo and Lamberti had been hired by Joyce Cohen. He had seen her once when she met with Caracciolo. And there was a boyfriend, Zuccarello claimed, who helped plan the murder. He identified Joyce Cohen from a photograph, but Spear wasn't impressed. Her picture had been plastered all over the newspapers and television for weeks. Zuccarello could have seen it anywhere. But he was impressed when Zuccarello chose another photograph from among several Spear showed him. This, Zuccarello claimed, was the boyfriend. The man in the photograph was Lynn Barkley.

It was the break investigators had been waiting for.

But over the next three months, during interminable hours of interviews, Zuccarello continually revised his story. First he said he had seen Joyce Cohen and Lynn Barkley meet Caracciolo at a surf shop in Coconut Grove in January 1986. Impossible. Joyce had been in Steamboat Springs that entire month, Spear knew. Then Zuccarello said the meeting had taken place at a 7-Eleven in North Miami in February. As his stories progressed, Zuccarello was careful to emphasize that he did not participate in the crime. He was nowhere near the Cohen house that night, he insisted.

A typical "snitch," Spear thought. Gradually an informer gives up more and more of the truth. He places himself closer and closer to the crime. But he never, of course, admits committing the crime. It was always someone else. Spear wasn't convinced that Zuccarello was telling the truth. He seemed to have information that only the murderer would know, yet he flatly denied any involvement in the crime.

Spear arranged for Miami homicide detective Ron Ilhart to polygraph Zuccarello on June 7, 1986. Ilhart immediately pegged him as a slick character, a smooth talker who had spent lots of time around crime and criminals. He prepared a series of test questions based on Zuccarello's story.

"Did you fire the shots that killed Stan Cohen?"

"Did you kill Stan Cohen?"

Zuccarello answered no to both questions when he took the test, and Ilhart scored those responses: "No psychological reaction indicative of deceptions." He thought Zuccarello was telling the truth—so far.

Then Ilhart asked:

"Were you present inside or outside the house when Stan was killed?"

"Were you at Stan's house the night he was killed?"

"Do you know for sure who killed Stan Cohen?"

Zuccarello answered no to each question. But this time Ilhart saw that he was trying to distort the polygraph charts. He had pressed his toes tightly together and "puckered up his rear end," common attempts to throw off a polygraph. The responses on the chart were inconsistent. Ilhart marked it "inconclusive." But he thought Zuccarello was lying. Finally he discontinued the test. Zuccarello's story didn't hold up. He was still trying to deceive the detectives. He shouldn't be tested further, Ilhart felt, until he settled on a final version of the crime.

Over the next few weeks, Spear became Frank Zuccarello's frequent companion. He signed him out of jail for drive-bys of the surf shop and the 7-Eleven store where he claimed to have seen Joyce Cohen and Lynn Barkley meet with Caracciolo. Spear drove him through the Cohen neighborhood, where Zuccarello excitedly pointed out the Cohens' big limestone house on the corner. He took Zuccarello out for a haircut and for dinner. And once Spear chauffeured him to visit his girlfriend, Gina.

After days of interviews eleven or twelve hours long, Spear felt Zuccarello was ready for another test. This time they would do an interrogation polygraph—use the test as an investigative tool to find the truth. Lieutenant Robert Rios, from the Broward Sheriff's Department, would administer the polygraph.

Around 1 P.M. on Saturday, June 21, Rios took Zuccarello into the polygraph room at the Miami Police Department. Spear watched through a two-way mirror. After he obtained some background information from Zuccarello, Rios launched into his standard pretest spiel.

"Let me explain to you a little bit about the polygraph. My suggestion is, if you can't pass it, don't take it. Don't waste your time, don't waste my time."

But Zuccarello insisted he was telling the truth. He wanted to be tested. He knew he would pass.

Rios hooked Zuccarello up to the machine. Then he read aloud Zuccarello's latest version of the crime. "Now," he asked, "is everything you're telling me in this statement true?"

"Yes," Zuccarello responded.

Rios looked over the chart. Deceptive. "You didn't do too well," he told Zuccarello, shaking his head.

Zuccarello said nothing. Rios took him off the machine. Then he began the painstaking process of working back through the details of Zuccarello's statement. "What specifically were they saying?" Rios asked about conversations Zuccarello claimed he overheard.

"Well, I don't know," Zuccarello hedged. "I don't know if I was in the room at that time."

Rios shook his head back and forth to let Zuccarello know he wasn't buying it. "Don't give me something that's not true," he warned. "You already know that you can't beat the thing. You already stumbled once."

Zuccarello revised his story slightly. Rios hooked him up and tested him on his new version. Deceptive again. Rios took him off the machine.

Throughout the long afternoon and into the evening, Rios patiently worked Zuccarello. The young man was an intelligent, skilled opponent in the verbal cat-and-mouse game they played. But eventually Zuccarello backed down. He didn't tell the truth on the first polygraph, he admitted finally, because he *had* gone into the Cohen home that night with Lamberti and Caracciolo. He remembered planters on the patio outside the front porch, an arch inside the front door, steps leading up to the master bedroom. He had followed Caracciolo upstairs. It was Caracciolo who shot Stan Cohen. Zuccarello ran into the bedroom right after he did it.

How many shots, Rios asked.

Zuccarello wasn't sure. Maybe two, three. Rios hooked him up to the machine again, and this time he concluded that Zuccarello was telling the truth when he said he didn't know how many shots were fired. It was the only portion of the polygraph that Zuccarello passed.

They took a break for pizza and Cokes. Zuccarello was exhausted. He didn't want to be tested any more that night, he said. It was after 11 P.M. He had already spent more than ten hours with Rios. But Spear was elated. At last, he thought, they were getting the truth out of Zuccarello. He called prosecutor David Waksman, who hurried down to the homicide office, despite the late hour. It was near midnight when they brought in a stenographer. They wanted a sworn statement from Zuccarello right then. They finally had the truth, and they didn't want to lose it.

Frank Zuccarello was granted complete immunity from prosecution in the Cohen homicide. He started talking at 11:51 P.M. and finished about two hours later. When it was transcribed, his sworn statement went ninety-seven pages. Zuccarello said he first heard of Stan Cohen in December 1985, when Anthony Caracciolo, Tommy Lamberti, and Jay Richitelli were discussing a "hit," or home invasion robbery. It was an inside job—Stan's wife, Joyce, had hired them to rob him. She would pretend to be a victim.

In late February 1986, the plan changed from robbery to murder. "I'm going to lay it on the line," Caracciolo had told them. "We're going to have to yoke this guy. There's a lot of money involved."

"What's the guy got?" Zuccarello asked. "A healthy life insurance policy?"

"As a matter of fact, he's got two," Caracciolo replied.

They would be paid at least $10,000 each for the job, Caracciolo had said. It wasn't a lot, Zuccarello thought, considering how rich the Cohens were.

Jay Richitelli wanted no part of the new plan. He dropped out. But the others stayed in. They would make the killing look like a home invasion robbery gone bad.

As Zuccarello watched from his blue Camaro Z-28, Caracciolo waited on his motorcycle for a planned meeting with Joyce Cohen in the parking lot of a 7-Eleven store in North Miami. Finally she drove up in a white Jaguar accompanied by a man with graying blond hair. She jumped out of the car and hugged and kissed Caracciolo as if they were old friends. Then her companion handed Caracciolo a map of her home showing the layout, the stairs, and the location of the alarm system's panic buttons in the master bedroom. Although Zuccarello couldn't hear what was said, Caracciolo told him later that Joyce said she would let them in the house, turn off the home's burglar alarm, and pen up the dog. "This is how [I] want it done," Joyce's companion had said to Caracciolo. Or, "This is the way it's supposed to be done."

Zuccarello identified a photograph of Joyce Cohen as the woman who met Caracciolo in the parking lot. Then he picked out a photograph of her companion, Lynn Barkley.

The plan was to use the victim's own gun to kill him, Zuccarello continued. Joyce was going to give it to Caracciolo or tell him where to find it. But just in case, they took their own weapons along and brought a dart gun to use on the dog if necessary. The three men arrived at the Cohen house shortly after 2 A.M. on March 7. Zuccarello recalled seeing the time on the digital clock on the dash of the black El Camino he was driving. Joyce Cohen met them at the door. She was wearing a light-colored robe. "Let's get this over with as quick as possible," she said as she let them in. "Get it over with."

Once inside, Lamberti's job was to show Joyce Cohen how to fake a break-in so she could claim intruders had killed her husband. Then while Zuccarello stood guard at the front door, Caracciolo went upstairs and shot the sleeping Stan Cohen. Zuccarello ran up the stairs and into the master bedroom just as the last shot was fired. Then they fled in the El Camino.

Driving back to Broward County, they had argued. "Anthony,

what happened? Why so many shots?" Zuccarello demanded. "I thought I heard two. . . . I panicked!"

"*You* panicked!" Caracciolo yelled back. "*I'm* the one that had to pull the trigger! I could have missed him one time!" He thought he had dropped the gun somewhere as they fled.

After leaving Caracciolo and Lamberti at Caracciolo's apartment, Zuccarello drove himself home, smoked a joint, and went to bed. When he awoke, he went to the beach to play paddleball.

"Did Anthony Caracciolo tell you why Joyce Cohen wanted to have her husband killed?" Spear asked finally.

"For two reasons. He stated for the reason she didn't love him anymore. And for the money. She got everything."


It was nearly two o'clock in the morning when Waksman telephoned Gerri Cohen Helfman at home. She was probably sleeping, but he knew she wouldn't mind being awakened when she heard what he had to say. He told her about Zuccarello's statement.

"This could be it!" he said excitedly. "I think we've finally got the breakthrough we've been looking for!"

Gerri had trouble getting back to sleep that night. After four long months, her suspicions about her stepmother had finally been confirmed. If she had not actually pulled the trigger of the gun that killed her father, she had hired somebody else to do it. She would pay for that crime, Gerri thought. And then this nightmare would be over.

# *Sixteen*

•

When Sergeant Tom Waterson heard about Frank Zuccarello's story, he was stunned. From his first minutes in the Cohen house on the morning of the murder, he had suspected that Joyce was the killer. But he never envisioned anything more complicated than her shooting her sleeping husband in the back of the head and throwing the weapon in the yard. "When are you going to arrest her?" Waterson asked Spear. It looked as if the case was solved.

Spear just smiled and shook his head. Zuccarello's story alone wasn't enough, Spear and Waksman had agreed. Zuccarello had, as they put it, "a lot of baggage." He was an admitted home invasion robber, a career criminal at age twenty-one. If a jury had to choose between Frank Zuccarello and Joyce Cohen, society woman and grieving widow, Zuccarello would lose. And Joyce would walk.

But Waksman had a plan. Now that they had Zuccarello, they would arrest Caracciolo and Lamberti and persuade them all to testify against Joyce Cohen in exchange for plea deals. With all three gang members, they would have a stronger case against Joyce. Then they would arrest her and try her for the contract murder of her husband. She was the one they really wanted.

At first it looked easy. They already had Anthony Caracciolo, it turned out. He had been arrested on April 24 for a string of home invasion robberies. Spear went to interview him in jail. Caracciolo was in his twenties, with dark, curly hair and classic Italian features. He was taller than Zuccarello and much heavier. His bulk and his full features gave him the incongruous appearance of a big teddy bear—with a slightly menacing air.

Caracciolo knew Zuccarello and Lamberti, of course, and he admitted participating in some home invasions. But when Spear brought up the Cohen homicide, he hit a blank wall. Caracciolo flatly denied any involvement in the murder. He had never even met Joyce Cohen, he claimed. Never heard of Stan Cohen. Never saw the Cohen house in Coconut Grove. Spear left disgusted.

Waksman decided to interview Caracciolo himself. Spear brought him into the interview room, still in handcuffs. Then he read Caracciolo his Miranda rights from the printed form and asked him to sign it.

"I'm not talking to you," Caracciolo replied sullenly. He refused to sign the form.

Waksman decided to give Caracciolo a little speech. "I don't know why you're protecting this woman," he began. "She's going to jail. She's not going to have any money. And *you're* going to jail."

Caracciolo tried to interrupt, but each time Waksman stopped him. "You're not allowed to talk. You didn't sign the Miranda form, you're not allowed to say nothing." He tried to goad Caracciolo into signing the rights form, but it was futile. Finally Spear took Caracciolo back to the Dade County Jail.

Waksman decided not to charge Caracciolo with the Cohen homicide—yet. After all, he wasn't going anywhere with the home invasion charges pending. Maybe they would have better luck with Tommy Lamberti. There was an arrest warrant out for him on the same home invasions, Spear discovered, but Lamberti was nowhere to be found. It looked as if he had skipped the state. Now Spear would have to go out and find him.

While detectives worked to track Lamberti, Waksman wondered how else they could connect this Miami society woman, this Mrs. Joyce Cohen, with three goons in Broward County. Perhaps through long-distance telephone calls. Waksman subpoenaed telephone records from any telephone that Joyce had access to—her home, her office, her hairdresser, her manicurist, Buccione's, Biscayne Baby. He spent countless hours staring at voluminous printouts of long-distance calls. But he came up with nothing.

Waksman took another tack. How did Joyce Cohen ever meet these guys in the first place, he asked Zuccarello? Zuccarello named Josephine Macaluso, a former girlfriend of Anthony Caracciolo's, who lived in the Grove, near the Cohens. She and Joyce partied together at Biscayne Baby, he said. Macaluso had called the cops on Caracciolo once or twice for beating her up, so she owed him no allegiance. This could be the connection, Waksman thought. This could be a break.

Spear found Josephine Macaluso and brought her in. She was a heavyset, squat, blunt-featured woman whose most memorable feature was her mouth. It was big. She used rough language, in a loud, abrasive Brooklyn accent. She sounded like a longshoreman and acted like one, Waksman thought.

Waksman asked her about Caracciolo, Lamberti, and Zuccarello. She knew Caracciolo, Macaluso admitted. Yes, she had had him arrested once. But she never heard of Lamberti or Zuccarello. How about Joyce Cohen?

"No, I don't know her," Macaluso insisted in harsh Brooklynese. "I don't know what you're talking about. I don't know nothing." She marched out of Waksman's office.

Spear stopped by Biscayne Baby and spoke with John Loehle, the doorman, who remembered Joyce Cohen well. He also recognized a photograph of Josephine Macaluso. "A mouthy New York broad," Loehle said. She had tried to bluff her way into the Champagne Room one night by claiming to be Joyce Cohen. "I said no, you are not Cohen, and she raised a bitch," he told Spear. He wouldn't let her in until the real Joyce Cohen showed up.

"Mrs. Cohen, is this your guest?" Loehle had asked Joyce when she arrived.

"Yes, it is," Joyce had answered.

"Okay, come on in," Loehle said. Joyce Cohen and Josephine Macaluso went up to the Champagne Room together.

When Waksman had John Loehle's sworn statement in hand, he invited Josephine Macaluso in for another chat. And this time he had

Frank Zuccarello stashed out of sight in an interview room. Waksman asked Macaluso again: Do you know Frank Zuccarello? Tommy Lamberti? Joyce Cohen? Ever been to Biscayne Baby? No, no, I don't know nothing about nothing, she insisted again.

Waksman called Zuccarello into the room. He walked right over to Macaluso and looked her up and down. "Josephine, they know the whole story," he said.

"Waksman, who the fuck is this guy?" Macaluso demanded loudly.

"Josephine, it's all over. It's all over," Zuccarello continued. "They know the whole story. I told them the whole story. They're going to give you immunity. Don't worry, they'll take care of you."

"Waksman!" Macaluso screamed. "Get this fuckin' guy away from me!"

Josephine Macaluso came back once more, this time with her lawyer, Michael Chavies. Waksman placed her under oath and then asked her again whether she knew Joyce Cohen. Again she denied it. Waksman turned to Sergeant Steve Vinson, who was standing nearby. "Sergeant Vinson, have you just seen a felony committed?" Waksman asked.

"Yes," Vinson replied soberly.

"Do your duty," Waksman instructed him.

Vinson arrested Josephine Macaluso for perjury. That ought to do it, Waksman thought, now she'll talk. But Macaluso said nothing.

As Sergeant Vinson slapped handcuffs on her, Macaluso's lawyer, Chavies, started yelling. "David, come on! I'll surrender her next week! Get an arrest warrant!"

"No, she's going to jail," Waksman replied, fuming. "We've given her like three chances already."

Josephine Macaluso went to jail. But she was soon released on bond, and while the perjury charge was pending, she jumped bail and took a trip to New Jersey. There she and her three young children were picked up in a car with two Colombians and forty taped packages of white powder: forty-two kilos of cocaine with a street value of $2.3 million. She told cops her "Colombian" boyfriend Anthony Caracciolo had arranged the ride for her, and she had no idea there were drugs in the car. And she didn't know the two men in the car with her. Macaluso was arrested and eventually was returned to Dade County on a fugitive warrant for jumping bail on the perjury charge. She sat in jail for months, but she wouldn't give in.

Finally prosecutors dropped the perjury charge. Eventually the drug charges against Macaluso in New Jersey were dismissed also. But Waksman could never understand why Josephine Macaluso wouldn't roll over. During his long career as a prosecutor, he had flipped a lot of people. And generally, he knew, when push comes to shove, you let someone else go to jail. You don't go to jail yourself. So why would Macaluso sit in jail for months in Miami to protect Joyce Cohen? For money? It made no sense. Were Anthony Caracciolo, Lynn Barkley, and now Josephine Macaluso all protecting Joyce? And if so, why?

Waksman was frustrated. He believed Zuccarello's story about Stan Cohen's murder, but it wasn't enough to take to a jury. They needed a connection, and they hadn't been able to find one.


Gary Cohen and Gerri Cohen Helfman came to see Waksman. When, they asked, are you going to do something? When will Joyce be arrested? Stan Cohen's children lived with the daily torment of seeing their stepmother, the woman they believed was their father's killer, alive and well and apparently enjoying her life. Although they had managed to freeze their father's estate pending the criminal investigation, Joyce was still living at Wolf Run Ranch in Steamboat Springs. And sooner or later, unless the prosecutors did something, Joyce and her lawyers would succeed in getting Stan's estate distributed. Except for modest bequests to Gary and Gerri and a few others, the entire estate would go to Joyce. And then she could just disappear, a rich woman.

"Let's wait until something develops," Waksman told Gary and Gerri, "because at this point, we put it on and if a jury doesn't believe Zuccarello, Joyce is gone. We need something to convince a jury that Zuccarello is telling the truth. . . . All you've got is Zuccarello. It might not be enough, and if we put her on and lose, it's history, it's gone.

"You put a guy on the stand like Zuccarello and he's going to say,

I did a hundred robberies with the boys. And by the way, I did this murder and I'm getting nothing for the murder. And by the way, it's this nice society woman here who paid us or offered us money to do it. And she's miss prim and proper.

"Look," Waksman continued, "I just got a call from a North Miami Beach detective who got some new evidence on a 1984 case. And I said, it really doesn't matter what you found now—the guy's free as a bird. That's what I'm trying to tell you. We just have to wait until something develops."

Gary and Gerri were heartsick.

Alan Ross heard rumors like distant thunder from friends among the Broward County criminal defense bar. They said that the Miami detectives were now focusing on a Broward home invasion gang in the Cohen case. There was an informant named Zuccarello, and he and his buddies were all pointing fingers at each other as to who committed the murder. No one mentioned Joyce Cohen.

Ross was relieved. Finally, he thought, the police were onto something other than their suspicions about Joyce. He called his client in Steamboat Springs with the good news. "Thank God, Joyce, they're going to solve this crime," Ross told her. Then he asked her if she knew someone named Zuccarello.

She had never heard of him, Joyce replied. Never met him.

Then Ross called Waksman. "Hey, I still represent Mrs. Cohen. We are aware of your investigation. If you ever want to talk to her, please call me first." Waksman said nothing. Ross would keep tabs on the investigation, but he thought Joyce Cohen was finally free to get on with her life and put the tragedy behind her.

Out in Steamboat Springs, Joyce and Shawn Cohen had settled into the big house at Wolf Run Ranch. Shawn had been kicked out of Tennessee Military Institute in May. He had sneaked out of the dorm once too often and wound up in a high-speed car chase with the local cops. With nothing else to do, he decided to hang out in Steamboat with his mother.

One day Shawn told his mother about the package he had removed from the secret cupboard in her bathroom in the house on South

Bayshore Drive. It was cocaine. "Oh, good, I'm glad you took it," Joyce said. "If the police had found it, they would have charged me with drugs."

Shawn never asked his mother how it got there or whose coke it was. He assumed it was hers. Besides, the coke was long since gone—Shawn had used it himself. It wasn't the first time he had found cocaine in that house. Actually, the first time it was "cut," an inert subtance used to dilute cocaine before selling it. It was in his mother's dresser, and Shawn still laughed when he remembered snorting "cut." After that, he knew the difference.

Despite "borrowing" from various friends, Joyce was running out of money. She asked her friend Kathy Dickett to stay with her at the ranch and help out with expenses. Soon the women were bringing friends home to party. Shawn noticed that the men were mostly young, closer to his age than his mother's. Joyce made it clear that she didn't want her new friends to know how old she was. Shawn was disgusted to see his mother with all these different guys. Night after night it was parties and men. Kathy Dickett, Shawn thought, was not a good influence on his mother.

One night Shawn heard his mother sobbing in her bedroom. He peeked in the door and saw her with a man, a low-class cowboy with a thick country accent. This was not the kind of guy Shawn expected to see his mother with, not after Stan. His mother was drunk, the guy was drunk, and they had been fighting. Shawn felt sorry for her. But he wondered how his mother could carry on this way, so soon after Stan's death. "It just really left a bad taste in my mouth," he said.

Shawn decided to move out of the house. He got a job as a dishwasher in a restaurant in town and began to hang out with a fast crowd. Soon he moved into a house trailer with some of his new friends. Joyce forbade him to bring them to the ranch. She was afraid they would steal something, she said.

One weekend when Joyce was out of town, Shawn took several friends to the ranch house for an impromptu party to celebrate his eighteenth birthday. They ate, drank, smoked pot, danced most of the night. Upstairs, the girls tried on Joyce's fur coats and jackets, giggling, preening, posing in front of the mirrors and parading around the house in her finery. Shawn thought it was hilarious. He knew his mother would have been furious, but she never found out.

To pick up a little cash, Joyce began to work as a hostess on occasional evenings at Mattie Silks, a trendy Victorian restaurant in Ski Time Square, the resort district of Steamboat Springs. She knew the owners, Bill Gander and Jerry Stanford, and the restaurant had always been one of her favorites. It was named for Mattie Silks, a/k/a Martha Ready, Denver's famous turn-of-the-century madam.

Stan and Joyce and their friends had spent many happy evenings at Mattie Silks. Some nights the stools at the bar were piled high with their furs as they sat in a laughing group at a table near the window, watching late skiers drift down the slope. But it seemed those good times had died with Stanley Cohen. Now Joyce was working there, and the people who knew her story felt sorry for her.

Although most of her old friends in Steamboat Springs stood by Joyce, there were occasional ugly scenes. One evening a customer at Mattie Silks handed Joyce a tip while she was working as hostess. "Don't give her any money!" the customer's wife said loudly. "She doesn't need it. She killed her husband—now she's rich!"

But in fact money was still a very big problem for Joyce. Back in Miami, there was a buyer for the house on South Bayshore Drive. The price was only $225,000—just half of what Stan had hoped to get from the sale. But Joyce was ready to take it. She simply had to have some money. She had expenses, and lawyers to pay.


Gary and Gerri had other ideas. Frustrated at the slow progress of the investigation into their father's murder, they took another bold step. They filed a civil suit against their stepmother for the "wrongful death" of their father. They accused her outright of conspiring "with other persons, known and unknown," to kill Stan Cohen. Damages claimed in the lawsuit: $5 million.

The civil suit was a kind of private prosecution that would produce its own investigation. Joyce and her friends could be questioned under oath. Leads could be pursued. And it was another mechanism through which to keep Joyce's hands off Stan's property. The attorneys who came up with this strategy were Irwin Block and Joseph Serota, both litigation partners at Fine Jacobson, the firm where

Gary Cohen and Steve Helfman practiced law. Block was a savvy, experienced former prosecutor, and Serota was his protégé and a rising star in the courtroom.

About a month later, Joyce Cohen struck back. Her lawyers filed a counterclaim accusing her stepchildren of conspiring to "slander, shame, and humiliate" her. She sought damages of her own: $50 million.

The litigation sparked a flurry of activity. The parties all noticed each other for deposition. Then each refused to be deposed. The prosecutors sought a stay of discovery in the civil case, claiming that the criminal investigation would be jeopardized. A stay was granted, and finally a compromise was worked out to permit the sale of the Cohen house. But before the house changed hands, Gary and Gerri wanted one last chance to investigate the murder scene. They were still hoping for the breakthrough that David Waksman said they needed. Gerri remembered a fascinating private detective who had testified at a murder trial that she reported on the television news. He was Rod Englert, a homicide detective with the Portland, Oregon, Police Department and a specialist in reconstructing crime scenes and tracking serial killers. They contacted Englert, and he agreed to come to Miami.

Englert began by guiding them in preparing an outline of every incident, no matter how apparently insignificant, which had occurred on March 6–7. On large sheets of white paper tacked to a wall, they constructed a meticulous time line, pinpointing the sequence of each incident, looking for a pattern, a clue that might be hidden there. Next he suggested that they reenact the crime at the actual scene, the now-deserted Cohen house on South Bayshore Drive. They would need more professional assistance for that phase of the investigation. At the Broward County Sheriff's Office they found Chuck Ebel, a specialist in blood splatter analysis. Ebel agreed to assist in their investigation.

Of course, Gary and Gerri needed permission to enter the house, and they had to go back to court to get it. Their investigator could examine the house, the judge ruled, but Joyce Cohen's attorney also had a right to be present to ensure that no damage was done to the property. The judge also appointed attorney Gerald Richman to act as a referee in case any problems developed during the investigation. Neither Rosenblatt nor Richman would be permitted to interfere in the investigation, however, or even follow the investigators around.

They came up with a plan. The investigation would begin at 5:30 P.M., Joe Serota notified Gerald Richman and Joyce Cohen's lawyer, Robert Rosenblatt. They would start with some measurements for an architectural model of the house. Then they would go upstairs to the master bedroom—without Rosenblatt.

When everyone arrived at the empty house, an architect hired by Gary and Gerri began the tedious task of measuring and making detailed drawings of the entire house, inside and out. Finally bored, Rosenblatt suggested that he and Richman share a pizza while they waited for the investigators to finish. When they sat down to a snack, Joe Serota, Chuck Ebel, and his assistant headed for the stairs to the master bedroom.

By now it was dark, and the old house took on the ominous atmosphere Gary Cohen remembered from years earlier. It had been closed up since the murder, and a musty stench hung in the still air. The stairs creaked and groaned as the small group moved toward the master bedroom where Stan had been killed. They clustered together in silence as Ebel examined the empty, cavernous room. Then he set to work. First he sprayed the entire room with Luminol, a substance that glows in the dark wherever it comes into contact with blood residue. Then he turned out the lights. Like phosphorescent paint under black light, eerie trails glowed in the pitch-dark room, illuminating the deadly spatter—across the floor, on the mirrored wall, everywhere. It pooled on the floor and speckled the walls, mute testimony to Stan Cohen's violent death. Ebel pointed to a deep pool of phosphorescence on the floor. "That's where his head drained blood," he said. It was a scene that none of them would ever forget.

Downstairs, Ebel and an assistant conducted a meticulous videotaped reenactment of Joyce's statement—where she said she was standing when she heard the noise in the kitchen, how she turned on the burglar alarm and ran back to the dining room, exactly where she was when she saw the shadowy figures run out the front door. At the end of his investigation, Chuck Ebel came to the same conclusion Detective Jon Spear had reached months before. Joyce's story was a lie.

It simply couldn't have happened that way. She couldn't have done what she claimed to have done, seen what she claimed to have seen, from where she said she was standing. It was a physical impossibility.

But they learned nothing new. Their investigation didn't answer the all-important question of what Joyce had, in fact, done before, during, and after her husband's murder. There was no new evidence. And without some concrete evidence linking her to the crime, she couldn't be arrested, let alone convicted.

Things began to look up for Joyce. Two suitors appeared in Steamboat Springs. One was a businessman from Philadelphia, a clean-cut man who reminded Shawn of Stan. He shook Shawn's hand when they were introduced and said, "Hi, how are you doing?" Shawn liked him. He seemed like a nice guy. And Joyce said he was rich. He lent her money.

The other possibility was Robert Dietrich.

One day when Shawn stopped by Wolf Run Ranch for food, he heard his mother and Kathy Dickett talking about "picking up these studs from Virginia." They liked these guys, they said. And Shawn liked Robert Dietrich, too, when he met him. Shawn thought he was cool. Dietrich was definitely more into partying than the guy from Philadelphia. Maybe that was why his mother seemed more interested in Dietrich.

Joyce had met Dietrich one evening while she was hostessing at Mattie Silks. He was good-looking: graying dark hair, large, luminous dark eyes, and finely chiseled features. Dietrich had been married several times but was unattached at the moment. Women always found him attractive. He seemed sensitive and intense—and he was instantly smitten by Joyce. He asked her to have a drink with him after she finished work, and she agreed. Mattie Silks was perfect for romance.

Dietrich told Joyce that he lived in the small town of Chesapeake, Virginia, in the Tidewater area near Norfolk, Newport News, and Virginia Beach. His family owned property there—a large mobile home park and some duplex houses. Dietrich lived in a large brick house on the property and managed the business for his elderly parents, who had retired in Florida. Dietrich was also a pilot who flew his own small plane.

As their romance blossomed, Joyce told Dietrich about her marriage to Stan and his tragic death. She loved Stan very much and they had been happy together, she reminisced, and then he was murdered while she was right there in the house. The crime hadn't been solved, and now her husband's children were saying that she was somehow involved in his death. That was ridiculous, of course. She had had nothing to do with it. She herself was a victim of the tragedy, and she couldn't understand why her stepchildren were treating her so cruelly. It must be Stan's money they were after. He had left nearly everything to her, Joyce told Dietrich, and her lawyers in Miami were trying to straighten things out. It would be resolved soon.

At Christmas, 1986, there was a huge Christmas tree in the big room next to the fireplace, just as there had been every year at Wolf Run Ranch. In that year's Christmas photo, Joyce and Robert Dietrich cuddled in front of the tree. Dietrich looked like a happy Marlboro cowboy—he wore jeans, a lumberjack shirt, and an enormous smile as he drew Joyce close. She wore one of her stunning, stylized all-white outfits—pants, boots, and a sort of long, flowing cape. With her helmet of shining dark hair and immaculate makeup, she had never looked more beautiful. But her face was enigmatic. She stared down at the floor rather than at the camera, a half smile playing on her lips.

Soon after that, Joyce left Steamboat with Robert Dietrich and moved into his house in Chesapeake, Virginia. Her worries about money would be over now. And she had a man to protect her and take care of her. Alan Ross was right. It was time to put the tragedy of Stan's death behind her and get on with her life.

# Seventeen

·

**B**ack in Miami, the homicide investigation stalled.

David Waksman's further attempts to roll Anthony Caracciolo were fruitless. Tommy Lamberti was nowhere to be found. Waksman hadn't come up with any independent evidence to support Frank Zuccarello's story.

And there was a big problem with Zuccarello's story. He insisted that the murder had occurred between 2 A.M. and 3 A.M., rather than 5:20 A.M., when Joyce had told police she had seen intruders and discovered her husband's body. Days of careful neighborhood canvassing still hadn't located anyone who heard shots that morning, at any hour. Jerry Mandina, the neighbor who reported a possible gunshot shortly after 5 A.M., had recanted. He now said it had sounded more like glass breaking. Another neighbor had heard the burglar alarm go off about 5:15. But no one had heard any shots.

Could Zuccarello have told the truth about everything *except* the time of the murder? Or could he simply be mistaken about the time—by two or three hours?

On November 4, 1986, Detectives Spear and Luis Albuerne, Sergeant Vinson, and David Waksman met with Dr. Charles Wetli in the Dade County Medical Examiner's Office to discuss the time of Cohen's death. Because of the delay caused by obtaining a search warrant, Stan Cohen's body had been lying on the bedroom floor for at least eight hours before he was called to examine it, Dr. Wetli reminded them. He was told by police that the victim had died at approximately 5:30 A.M., and he saw no reason to disagree. So he hadn't performed any special tests to pinpoint the time of Cohen's death. In his autopsy report, Wetli estimated the time of death between midnight and 6 A.M. That was as close as he could come.

Albuerne told Wetli that he had observed lividity (pooled blood staining the body after death) on Cohen's right side as paramedics moved the body from the bed to the floor about 6 A.M. on the day of the murder. Albuerne also thought the blood on the bed was not fresh but rather slightly jelled. His observations suggested Cohen had been dead for some time before police and paramedics were called to the scene by Joyce Cohen—and they supported Frank Zuccarello's version of the time of the murder.

Dr. Wetli listened intently. But while he felt Cohen was probably killed earlier than 5:30 A.M., he couldn't rule that out as the time of death. He simply had no basis for a more definite opinion.

"Sorry, guys, I can't help you," he told them.


In December 1986, David Waksman left the Dade County State Attorney's Office to join a personal injury law practice. He had one big regret: he still hadn't found the connection—a telephone record, a note, something—between Joyce Cohen and Frank Zuccarello and his gang. The case was unfinished, and it nagged at Waksman. His colleagues were sorry to see him leave. They predicted he would be back someday, that he wouldn't be able to stay away from the excitement of the prosecutor's office. They could be right, Waksman thought. But nevertheless the Cohen case had to be reassigned.

Assistant State Attorney Abe Laeser was in charge of major crimes. It was his job to reassign the case, and one day he was approached in the hall by Kevin DiGregory, an able, experienced prosecutor. DiGregory had his eye on the Cohen case. He had discussed it many times with David Waksman, and he found it fascinating. "Abe, if you need anyone to take Cohen, I'll do it," DiGregory offered.

The next day DiGregory was delighted to find the Cohen file on his desk. A short, fit man with curly brown hair, a bushy mustache, and friendly brown eyes, DiGregory was a career prosecutor who simply couldn't imagine himself practicing any other kind of law. He would never go into private practice to defend criminals. How could he feed his family with money that came from drug dealers and murderers? It was incomprehensible to him.

Since Cohen was a capital case, and highly publicized at that, DiGregory would need another prosecutor to assist him. His choice: John Kastrenakes, a smart young lawyer who had been prosecuting armed robberies. Handsome in a boyish, all-American way, Kastrenakes was something of a rarity in Miami—a native son. This would be his first homicide, a big step up the career ladder. DiGregory and Kastrenakes were good friends outside the office, and they relished their first opportunity to work on a case together.

By coincidence, Kastrenakes already knew Frank Zuccarello. Zuccarello had provided evidence to Metro-Dade detective Joe Gross on the Richitelli gang's home invasion robberies in Dade County. Kastrenakes was prosecuting those cases, and he had a good relationship with Zuccarello. And in all probability Zuccarello would be the state's main witness in the Cohen case.

Kastrenakes was happy with his new assignment. Although the lead attorney bears ultimate responsibility for the conduct of a case, assisting, or "sitting second chair," is a valuable training experience for a prosecutor. In the Dade County State Attorney's Office, the one who sits second chair is jokingly referred to as the "butt boy." But because of his relationship with Zuccarello and his compatibility with his friend DiGregory, "Butt Boy" Kastrenakes looked forward to playing a major role in the Cohen case.

DiGregory and Kastrenakes reviewed David Waksman's file on the Cohen murder and concurred with his "roll the co-conspirators" strategy. On January 7, 1987, they called a meeting to discuss the case. Sergeant Vinson and Detective Spear attended, as did Detective Joe Gross from Metro-Dade's robbery division. They all agreed that their next step was to arrest Tommy Lamberti. But first Spear had to find him.

Spear had interviewed Joy Ellefson, a pretty blonde who was Lamberti's girlfriend. Although Spear found her vague and uncooperative, he learned enough to conclude that Lamberti was probably in California, on the Monterey Peninsula. Soon he was flying west, hoping to locate the elusive Lamberti.

Spear's hunch was right. Lamberti had been working as a house-painter in Monterey. But although he managed to find several Californians who had met Lamberti, the fugitive had moved on, possibly using the alias Bobby Cimino. But Spear's time wasn't wasted. He learned that Lamberti had talked about the Richitelli gang's exploits with his new friends, including a beauty queen, Miss Artichoke of Castroville, California, the artichoke capital of the world. Miss Artichoke, a gorgeous eighteen-year-old of Mexican-American descent, had dated Lamberti briefly. On a later trip to California, Spear located another Lamberti girlfriend, a strawberry blonde who claimed to be a centerfold model for *Hot Rod* magazine. Spear couldn't imagine how Lamberti attracted such beautiful young women.

Gary Cohen and Gerri Helfman requested a meeting with the new prosecutors assigned to the case. They were accompanied by their lawyers, Irwin Block and Joe Serota, who were handling the civil case against Joyce Cohen. Kevin DiGregory and John Kastrenakes briefly described the case strategy and reviewed the status of the investigation. And although DiGregory sensed their frustration, he gave Stan Cohen's children his honest assessment. We still don't have enough to arrest Joyce Cohen, let alone convict her. If we arrest her prematurely, we're likely to lose the case. Under the law's double jeopardy prohibition, if we blow it, we lose her for good. She can never be retried. She would walk.

Gary and Gerri had heard it all before. Their despair showed on their faces. Their lawyer Irwin Block, a former prosecutor himself, understood what the prosecutors were up against, and he had to agree with their analysis. But he also knew how deeply discouraged his clients were. They believed their stepmother was getting away with murder. And they felt powerless to do anything about it.

Stan Cohen's death had sent a shock wave through his entire family. There were tangible physical consequences as well as emotional pain. Stan had always taken care of his family. Now his mother,

Frances, an elderly widow, fell into declining health. And Stan's younger brother, Artie, already ravaged by muscular dystrophy, was growing weaker and losing some of the few self-care skills he had left. He had more trouble shaving, dressing, and feeding himself. His independence was fading, and without his brother to take care of him, he faced an uncertain future. The Cohen family was devastated by Stan's death.

After the meeting with the new team of prosecutors, Gary and Gerri sank to a new low. It looked as if Joyce might never be charged in their father's murder—but they were more convinced than ever that she was guilty. After much soul searching, they reached a difficult decision. They would pursue their stepmother in the civil case just as if there were no criminal investigation. They would persevere, no matter how long it took, no matter what it cost. They were determined. They turned to Joe Serota for help. Serota was more optimistic about the case than Block had been. He always felt he could win a jury trial in the civil case, regardless of the obstacles. He assured Gary and Gerri that he would help them with whatever they decided to do.

From time to time, Joyce Cohen's lawyers approached attorney Joe Serota with proposals for settling the litigation. Serota was obligated to convey each proposal to his clients, but he always dreaded it. "Let me understand this," Gary would interrupt angrily, his mouth hardening into a tight line and his jaw jutting out defiantly. "They want to give us some more money from the estate and we should forget about the case? We should take *money* and forget Joyce murdered my father? Is that it? Never! Never!"

In October 1987, Anthony Caracciolo was arrested for the murder of Stanley Cohen. It was the first arrest in the Cohen case, but Caracciolo was really old news. Zuccarello had named him as the triggerman more than a year earlier. And Caracciolo was already in jail for home invasion robberies. Although Caracciolo still vehemently denied any involvement in the Cohen homicide, the prosecutors felt they had little to lose by arresting him now. Spear hadn't caught up with Tommy Lamberti yet, but he was still on the trail. In the meantime, the arrest might put some pressure on Caracciolo to turn against Joyce. He had already negotiated a plea on his home invasions: twenty-seven years in jail. But the Cohen murder added the possibility of the death penalty. That might get his attention, the prosecutors reasoned. It was all they had left.

When he heard about Caracciolo's arrest, Alan Ross was alarmed. He had caught vague rumors that Zuccarello was somehow implicating Joyce Cohen, but he hadn't learned anything definite. Now that Caracciolo had been arrested, it was obvious Zuccarello had fingered him, too. Ross guessed the prosecutors' strategy. Charge Caracciolo, offer him a deal, and roll him against Joyce.

But Ross still didn't know what Zuccarello had said about Joyce. When he asked her, Joyce had assured him that she had never heard of either Frank Zuccarello or Anthony Caracciolo. And the attorneys representing the two men weren't cooperating with Ross. They were busy watching out for their own clients. Detective Spear and the prosecutors certainly wouldn't help him out. His usual intelligence-gathering method—private investigators interviewing witnesses right after the police—hadn't turned up Zuccarello's story, either. But Ross desperately needed to know what Zuccarello was saying about his client.

Ross came up with a creative tactic. He would file a request to examine "public records" in the case against Caracciolo. Under Florida law, anyone is entitled to obtain a copy of certain public records, including materials that prosecutors have provided to a defendant in a criminal case. Ross made good use of that law. He got a copy of Zuccarello's ninety-seven-page statement about the Cohen homicide as a public record, since Kastrenakes and DiGregory had provided the statement to Caracciolo.

As soon as he started reading the statement, Ross knew Joyce Cohen would be arrested for murder. It was inevitable. When he called her in Chesapeake, Virginia, with the bad news, Joyce was stunned. Ever heard of any of these guys, Ross asked her again. Frank Zuccarello? Anthony Caracciolo? Tommy Lamberti? No, no, no, Joyce insisted. How about Josephine Macaluso? Absolutely not, she replied.

Then Ross got to work. He had witnesses to interview, a bond hearing to prepare for, a defense to plan. He knew he didn't have a minute to waste. He was going to need a lot of help from his law partners—and a lot of money from his client.

In May 1988, Tommy Lamberti was finally arrested back in his old New Haven neighborhood. When he first saw Lamberti, Spear was disappointed. The guy was good-looking—curly dark hair, nice build—but nothing special that he could see. Not the stud he had imagined. But, incredibly, women were still lining up for Lamberti. His pretty blond Florida girlfriend, Joy Ellefson, flew to New Haven to marry him—in jail.

Lamberti was returned to Miami to stand trial for the murder of Stan Cohen, as well as a long string of home invasion robberies. Spear was anxious to talk to him about the Cohen case. The prosecutors wanted to offer him a deal to testify against Joyce Cohen—the last hope for their "roll the co-conspirators" strategy. But like Caracciolo, Lamberti swore he had never seen Joyce or Stan Cohen, knew absolutely nothing about the homicide. And he offered to take a polygraph to prove it.

DiGregory and Kastrenakes reluctantly concluded that the roll the co-conspirators strategy had to be abandoned. Neither Lamberti nor Caracciolo would roll, and they had to come up with a new strategy if they hoped to convict Joyce Cohen of her husband's murder. Although they believed Zuccarello's version of the murder, they had nothing to corroborate his story—no co-conspirator testimony from Caracciolo or Lamberti, no medical evidence pegging the time of death at 2 or 3 A.M. rather than 5:20 A.M., no one who heard shots at 2 or 3 A.M., no map of the Cohen house given to Caracciolo, no canceled checks or records of phone calls between Joyce Cohen and the hired killers. Nothing. Zuccarello's story would have to stand alone.

But Zuccarello as a state's witness was a prosecutor's nightmare—a career criminal who admitted participating in a string of violent home invasions and at least one murder, a witness who had changed his story several times and had everything to gain by his testimony against others. The prosecutors knew Alan Ross could tear Zuccarello apart on cross-examination. A jury would hate Zuccarello—and that might keep them from convicting Joyce Cohen.

DiGregory finally concluded that since they couldn't count on Zuccarello's eyewitness testimony to persuade a jury, they should treat the case as one based only on circumstantial evidence. They would have to assemble the many small pieces of the puzzle and lead the jury to draw the correct inferences.

It would be painstaking work, but this was DiGregory's favorite kind of case—one that required investigation, imagination, and creative preparation by the prosecutor. He found it much more challenging to assemble a circumstantial case than to argue about the voluntariness of a defendant's confession or his mental state. DiGregory couldn't wait to dig into the voluminous files on the Cohen case. And he knew John Kastrenakes would be a valuable asset. He was the best investigative prosecutor DiGregory had ever met.

Together the two men summarized the physical evidence in the case. They had the murder weapon, Stan Cohen's own gun—no fingerprints were found on it, but there were two tiny bits of tissue jammed in the grip. They had samples of facial tissue taken from the Cohen house similar to the pieces on the gun butt, but the bits were too small to make a definite match. There was gunpowder residue on swabs taken of Joyce Cohen's hands on the morning of the murder, but the type of particles indicated she hadn't fired the weapon. They had facial tissue found in the wastebasket of Joyce's bathroom with traces of nasal mucus and a dark stain on the tissue.

But how to put those pieces of evidence together to convict Joyce Cohen? They weren't sure.

By August 1988, Alan Ross was more certain than ever that Joyce Cohen was about to be arrested for her husband's murder. He suspected that DiGregory and Kastrenakes were busy presenting their case to the Dade County Grand Jury to get an indictment against her, but they wouldn't tell him. He knew the grand jury met every Wednesday, and every Thursday he held his breath all day, waiting to hear that Joyce had been picked up in Chesapeake.

Ross wanted to surrender his client without the embarrassment of an arrest. He called DiGregory. "Look, I know the grand jury meets every Wednesday," he said. "Why do I have to spend every Thursday waiting for the inevitable? Why are you ruining my life? Just tell me when it's going to be. I'll bring her here. She'll surrender."

But DiGregory refused to play ball.

Finally Ross decided that indictment and arrest were likely during the month of September. He called Joyce at Dietrich's house in Chesapeake and reluctantly advised her to return to Miami to be available for arrest.

Joyce was incredulous that after more than two years she would actually be charged in Stan's murder. She knew that neither Caracciolo nor Lamberti had backed up Zuccarello's story about her. And she had passed two separate polygraph tests to prove her innocence. It just didn't seem possible that she could be arrested. But she trusted Alan Ross—and she was resigned to taking his advice. Joyce came back to Miami.

Ross sent a letter to DiGregory confirming that Mrs. Cohen would spend the month of September in Miami and that she would surrender voluntarily at any time. But there was no arrest. At the end of the month, Joyce returned to Chesapeake.

On October 23, 1988, Lieutenant E. M. Pietrucci, commander of special investigations for the Chesapeake Police Department, took a call from the Miami Police Department. Assistance was requested in Chesapeake to arrest a suspect wanted in Miami for murder. The suspect was living in Chesapeake at a known address. Could the lieutenant arrange for assistance to the Miami detectives coming up to make the arrest? Of course.

Lieutenant Pietrucci pondered a moment. He needed reliable officers to assist the Miami cops in the arrest—but the job also called for good social skills. Like police departments around the country, the Chesapeake Police Department adhered to the unwritten rules of the brotherhood of law enforcement, one of which is proper hospitality for officer-guests. Whom to assign? The unofficial hospitality committee of the Chesapeake Police Department: Detectives Buddy Barber and Ronnie Young.

Friends and partners for several years, Barber and Young were undercover narcotics detectives. Young was blond and cherubic, Barber dark and lean. They wore their hair long and sometimes didn't shave before coming to work. Their daily uniform was jeans, T-shirts, sneakers, and shades. They drove cars confiscated from dope dealers—Camaros, mostly. Barber and Young could give the Miami detectives all the help they needed in setting up the arrest. And they were friendly, outgoing, personable. They could show the Miamians a good time while they were off-duty.

Barber and Young were dispatched to meet with the Miami detectives at their motel, the Holiday Inn Chesapeake. It was a new motel, one of the nicest in town, with a bar that would make the Floridians feel right at home: the Key West Lounge.

When Barber and Young met Detective Jon Spear and his Cuban partner, Nelson Andreu, they were startled to find the Miami detectives in shirts, ties, jackets, and spit-shined shoes. Barber stared at Jon Spear's hair. It looked slicked back or something. Mousse? Hair spray? And he noticed that Spear wore two gold bracelets on his right wrist. Definitely not the Chesapeake undercover cop look.

But once they started discussing the arrest, the Chesapeake detectives were fascinated. Spear told them that they were there to arrest a Miami woman, Joyce Cohen, for the contract murder of her husband. Spear knew she was living with a local man, Robert Dietrich. Did Barber and Young happen to know Dietrich?

As it happened, Barber and Young did know Robert Dietrich. He flew his own plane and seemed to have a lot of money to throw around for someone who managed a trailer park. The two detectives drove Spear and Andreu to a location a couple of blocks from Dietrich's big brick house at 1120 Main Street. Then they called Dietrich's home phone number from their mobile phone. When a woman answered, they hung up. A few moments later, they moved into position outside Dietrich's house. While Barber, Young, and Andreu hid in bushes in the yard, Spear knocked on the front door. No answer. They called the phone number again. No answer.

Just then a scruffy-looking dark-haired man rode up on a bicycle. "What do you want?" he demanded.

Barber and Young immediately recognized Robert Dietrich. They stalled. "Was there a robbery at this house?" Barber asked. "Did someone here call for assistance?"

But Dietrich had been anticipating the police for months. "Do you have a search warrant?" he said. "If not, get out."

Just then a BMW pulled into the driveway. It was Robert Byrum, Joyce Cohen's local lawyer, alerted by Alan Ross. Spear introduced himself, showed his badge and the warrant, and told the lawyer he was there to arrest Joyce Cohen for murder.

"I don't believe she's in the house," Byrum said, "but I think I can find her. Can I surrender her tomorrow morning?"

"No way," Spear replied. "I want her now."

"Well, I have to find her. How about if I bring her in to the Chesapeake P.D. in about an hour?"

Although Spear was reluctant, Barber and Young knew the attorney well. He could be trusted to surrender his client as promised. So it was agreed.

One hour later, Joyce Cohen walked into the Chesapeake Police Department with her attorney and a teary-eyed Robert Dietrich. Spear noticed that she had put on some weight. She was wearing baggy, shapeless pants and a droopy top. She looked dumpy, he thought, not flashy, as she had looked in Miami. But Joyce seemed controlled, confident. She acted as if this was some terrible mistake which would soon be corrected. Spear showed her the warrant and Detective Young read her the Miranda warning. "Do you want to talk to me, Joyce?" Spear asked her.

She shook her head no, and Spear turned her over to the Chesapeake Police Department for processing and booking.

News photographers showed up. They snapped pictures of Joyce Cohen under arrest, in handcuffs, her head covered by a coat just like a Mafia don. As Detective Barber walked her across the street to the women's jail, he asked, "Where were you when we came to the house?"

"Oh, I was there," she replied. "I saw you."

That night Detectives Barber and Young enthusiastically took up their duties as the hospitality committee. Dressed in their usual jeans and T-shirts, they went to pick up Spear and Andreu at their motel and were transfixed by the Miami detectives' off-duty attire. They looked like something out of "Miami Vice." They wore tight pants, shirts open halfway down their chests, and gold chains—a "Mr. T starter set," Ronnie Young called Andreu's gold. "Spear wears Bally shoes and he smells like cologne," Barber grumbled to Young.

They started with the seafood buffet at the Key West Lounge, washed down with plenty of beer. After dinner, Spear ordered a White Russian, light on the Kahlúa. It was a drink neither Barber nor Young had ever heard anyone order. Then they moved on to waterfront spots in Virginia Beach and Norfolk, where Barber and Young discussed the local narcotics scene with their guests. Listening to Spear and Andreu talk about Miami, Barber and Young concluded that Chesapeake was about six years behind Miami in drug trafficking but headed down the same road. They were already seeing violent Jamaican posses in their area, and the trade was moving from marijuana to cocaine.

The next day Alan Ross flew in for Joyce's bond hearing. He was anxious to get bail set for his client, so she could remain in Chesapeake with Robert Dietrich until her trial in Miami. But despite Ross's best efforts, and some sympathetic comments from the Chesapeake judge, Joyce remained in custody. That meant she might as well return to Miami immediately so that Ross could try to get bail set by the Miami judge assigned to the case, Judge Tom Carney.

Barber and Young had been excellent hosts, and the Miami detectives had enjoyed their off-duty time in Chesapeake. Young gave Spear a SWAT team T-shirt as a souvenir. And when Spear told Buddy Barber he might have to return to Chesapeake later, Barber had only one comment: "Next time wear jeans."


Joyce Cohen came back to Miami to face first-degree murder charges in the death of her husband. Videotapes and photographs of her return shocked Miamians, not because she was under arrest, which had long been anticipated, but because of her appearance. She was virtually unrecognizable. The sleek brunette with the bedroom eyes had become an overweight, frumpy hausfrau, her fleshy face obscured by thick glasses and an unruly mop of hair streaked with gray.

The change was so radical that most believed it was deliberate, an effort to replace the sexy, jet-setting, coke-snorting party girl with a dowdy, demure, uninteresting, and unattractive matron, someone who couldn't be imagined plotting her husband's murder. Tyrone, Joyce's Grove Isle hairdresser, was stunned. "She looks like a Sunday school teacher," he stammered.

At the Channel 10 television news desk in Miami, Gerri Helfman sat silently off-camera while her co-anchor ran the videotape and announced the arrest of her stepmother for the contract murder of her father. Then she was back on-camera, poised, professional, delivering the news as usual. Inside, she was elated.

Ever since March 7, 1986, Gerri had lived every day in the shadow of her father's murder. Even her wedding day held sad memories. For two and a half years, Gerri, Steve, and Gary had spent hours every day working on the investigation and their civil suit against Joyce. They had kept a daily log of their progress, and the mountain of paper poignantly reflected their pain. But now it looked as if it had all been worth it. The tide was finally turning in their favor.

Later, Gerri was on assignment interviewing Marta Villacorta, chief administrator of South Florida's maximum-security prison for women, the Broward Correctional Institution. The subject of the interview was the high turnover rate among guards at the prison.

As the cameraman worked to set up the shot, Gerri chatted with Ms. Villacorta. "You may meet my stepmother someday," she said.

"Oh? Will she be applying for a job as a guard at the prison?" Ms. Villacorta asked.

"No. We hope she'll be an inmate," Gerri replied with a grim smile.

# *Eighteen*

•

Alan Ross's immediate priority was to get his client out of jail—the Dade County Women's Detention Center. The struggle took the case to the Third District Court of Appeal, the courthouse Stan Cohen had been so proud to build. Ross managed to get a $1 million corporate surety bond set for his client. It was a resounding victory. Since she had no money, Joyce's Miami friends and Robert Dietrich and his elderly parents had put up their homes and assets as collateral to guarantee her appearance at trial.

Ross had the paperwork prepared months in advance. And once he got the appellate court's ruling, he walked the papers over to Judge Tom Carney and asked him to arrange for Joyce's immediate release from the nearby Women's Detention Center. Television news crews filmed Ross triumphantly driving Joyce away from the jail in his white Porsche. Joyce was ecstatic. She had spent a dreary month in jail, and she couldn't wait to get out of Miami. "One step at a time," Ross cautioned her. "Let's let the dust settle. Then we'll get you back to Chesapeake. Right now we have to concentrate on the case."

The $50,000 retainer Joyce had scraped up for Alan Ross had long since been exhausted, and the trial that lay ahead was going to be very expensive. Ross would have to work nearly full-time preparing for trial. He would need the assistance of lawyers in his firm as well as private detectives and expert witnesses. They all had to be paid.

Since Joyce had no money, she signed over all her rights to her husband's estate to Ross to fund her defense—her right to life insurance proceeds, property, cash, everything. If she won at trial, Ross would also win—big. Stan Cohen's estate was still worth several million dollars, Ross thought, although the original $12 million estimate was probably too high. But if Joyce was convicted, she would be disinherited under Florida law, and Ross wouldn't get a dime.

Ross was willing to let his legal fees ride on the outcome of the trial. But he still needed cash to pay expenses—expert witness fees, deposition transcripts, and all the other pretrial procedures. He set up funds for various expenses and asked Joyce's friends to contribute—so much for a forensic pathologist consultation, so much for the deposition transcript of a crucial witness, so much for a private investigator. Joyce's loyal friends came through for her again, putting up cash in addition to the assets they had already pledged for her bail.

But it wasn't enough. To raise more cash, Myra Wenig, Shu Sampson, and Sam Smith held a giant yard sale of Joyce's household goods and furniture, those items she was willing to part with.

It still wasn't enough, and eventually Ross had Joyce declared temporarily indigent by the court. That way the state of Florida paid for her necessary expenses of defense—but not Ross's fee. If the state paid his attorney's fee, there would be a cap on the amount—a predictably low cap. But he preferred to bet his entire fee on the outcome of the trial. Alan Ross was a high-stakes gambler.

After Joyce's release from jail, Robert Dietrich came to Miami until Ross obtained a court order allowing Joyce to return to Chesapeake, just as he had promised. There they resumed a life far different from the Coconut Grove fast lane where Joyce had groomed her Joan Collins persona. Dietrich's trailer park was filled with battered pickups and dusty cars; women hung wash on outdoor lines, and children played in puddles in the rutted dirt roads. Dietrich's grown son, Robbie, lived in a duplex nearby. For entertainment, he liked to take his small boat out fishing for flounder on Chesapeake Bay, and sometimes Robbie went with him. Joyce usually stayed at home.

But at least Dietrich's big brick house was the nicest in the neighborhood of small frame houses. And inside, Joyce had re-created a miniature version of the Great Room she had left behind at Wolf Run Ranch. Walls had been removed between the living room and dining room to make one large room, which was carpeted in deep-green pile. There was a small fireplace at one end of the room, with the 1986 Colorado Christmas picture of Dietrich and Joyce standing on the mantel next to Joyce's antique clock.

The russet-accented sofas and love seats from the ranch house were there, arranged before a picture window. Victorian leaded glass panels hung from chains across the windows. Also transplanted from Colorado was the big dining table with the carved wood captain's chairs, which were now crowded into the kitchen. And in the corner of the new Great Room stood the baby grand piano from the house on South Bayshore Drive.

Joyce was now home and free on bail, but she behaved like someone still imprisoned. She spent most of her time in the house, watching soap operas on television or devouring romance novels, one after the other. She seemed moody, depressed, as if she were living under a black cloud. Sometimes Dietrich tried to get her out of the house—to dinner, to night spots on Chesapeake Bay—but she usually refused.

Shawn Cohen had followed his mother to Chesapeake. He and his new wife, now pregnant, lived in one of Dietrich's nearby duplex houses. Joyce began to confide in Shawn about her increasing irritation with Dietrich. The man was uneducated, she complained, he just wasn't up to her standards. His beer drinking disgusted her—so lower class, she said. She was still doing a little coke, but he complained whenever he caught her—just as Stan had. And Dietrich's nervous habits were driving her crazy, she told Shawn. He was a man in constant motion, fidgeting, running in and out of the house, slamming doors. "Why don't you just stay outside?" Joyce would yell at him irritably.

They had begun to fight about money, Joyce told her son. Dietrich thought she spent too much and tried to put her on a monthly budget of about $1,500. I can't afford you, he would shout at her. You're running it dry! He had already put out a lot of money for Joyce—

close to $100,000, Shawn estimated, for legal expenses alone. He was entitled to be a little resentful, Shawn thought.

Joyce told Shawn that she had asked Dietrich to change his will to make her the beneficiary. What if something happened to you? she said. What would happen to me then? I have nothing, no one. I can't even pay my lawyer!

Dietrich seemed willing to rewrite his will for Joyce, but his parents objected, Shawn recalled. It was their property Dietrich was managing, and they planned to leave it to him when they died. They didn't trust Joyce. She was, after all, accused of murdering her husband in his sleep. When Dietrich told his parents that he wanted to marry Joyce, they insisted on a prenuptial agreement. But Joyce refused. There was no wedding.

She also refused to sign promissory notes for the money she borrowed from Dietrich. "My mother was always against signing anything for Robert," Shawn commented.

The quarrels worsened. One night Joyce went to Shawn's duplex looking for Dietrich. He had left early that morning, and she hadn't heard from him since. Shawn and Robbie, Dietrich's son, walked the trailer park twice that night, looking for him. But they never found him. When he showed up the next morning, Joyce started yelling at him. Dietrich yelled right back. She could leave if she was going to yell at him! He didn't need the hassle!

Shawn knew his mother was just biding her time. She fully expected to be acquitted at trial. Alan Ross called almost daily, reassuring her. "You have nothing to worry about," he always said. She would collect her inheritance from Stan's estate and pay off her lawyers. And then, Shawn was certain, she would leave Dietrich and Chesapeake far behind.

"She'll hit that high lifestyle again and be gone," he predicted confidently. "And I know that money will be gone quick, too. The first thing she'll have to buy is a couple of Jaguars and a new wardrobe." Joyce would need the new clothes. Since she had gained so much weight, she couldn't wear her designer outfits anymore. At home she usually settled for baggy pants with loose shirts flapping over the waist.

Shawn worried that his mother might leave him behind, too.

"Mom, when you get all that money, you're not going to forget about me, are you?" he asked her. Joyce wouldn't answer her son. But he still believed she would look out for him.

In Chesapeake, Joyce cultivated few friends. Donna Brown, Robert Dietrich's business manager, was an exception. Donna was a small, slender woman in her fifties who moved into the trailer park to help Dietrich, whom she had known for years. She was good with figures. She managed the accounts and kept Dietrich's affairs in order. And she was genuinely fond of Joyce. When Donna's husband died shortly after Joyce moved in with Dietrich, Joyce was very kind to her, sitting with her for hours, comforting her. She knew how Donna felt, Joyce told her, since she had lost her own husband.

As the trial drew closer, Joyce spent hours on the phone with her attorneys preparing for her ordeal. Sometimes they even discussed her wardrobe. As every trial lawyer knows, a defendant's physical appearance and demeanor are critical in a jury trial, and great care must be taken to project the right image.

One day Joyce asked Donna Brown to look at some clothes she might wear at trial. Several outfits were spread out on the bed. "What do you think?" she asked.

Donna surveyed dresses with big, white bib collars, suits and jackets buttoned up to high necks. They looked like costumes for a play— prissy ensembles for a matronly schoolmarm, not for Joyce. Donna thought Joyce dressed very well—expensive, tasteful, tailored clothes that were becoming to her short figure: longish skirts, boots, sweaters. "Joyce, these clothes just aren't you," she said. "There isn't one outfit that's really you. Where did you get this stuff?"

"Alan Ross told me to wear these. He said the psychologist recommended them."

"Joyce, I think it's a mistake. Why don't you just be yourself?"

"Well, I have to follow Alan's advice," Joyce sighed.

As a condition of her bond, Joyce had to report every Monday morning to Detective Ronnie Young at the Chesapeake Police Department. She was always there, always on time, always with Dietrich in tow. His mood was usually black, but every Monday morning Joyce was cheerful and friendly, joking with Young about how this was all a mistake and would soon be resolved. She was so positive, so confident, that eventually Young began to wonder whether the Miami detectives had the right person after all.

Back in Miami, Kevin DiGregory and John Kastrenakes were in the midst of feverish trial preparations. They needed help locating and reinterviewing their witnesses and preparing them to testify at trial. Spear couldn't give the prosecutors as much help as they needed. His homicide case list grew nearly every week—the murder business was still booming in Miami.

Kastrenakes suggested they ask Special Agent Steve Emerson to help. Emerson was a detective with the FDLE, the Florida Department of Law Enforcement, an agency with statewide jurisdiction. Kastrenakes already knew him and liked him. Emerson had been working home invasion robberies in Dade County and Broward County. He was well acquainted with the Richitelli gang and had interviewed Frank Zuccarello many times. When Kastrenakes called him, Emerson was anxious to help. He got authorization to "detach" from the FDLE's Miami office so he could work full-time with the prosecutors.

DiGregory and Kastrenakes heaved a sigh of relief. Emerson was one of the new breed of detectives—young, smart, college-educated. With his help, they just might get their case together on time. Emerson's first assignment: find witness Frank Wheatley—again. Stan Cohen's former project manager had disappeared from his Atlanta job, and this time he didn't intend to be found.

One witness the prosecutors didn't have to search for was Officer Catherine Carter, the first person to arrive at the Cohen house on the morning of the murder. She was still riding patrol at the Miami Police Department, although she had recently earned a law degree in the night school program at the University of Miami Law School.

When Carter came in to prepare her testimony, DiGregory and Spear gave her a copy of the sworn statement she had made to her supervisor about the events of March 7, 1986. Carter read her statement, they discussed it briefly, and when they finished, she got up from the table and headed for the door. Then she turned back to Spear, a quizzical look on her face.

"What's the matter?" he asked her.

"There's something missing from my statement," she replied. "I thought it was there, but it isn't."

"What? Did you forget to mention that Joyce Cohen confessed to you?" Spear joked.

"Well, Joyce said, 'I shouldn't have done it.' I know she said it. I thought I put it in my sworn statement but it's not there."

DiGregory and Spear stared at each other speechlessly.

"Cathy," Spear said, "think about it. Are you positive—absolutely positive—that's what she said?"

"Yes, I am."

"But why isn't it in your statement?"

"I thought it was. I just noticed that it's not there."

"Well, then, tell us just what happened."

"She was sitting with me on the sofa, rocking back and forth, just sort of staring off into space. She said something about Stan's daughter getting married on Saturday, then she said, 'What am I going to tell the kids?' Then she said, 'I shouldn't have done it.' That's all."

"Shouldn't have done what? Did you ask her what she meant?"

"No, I didn't."

"Why not?"

"Because the phone rang or one of the detectives walked up just then."

"Did you tell the detective what you heard?"

"Nope."

"Cathy, you're positive—positive—about this?"

"Yes, I am."

Officer Carter left. Spear and DiGregory looked at each other for a moment. "You know Alan Ross is going to tear her ass," Spear said.

"Yeah, I know," DiGregory replied, shaking his head.

Everyone described Alan Ross as a showman in the courtroom, with his booming, melodious voice and commanding presence. He considered a trial to be high theater—just as he thought of life in general. In fact, Ross was the child of professional entertainers. His father, Milton Ross, was a stand-up comic and musician who had performed in the big hotels on Miami Beach. His mother was a singer. Some nights when they couldn't find a baby-sitter, they took young Alan along to work with them. And hanging around backstage, watching his parents work, he met the great entertainers who played the Beach—Dick Shawn, Buddy Hackett, Jerry Lewis, Jan Murray. He was hooked.

Ross got his start as a performer when he was twelve or thirteen years old, playing drums six nights a week in nightclubs. He thought he was headed for stardom, and he loved the life. He had visions of playing with the Allman Brothers Band, his idols. After college, he and a couple of friends took their band on the road, looking for glory. It lasted eight months.

Ross finally decided "it wasn't the Jewish thing to do." He headed back to Miami and, as the result of a dare, wound up at the University of Miami Law School. He claimed it took him only thirty seconds in law school to choose criminal law as his legal specialty. It was the only subject that seemed to have anything to do with real life. Conditions precedent to contracts, the Rule in Shelley's Case, the Rule Against Perpetuities—it all seemed like a meaningless intellectual exercise to him. Getting arrested, going to jail—now that was something he could understand.

Ross decided he wanted to clerk with the best criminal defense lawyer in Miami. He asked around and everyone gave him the same name: Gerald Kogan. But Kogan received dozens of résumés each year from law students with better grades than Ross's. Then Ross hit upon a foolproof idea: he offered to work free.

"Well, hmm. Free, I can afford. Free, I'm in the market for. Free, I can't pass up. You're on," Kogan responded.

Ross worked hard, learned a lot, and absolutely revered Gerald Kogan. He churned out 140 appellate briefs for Kogan over the next few years on every conceivable criminal law topic. But the most valuable thing he learned from Kogan was that there was something honorable about being a defense attorney. "You don't have to be a criminal to be a criminal defense lawyer," Kogan admonished.

Ross had chosen his mentor well. In 1986, Gerald Kogan was appointed to the Florida Supreme Court, and Ross had become one of

Miami's leading—and most highly paid—criminal defense attorneys. He had made his reputation—and most of his money—defending suspected drug dealers. And his acquittal record was impressive. But it had been nearly ten years since he had tried a murder case—and he lost that one.

Ross insisted that Joyce Cohen was innocent, a good person caught in difficult circumstances. He was reassured by the results of the polygraphs she had taken. He argued that the prosecution was entirely political, that the prosecutors were being pressured by Gary Cohen and Gerri Helfman and their influential friends. Gary and Gerri—"the vultures"—must be motivated by hatred of their stepmother and greed for their father's estate.

Zuccarello, Ross said, had merely invented a plausible story about the Cohen homicide from newspaper and television accounts of the crime. He saw a chance to cut himself a better deal on the long stretch of time he was facing on the home invasion robberies, and he took it. In fact, Zuccarello had cut himself a great deal. He could have gotten a total of twenty-three life sentences for his crimes, but his plea bargain with the prosecutors put him in jail for only two years and three months. By the time Zuccarello testified against Joyce Cohen at trial, he would be out on the street, a free man again. And he would never be charged in the Cohen murder.

As he was preparing Joyce's defense, Ross got depressing news. The prosecutors would seek the ultimate penalty against his client, death by electrocution in "Old Sparky," Florida's electric chair. Another political decision, he thought, and one that put a heavy burden on him. Now he was responsible not just for his client's freedom but for her very life.

Under Florida law, Ross and the prosecutors would have to select a "death-qualified jury"—jurors who state they could vote for the death penalty in a proper case. Ross always felt that a death-qualified jury put the defendant at a terrible disadvantage from the start. Jurors who could vote for the death penalty were likely to be punitive people, he thought, with few qualms even about putting a fellow human being to death.

Ross hired a psychologist to help him develop a profile for jury selection, an outline of which traits to look for and which questions to ask potential jurors on voir dire examination. But because of the complexity of the case, the psychologist couldn't come up with a clear profile. The psychologist's final advice: avoid old Jewish women.

Not much help, Ross groused. I could have thought of that myself. His general view, like that of many old-school trial lawyers, was that he could take the first twelve people off the street, put them in the jury box, and convince them that there was at least one "reasonable doubt" in the state's case. But he knew that the death penalty would make jury selection, as well as his defense tactics, far more difficult than that.

The prosecutors' decision to seek the death penalty also meant Ross would have to divide the trial responsibility into two phases: the guilt-or-innocence phase, which he would handle himself; and the penalty phase (if there was one), which he asked his young partner, Robert Amsel, to take. It is considered bad karma with a jury to have a lawyer assure the jury that his client didn't commit the crime, then, if there is a conviction, have that same lawyer argue that his client was under stress when the crime was committed and so shouldn't get the death penalty. It destroys the lawyer's credibility. Better to have two different lawyers for the separate phases of trial.

But despite his misgivings about the death penalty issues, Alan Ross was confident of victory as the trial approached. He knew the state's case, and he could deal with it. Zuccarello, he was sure, would be seen by the jury as the sleazebag he was. The prosecutors had no real support for Zuccarello's self-serving testimony about the crime. And the state had a real problem with Zuccarello's claim that the murder happened between 2 and 3 A.M. Even Dr. Wetli, the medical examiner, could only say that the time of death was between midnight and 6 A.M.

Ross had a hotshot forensic pathologist from New York, Dr. Michael Baden, who would testify that death must have occurred shortly after 5 A.M., just as Joyce Cohen said. If Cohen had died at 2 or 3 A.M., lividity would have been visible on his body by 5:30 A.M. It would still have been there at 3 P.M. the next day when Dr. Wetli took his photos of the body. Dr. Baden had examined copies of Dr. Wetli's crime scene slides. He saw no lividity on Cohen's body.

As the trial approached, Ross confidently predicted victory. After a pretrial hearing he joked to the prosecutors, "When this trial is over, I'm going to buy myself a new boat. And I'm going to name it the *ReJoyce*, in honor of my client." He already had his eye on a new Bertram forty-six-footer—a very expensive boat.

"Alan," John Kastrenakes responded. "You may be right. You may win. But I just hope this: that by the end of the trial, Kevin and I will have created a reasonable doubt in *your* mind that your client is *innocent*."

# *Nineteen*

•

As Joyce Cohen's trial approached, the prosecutors gave themselves no better than a fifty-fifty shot at convicting her. But that was all right with Kevin DiGregory. He liked being the underdog. It kept him from losing his competitive edge, motivated him to keep plugging along. He hated overconfidence, and he urged John Kastrenakes to train physically for the long ordeal ahead. He knew they would be tired and overworked, and he feared they might get sick. DiGregory always made it a point to keep up with his physical fitness program, especially during trial. He ran every day and often worked out with weights.

DiGregory and Kastrenakes had made substantial progress in rounding up witnesses, with the help of Special Agent Steve Emerson, who had even managed to find Frank Wheatley. And they had finally found a way to use the physical evidence to convict Joyce. They had worked out a scenario that placed the murder weapon in her hand on the morning of March 7. Although the physical evidence had been available to Ross all along, the prosecutors guessed he hadn't yet figured out their plan. So far, they thought they had succeeded in keeping Ross's attention focused on the informant Frank Zuccarello, hoping that he wouldn't realize how important the physical evidence was to the state's case.

Zuccarello's insistence that the murder was committed between 2 and 3 A.M. was still troubling. If he was telling the truth, what was Joyce Cohen doing for two or three hours, from the time Stan was killed until she called 911 at 5:25 A.M.? Was she coked up, in a daze all that time? Was she asleep? Or was she staging evidence at the murder scene—throwing a rock through the kitchen door to fake a break-in, flushing coke down the toilet? Anything they could think of would have taken only a few minutes, not hours.

Then there were those late-night phone calls from Joyce's friends in Colorado at *exactly* the time that Joyce later said she saw intruders and her husband was shot. Apart from the lateness of the hour, there was something fishy about those calls. The prosecutors had subpoenaed phone records from the Carrolls' condominium in Steamboat Springs as well as the Cohens' house in Coconut Grove. They found calls to Joyce from the Carrolls at 5:18 and 5:20 A.M., presumably from Kathy Dickett and Kimberly Carroll. Then at 5:25 there was a call from the Carrolls to the Metro-Dade Police Department, at the same time Joyce called 911 in Miami. But there was another call at 5:27 from the Carrolls to Joyce—collect. The Cohens' phone records showed that the charge was accepted and that the call lasted about two minutes. Neither Kimberly nor Joyce had mentioned it in their statements. Why, John Kastrenakes wondered, would someone place a collect call during such an emergency? Were all these calls just coincidence—or had they somehow been prearranged?

Pursuing that line of thought, Kastrenakes had worked out another scenario. Kathy Dickett was Joyce's best friend in Steamboat Springs. Suppose Joyce had asked Kathy to call her at that hour of the morning. Then, by accident or on purpose, Kathy had bumped into Geri and Kimberly Carroll that night, and once they arrived at the Carrolls' condominium, Kathy suggested the "impromptu" early-morning phone call to Joyce in Miami.

But why would Joyce want to receive a phone call from anybody that morning? Because she needed it as her alibi. Did Joyce arrange for her friends in Colorado to become unwitting participants in her scheme? He had no proof, but Kastrenakes suspected that Joyce had set up her own alibi by asking Kathy to make sure she got a call at a certain time that morning. Then, Kastrenakes reasoned, Kathy had Kimberly Carroll make those phone calls. Perhaps Joyce thought Kimberly, a Miami attorney's daughter, would be a more believable witness than Kathy. If she couldn't have gotten Kimberly to call, maybe Kathy would have done it herself.

In her statement, Joyce said she told Kimberly Carroll, "I hear a noise. I've got to go now." When Kimberly called back, Joyce was screaming that Stan had been shot. Kimberly apparently believed that someone had broken into the Cohens' house while she was on the phone with Joyce and that Stan was shot just before she got Joyce back on the phone in her second call. Because Kimberly had been on the phone with Joyce at that crucial time, she could verify that Joyce told her about the break-in and the murder as they were occurring— or at least as they *seemed* to be occurring. As soon as Stan was dead, Kastrenakes's theory went, Joyce had only to wait for her alibi phone call from Colorado. When the call came, she could "discover" the murder, raise the alarm, call the cops, and play the hysterical widow.

But if Joyce and her hired gun Anthony Caracciolo planned the murder to occur between 2 and 3 A.M., why did the alibi phone call come shortly after 5 A.M.? Here Kastrenakes found a clue in Joyce's sworn statement to Detective Spear. When Joyce first mentioned the call from Kimberly Carroll, Spear had asked her what time it was then. About 3 A.M., she had replied. Since Joyce expected Stan to be killed between 2 and 3 A.M., Kastrenakes reasoned, she must have asked Kathy Dickett to arrange the alibi phone call for 3 A.M., when she could be sure Stan was dead. And the call did come shortly after 3 A.M.—*Colorado* time. But with the two-hour time zone difference, by then it was just after 5 A.M. *in Miami*.

A failure to communicate, Kastrenakes thought. It was like a bad joke. Joyce had told Kathy, "Call me at 3 A.M." But she didn't say whose time, hers in Miami or Kathy's in Colorado. But if Kastrenakes's scenario was right, two questions remained. What was Joyce doing, alone in the house with her husband's corpse, for *two or three hours* while she waited for that alibi phone call from Colorado?

And what would she have done if the call had never come?

Although Kastrenakes had no evidence that Kathy Dickett knew about Joyce's plan to murder her husband, he did have lots of questions for her and tried to subpoena her again, but it was too late. She was the one witness even Special Agent Steve Emerson couldn't get. She had moved to Australia, far beyond the reach of the state of Florida. So what they still lacked, DiGregory and Kastrenakes agreed, was that final, indisputable link tying Joyce Cohen to her husband's murder—something tangible, something from an independent source, something that even Alan Ross couldn't explain away.

One week before trial, John Kastrenakes was working late, poring over stacks of telephone records again, still trying to match up even one call between Joyce Cohen and her hired killers. No luck. Kastrenakes beat his fist against the stack of records in frustration. He knew Joyce had hired the men who murdered her husband, but the volumes of Southern Bell printouts refused to yield that tangible link he so desperately sought.

He turned the problem over in his mind for the thousandth time, and for the thousandth time he thought about Stanley Cohen. Sometimes he almost felt he could communicate with the dead man, the man whose life and death had been his preoccupation for nearly two years. "Stanley, damn it! We know she did it—and we're trying to prove it for you. But we just can't find the link. Help me, Stanley! Give me something! Show me something!" Kastrenakes waited, feeling foolish. He didn't really believe the murdered man could somehow help him. Maybe he had been working on the case too long.

Frustrated, angry, and depressed, Kastrenakes drove home slowly that night. It was nearly 10 P.M. when he arrived at his suburban Coral Gables home and saw a car in his driveway. Whose? Oh, yes, that realtor friend of his wife's, Charlotte Miller, no doubt trying to interest his wife in a new house. Bad timing—the last thing he cared about was house hunting, with the Cohen trial just a week away.

Kastrenakes walked into the house, kissed his wife and, greeted Charlotte with a tired wave.

"Oh, John, were you still at work? What are you working on so late?" Charlotte asked.

"The Cohen trial," he said. "It's starting next week."

"I've heard about that," Charlotte said. "You know, we lived right down the street when Stan Cohen was killed."

"Yes," Kastrenakes answered. "And in that whole neighborhood no one heard any shots that night."

"What? Well, that's funny," Charlotte said. "I know one person who heard something that night."

"Oh? Who?"

"We had a guest. He told my husband that he heard something that night. I think he said it was gunshots."

Kastrenakes's heart began to pound. "Who was it?" he asked carefully. "Where is he now? Do you know?"

"His name is Ahouse. Call my husband, he'll tell you about him."

Kastrenakes went to bed that night, but sleep wouldn't come. Charlotte had given him Bernard Ahouse's New York phone number. "Call him early in the morning," she had suggested. What Kastrenakes hoped, of course, was that Ahouse would recall hearing exactly four shots between 2 and 3 A.M., in line with Zuccarello's story about the time Stan Cohen was shot. But what if he had heard nothing? Or two shots, or six shots—any number but four? Then he would be useless. And what if Ahouse had heard four shots at 5:20 A.M., the time Joyce Cohen claimed her husband had been shot? Of course, Kastrenakes would have to notify Alan Ross about a witness favorable to the defense.

Lying awake in the dark, Kastrenakes understood that what he was about to do could make or break the state's case against Joyce Cohen. He knew he would have to take that chance. He had to talk to the only witness who might have heard gunshots ring out that night—and he couldn't tell Kevin DiGregory until it was over.

It was still very dark at six o'clock the next morning when Kastrenakes called Bernie Ahouse from his kitchen phone. His hand trembled as he waited for an answer. Finally he was talking to Ahouse and yes, Ahouse had been staying with his friend Frank Miller in Miller's Coconut Grove condominium on the night of March 6, 1986. He left Miami early the next day. Yes, he remembered the night. And he remembered hearing something unusual.

Kastrenakes had to clear his throat. "Mr. Ahouse, please tell me what you heard."

"Well, I remember I was asleep and . . ."

"Thank you, sir," Kastrenakes said when Bernie Ahouse was finished. "Someone will be in touch with you later."

John Kastrenakes hung the phone up gently. Then he sat down at the kitchen table, dropped his head in his hands, and stifled a sob.

# IV
·
## Judgment

# *Twenty*

**J**oyce Cohen would be tried in the Metropolitan Justice Building—the scene of nearly all criminal trials in Dade County, from traffic offenses to capital murder cases. Nine stories of dingy, moldy limestone housed the Dade County State Attorney's Office, the Dade County Public Defender's Office, the criminal courtrooms, and the judges' chambers. The building nestled against grimy expressway overpasses, alongside Miami's seedy hospital district, hard by the black, oily Miami River. It was a cheerless place, despite Miami's abundant sunshine and the straggly palms that lined the cracked sidewalks and the huge municipal parking lot across the street. An enclosed overpass connected the Metropolitan Justice Building with the Dade County Jail immediately behind it. The side streets were clogged with prisoner transport vehicles and jailhouse catering trucks that bore an ironic warning: JUST SAY NO TO DRUGS AND YOU WON'T DINE WITH US TONIGHT.

Pedestrian traffic in front of the Metropolitan Justice Building was heavy five days a week. Hotdog vendors did a brisk business under their bright umbrellas, and occasionally turf battles broke out among rivals for the coveted front sidewalk. The hotdog wars would get so bad during the Cohen trial that the law finally intervened. Sidewalk vendors were permitted only in specifically designated areas. Police passed out maps and rules in English and Spanish to the vendors, many of whom had immigrated from Cuba, Nicaragua, or Guatemala and spoke little English. "If the police try to make me move, they'll have to take me to prison!" one anguished vendor declared in heavily accented English.

Inside the big gray building, long lines passed through airport-style metal detectors. Ancient, narrow escalators like conveyor belts moved the raw material of the criminal justice system through the building's first six floors. The human parade ran the gamut—swaggering teenage toughs, ageless black men with thick dreadlocks under grimy plastic shower caps or heavy wool hats, whining children clinging to distraught mothers, young pregnant women, down-and-out old men, well-dressed lawyers—and cops.

Especially cops. Cops from all of the twenty-four separate municipal jurisdictions in Dade County. A virtual smorgasbord of law enforcement: Miami cops in dark navy uniforms with the city emblem, a stylized gold palm tree; Metro-Dade cops, wearing dun-colored uniforms with patches reflecting a peaceful Everglades scene complete with a scarlet-clad Indian; cops from suburban Hialeah in blue uniforms with a colorful Seminole Indian extending an arm in blessing; cops from the city of Miami Beach, from Sweetwater, Opa-Locka, Coral Gables, Homestead, from the Florida Highway Patrol. They were all cops. And each, of course, drove a city vehicle, adorned in the manner prescribed by that municipality. The doors of some cars were emblazoned with city emblems. Others were generic: POLICE in big black letters on the sides, hood, and trunk.

The Joyce Cohen case was set for trial on October 10, 1989, more than three and a half years after Stan Cohen's murder. Codefendants Tommy Lamberti and Anthony Caracciolo would be tried later. The case had been reassigned from Judge Tom Carney to Judge Fredricka G. Smith, who would preside in Courtroom 4-2. Judge Smith had a well-earned reputation as an intelligent, conscientious, thoughtful jurist. She was also said to be a fervent feminist. In one story that made the rounds, she allegedly called a male prosecutor up to the bench and admonished him for calling her "Ma'am." Demeaning, she said—refer to me as "Your Honor" or "Judge," not "Ma'am." When the story was repeated to Judge Smith, she laughed good-naturedly. But she didn't deny it.

Judge Smith's courtroom was a large, high-ceilinged, echoing chamber with poor lighting and shabby decor. Everything seemed to be in shades of beige, brown, and mustard. Above the judge's bench was the carved and gilded motto: WE WHO LABOR HERE SEEK ONLY TRUTH.

The courtroom seated about forty spectators in worn, theater-style armchairs bolted to the floor. The first two rows on the right side were reserved for press. Since Florida allows television cameras in its courtrooms, a pool camera was set up next to the jury box. The Joyce Cohen trial would become a long-running nightly miniseries on Miami television stations.

To the left of the judge's bench was her private door, leading to her chambers. To the right, the back door that led to a small holding cell. There incarcerated defendants were held until they were admitted to the courtroom. That small cell was the first one a defendant would see after a guilty verdict. Joyce had never seen that holding cell. Free on bond, she entered and left the courtroom, along with her lawyers and the spectators and witnesses, through the front door.

October 10 dawned sunny, humid, and warm, Miami autumn. By 8:30 A.M., the steamy sidewalks were already crowded, dotted here and there with umbrellas raised against the sun, Caribbean-style. Promptly at 9 A.M., the curious few assembled in Courtroom 4-2 got their first close look at Joyce Lemay Cohen, the diminutive star of the six-week spectacle that was about to unfold. The woman who strode confidently into the courtroom was not the same dowdy hausfrau who was arrested in Virginia. Joyce had lost weight and pulled herself together for her ordeal.

She was noticeably short—barely five feet tall even in the high-heeled black pumps she wore. Her thick, shoulder-length dark hair, now dyed to cover the gray, was pulled back neatly at the nape of her neck with a black silk bow. She wore little makeup, only clear nail polish, and no jewelry except plain gold clip earrings. In black-framed glasses and a long-sleeved silk dress in a conservative plaid, Joyce looked exactly like what she might have been: a well-heeled, respectable young matron who shopped in expensive boutiques in the Grove. Or an actress in a soap opera.

Flanking Joyce were her attorneys: Alan Ross, wearing a perfectly tailored dark suit and red tie; and his young partner, Robert Amsel, whose long dark hair curled slightly over the back of his shirt collar. With Joyce in the middle, the three took their seats at the defense counsel table, just in front of the rail and facing the empty jury box.

Not three feet behind Joyce, close enough to touch her if they cared to, sat Gary Cohen and Gerri Cohen Helfman. Gary dressed like the successful young attorney he was, in a neat suit, white shirt, and tie. Gerri, now weekend news anchor for Channel 4, the local NBC affiliate, wore a casual denim dress and sandals. Her face, so familiar from the news desk, was prettier, softer in person than on television. But beneath her calm features was turmoil. After more than three and a half years, the end of her long quest was in sight. But what would be the outcome, she wondered nervously. Would her father's killer go to prison? Or walk out of the courtroom a free— and rich—woman?

The years since their father's death had brought some happiness to Gary and Gerri. Gary had married Carol Norris, his date at Gerri's bridal shower, and they had a nine-month-old son, Anthony. Gerri and her husband, Steve, also had a son, four-month-old Douglas. Brother and sister spoke together quietly. Neither even glanced at their stepmother, about to go on trial for her life—for the contract murder of their father.

Next the three young prosecutors filed into the courtroom: Kevin DiGregory, looking fit and composed; John Kastrenakes, smiling, self-assured; and Paul Mendelson, tall, studious-looking in his dark-rimmed glasses, a specialist in legal research and procedure, on loan from the Legal Department of the State Attorney's Office. Mendelson was also a top appellate lawyer. If the state got a conviction, it would be his job to hang on to it on appeal.

"All rise!" Alex Bosque, the young bailiff, announced the arrival of presiding Judge Fredricka Smith. The judge, a woman not much older than Joyce, had the same small stature. Her short-cropped, graying dark hair framed her elegant, expressive face and emphasized her large, intelligent eyes. A bright-red dress collar stood up just past the neck of her somber black robe. Seated at the massive judicial bench in Courtroom 4-2, Judge Smith looked poised and prepared.

"Please be seated."

The battle for Joyce Cohen's life had begun.

The first task was selecting a jury of twelve citizens capable of voting for the death penalty—if Joyce Cohen was convicted. The process of examining prospective jurors about their attitudes toward the death penalty is called "death-qualifying" the jury, a macabre term for an emotionally wrenching process. A panel of twenty prospective jurors was led into the jury box, a random selection of Miami citizens: men and women, black, white, Hispanic, in nearly equal proportions. They were dressed in a variety of styles: short-sleeved *guayabera* shirts worn outside the pants Cuban-style, blouses, skirts, low-heeled shoes, and an occasional jacket and tie.

Judge Smith welcomed the panel. Then Kevin DiGregory rose, faced the panel, and briefly summarized the charges against Joyce Cohen—contract murder, conspiracy to commit murder, and display of a firearm during the commission of a felony. A few jurors exchanged glances. Upstairs in the jury pool room, where hundreds of prospective jurors awaited assignment, there had been talk. If you're sent to Courtroom 4-2, they'd said, it's that big case, that murder trial.

"Ladies and gentlemen, look at this defendant, Joyce Lemay Cohen." DiGregory strode toward Joyce and pointed directly at her impassive face. She didn't flinch. "Can you assure the State of Florida that if I prove my case against her, and you find her guilty of first-degree murder, that you could vote for the death penalty for this defendant?"

Several jurors shifted in their seats; some looked away. Joyce Cohen watched them from behind her glasses without expression. Her face was a mask—or a shield.

"Juror in seat number four, Miss Weaver?"

Miss Weaver looked down at her lap and shook her head.

"Miss Weaver, could you vote for the death penalty for this defendant if the law required it?"

"No, no, I couldn't vote the death penalty—not for her, not for anyone." Miss Weaver twisted a tissue around and around, through her thin fingers.

Miss Weaver was excused. But at the end of six long days, after questioning one hundred prospective jurors, the prosecutors and defense attorneys agreed upon twelve jurors and four alternates who stated that they could, indeed, look at Joyce Cohen and promise to vote for either death in the electric chair or life in prison, depending upon the requirements of Florida law. Alan Ross made sure that they also promised, "Mrs. Cohen, I absolutely presume you innocent." He hoped it was more than an empty exercise.

Eight men and four women made up the jury. Attorneys on both sides were satisfied. It looked like a smart jury: a teacher, a school administrator, a production supervisor, a former air traffic controller, an insurance executive, a health care worker. Ross was particularly pleased with juror number eleven, Dr. Catherine Poole, a radiologist for twenty-two years and presently professor and chairman of the Radiology Department at the University of Miami Medical School. Ross pegged Dr. Poole as a natural leader. There's our jury foreperson, he thought. He was certain Dr. Poole would be impressed with his expert forensic pathologist from New York, Dr. Michael Baden. And he hoped she would find Dr. Wetli's work slipshod.

"Do you solemnly swear that you are qualified to serve as jurors in this cause and will render a true verdict in this case, so help you God?" In unison they swore.

John Kastrenakes gave the opening statement for the State of Florida. "This case is foremost about money," he began dramatically, pacing before the jury. "It's also about hatred, and about drug abuse, extramarital affairs, a failed marriage—and, ultimately, murder." He recited a tale already well told in the news media, that of a sexy young wife who tired of her older husband, who had a boyfriend in the Grove and a heavy cocaine habit that required lots of cash, who wanted to be rid of her husband without giving up any of his money in a divorce, and who hired the three men who killed her husband as he slept in his own bed.

Joyce stared at Kastrenakes, her face a blank expanse.

Later that morning, he continued, Joyce went to the police station and gave a statement under oath. She lied to them. But she didn't anticipate the witnesses and the physical evidence the cops would find. That evidence will show you that Stan Cohen had been dead for *hours* by the time she called for help, Kastrenakes told the jury. And she used that time to manipulate the crime scene, to create a false burglary.

Then Kastrenakes dropped his bombshell. Evidence never before made public showed that Joyce Cohen's hands were covered with gunshot residue on the morning of the murder; that the murder gun found in the Cohens' front yard had been wiped clean of fingerprints, but two tiny pieces of tissue still clung to the gun butt; and that the same type of tissue was found where it had been hidden—in Joyce Cohen's private bathroom on the other side of the house from the bedroom where her husband was murdered.

There was more. On that hidden tissue were gunshot residue, traces of makeup, and nasal mucus from a person with type B blood. Joyce Cohen's blood type? B.

Kastrenakes hammered out the conclusion. Joyce Cohen herself had wiped down the murder weapon with that tissue to remove her hired killers' fingerprints. She threw the gun off the second-floor terrace, and then hid the soiled tissue in her own private bathroom.

Joyce Cohen was guilty as sin.

As Kastrenakes returned to his seat, the courtroom was dead quiet. Joyce stared straight ahead, face composed, hands folded primly together.

Like an actor taking the stage, Alan Ross stepped confidently to the podium. "May it please the court," he thundered. "Ladies and gentlemen of the jury. I have listened to the state's suggestion of what the evidence in this case is going to be. It isn't. In a word, *bull*!" He bellowed the word and it hung in the air. Everyone knew what he had left off the end.

Ross described a farce of shoddy investigation, unreliable "evidence," and outright lies, strung together by investigators for one purpose: to nail Joyce Cohen for the contract murder of her husband, even though she had nothing to do with it. While detectives hounded her, he said, the real killers got away. "This murder remains an unsolved crime, and at the conclusion of this trial it will still be an unsolved case," he told the jury.

Joyce began to weep quietly. She wiped her eyes with a tissue.

Ross recounted the events on the morning of the murder. Everything started around 5:15 A.M., when Mrs. Cohen discovered a break-in in the kitchen and set off the alarm. As she ran toward the stairs, she saw a man dash out the front door. Upstairs, she found her husband in bed, bleeding from the head.

Joyce grew more upset as her lawyer spoke. Reliving the horror of that morning through his words, she began to sob openly, her face red and puffy, shoulders heaving. Robert Amsel, sitting beside her, seemed not to notice.

Uniformed officers and paramedics arrived at the Cohen home, Ross continued. The body was still warm. There was no lividity. "He's workable," the paramedics concluded. But the cardiac monitor showed a flat line.

Then, on the very morning of the murder, Miami homicide detective Jon Spear had bluntly accused the new widow: You murdered your husband, didn't you? "From that moment forward," Ross pronounced stentoriously, "the police were no longer interested in any leads unless they pointed to Joyce Cohen. . . . They followed one lead—we're going to prove Detective Spear is right." He had deftly supplied his answer to the jurors' mental question: Why would the police deliberately pursue the wrong person?

Neither Kastrenakes nor Ross mentioned that Joyce had refused the cops permission to search her house. The jury never knew they had to get a search warrant to finish their investigation. If the jury heard that, Kevin DiGregory believed, the case would be over in ten minutes flat. But Judge Smith had ruled that information inadmissible. The accused couldn't be penalized for exercising her Fourth Amendment right to have the state get a warrant before searching her home.

But Ross did tell the jury what he thought about Frank Zuccarello. He was a lying, conniving criminal who made up stories about Joyce Cohen to cut himself a better deal on his home invasion robberies. Ross gleefully detailed Zuccarello's cozy relationship with the cops. And what the police did for Zuccarello reached an all-time low when they took him to his girlfriend's house and waited outside while he had sex with her, in payment for testimony incriminating Joyce Cohen.

Ross finished on a softer note. "The state can't prove its case for one very good reason. In truth and in fact, Joyce Cohen is innocent. When this case is over, I'm going to stand in this same spot and count with you each reasonable doubt that exists in this case—and there'll be lots of them. . . . I'll ask you to return a not guilty verdict for the best reason possible: Joyce Cohen is *not guilty*. Thank you."

Ross looked at each juror, one by one, searching their faces. Finally he sat down beside his sobbing client.

After a short recess, the prosecutors called their first witness: Frank Wheatley, the SAC Construction project manager Stan Cohen had sent to Steamboat Springs. In his neat dark suit and tie, Wheatley looked clean-cut and sounded southern. "I'm from Miamuh," he began softly, using the city's old-time pronunciation. And Steamboat Springs was different from Miamuh, he told the jurors. "It had more of a party atmosphere." A party, the judge and jury soon learned, meant alcohol—and drugs.

It was at a party in Steamboat Springs that Wheatley learned to snort cocaine, he recounted. Both Joyce and Stan Cohen snorted coke at those parties. But "Stanley was real funny about who he did it in front of, so he wouldn't usually do it with a lot of people around that he wasn't close to." Sometimes Stan wore a chain around his neck, Wheatley recounted later on cross-examination, and on the chain was a "bullet," a vial of cocaine that dispensed measured doses.

Gary and Gerri, sitting in the gallery of the court, looked at each other in stunned silence. They had never heard this before. And they simply couldn't imagine their graying, middle-aged father in the hip Colorado party scene, sporting a bullet of coke around his neck.

Soon Joyce was doing lots of cocaine, especially when Stan wasn't around, Wheatley testified.

Where did she get the coke? DiGregory asked.

Sometimes "Stanley would have some and she'd get it out of his drawer and bring it," Wheatley said. "Then other times she would have her own that she had gotten from other places. . . . [Sometimes] it came through the mail to her from [a friend] in Miami."

Finally Stan had tried to make her cut down. "She told me that Stanley was watching her, how she spent her money, and that she didn't want him to know that she was buying cocaine with it," Wheatley continued. "On one particular occasion . . . she had gone out and bought a sweater that cost a little over a hundred dollars, or told Stanley that she had and that's why she had spent the money. She had actually bought a gram of cocaine with it."

"Did she ever tell you about a time when she took cocaine from [Stan] without his knowing it?" DiGregory asked.

"Yes," Wheatley replied. "She told me that she had got it out of the drawer . . . and that she would have to replace it and I was supposed to . . . get some to replace it with, and I wasn't able to so she had put some baking soda or something back in to replace the quantity taken out."

Prosecutor DiGregory led Wheatley deeper into the Cohens' private lives. The jury was rapt. Wheatley said that as he and Joyce partied together more and more—while Stan was back in Miami—she began to confide in him about her marriage. She was frustrated and bored with Stan. He was too old for her. She wanted to party, but Stan just wanted to go to bed early.

At a party at the Cohens' one night, Wheatley continued, Stan was obviously tiring, while Joyce was still going strong. She was afraid their friends would notice her husband's demeanor and leave. So "she crushed up a Valium and put it in his drink. . . . If he would go to sleep, you know, then we could stay there and party."

At the defense table, Joyce Cohen made furious notes on a yellow legal pad. Her grip on the pen tightened, her knuckles white and straining. Bold, sharp strokes bit into the paper. Her lips pressed together in a tight line.

With the Valium episode still lingering in the air, DiGregory moved to the heart of Wheatley's testimony: a conversation he had had with Joyce in October or November 1984. "She said to me one night, when we were talking, she said she wished she knew somebody that she could have kill him, or had the nerve to do it herself," Wheatley told the intent jury.

"When you heard her statement, what was your reaction?" DiGregory asked his witness.

"I laughed. Because I didn't think it was anything serious."

"Did there come a time when you changed your mind?" DiGregory asked.

Ross was ready for that one. He leaped to his feet, objecting. The objection was sustained. But the inference was inescapable. After Stan Cohen's murder, Wheatley thought back on that conversation. And then he took it very seriously.

The state continued its parade of witnesses. One by one, they supplied pieces of the case against Joyce Cohen, just as Kastrenakes had outlined it to the jury. Miami homicide detective Sergeant Luis Albuerne described the crime scene on the morning of the murder. He saw Stan Cohen's body lying on the floor next to the bed, where paramedics had left it. There was lividity, Albuerne testified, a light purplish color near the right armpit and on the right side of the body.

Jerry Mandina, a neighbor who lived directly across the street from the Cohens, told the jury what he heard on the morning of March 7. He was working at his desk before an open window from 3:30 A.M. to 5:30 A.M. The window faced the Cohens' house. It was dead quiet, he recalled, until he heard a noise from across the street. It was a sharp, loud noise, then tinkling glass. At first he thought it might have been a shot, but he changed his mind. It was more like slamming a door very, very hard, followed by glass breaking. He didn't look at a clock, but he thought it was around 5 A.M. About five minutes later a burglar alarm went off. He heard nothing else.

Miami police officer Edward Golden told the jury about finding the murder weapon, the Smith & Wesson .38, near the front door of the Cohen house. Kevin DiGregory handed Officer Golden the gun, its evidence tag still attached.

Is this the weapon you found? he asked.

Yes, Golden replied.

Stan Cohen's gun was admitted into evidence.

ID Technician Sylvia Romans described the two tiny pieces of white tissue that she found caught in the revolver's grip. No latent prints were recovered from the gun, she testified. Her partner, Guillermo Martin, told the jury how he collected swabs from Joyce's hands on the morning of the murder. "Well, I just washed my hands," she had told him. He saw no blood on her hands or clothes.

Then Kathy Moser took the stand. She looked neat, well groomed, and conservative in her checked jacket, white blouse, and black skirt, and she made an excellent witness. Moser worked for the Steamboat Springs Ski Corporation and had lived in Steamboat for the past fifteen years with her husband, Bill. The Mosers had met the Cohens about ten years earlier, she told the jury, and they became good friends. When they met, Joyce Cohen was quiet, shy, "a nice lady."

But over the years, Moser saw her become a coke-snorting party girl who wanted to be the center of attention.

"Do you see changes in Joyce Cohen's appearance today?" DiGregory asked Moser.

"Yes," she replied, looking at the defendant directly for the first time. "She's now wearing glasses and she was usually wearing contacts. And she generally doesn't dress quite that . . . matronly."

Kathy Moser admitted that she had used cocaine with Joyce at parties a few times—the first was Christmas, 1984. But a year later, Moser and her husband were worried that Joyce's drug use had gotten out of hand. There were rumors. Joyce was "causing a stir around town," Moser recalled. She and her husband tried to talk to Joyce about their concerns, but she told them, "Mind your own business."

Moser said she had talked with Joyce once more, in February 1986, right before Joyce returned to Miami for Gerri Cohen's bridal shower. The Cohens' marriage was "horrendous," Joyce told her friend. She wanted out. And she was furious with Stan about his affair with an old flame in Miami.

"What was the name of the old flame?" DiGregory asked.

"Carol Hughes," Moser replied.

Miami homicide detective Lieutenant Edward Carberry took the stand to identify the sworn statement Joyce Cohen gave on the day of the murder. While the jurors followed along on their copies, DiGregory and Carberry read the questions and answers aloud. Joyce described an ordinary evening at home until nearly midnight, when she had heard a noise in the backyard. Stan took his gun out of the drawer where he usually kept it, she said, and they went outside to investigate. Finding nothing, they went back upstairs for the night. Where was the gun at that time? Detective Spear had asked.

"He had laid it on the nightstand," Joyce had said, "and I had picked it up, and I said, why are you leaving this here? He said, leave it here for now. And it was in a case then."

The jurors heard Joyce tell Spear about the phone calls from Colorado and the banging noise that drew her to the kitchen. Then she saw somebody running out the front door, she said. She dashed up the stairs and found her husband bleeding on the bed.

"I ran over to him and I said, Stan! I put my hands on his shoulders and it was blood. The phone was right there, and I picked it up and I called 911. I said, My husband has been shot, please get me some help! After I saw the blood, I ran and got a towel and I tried to stop it. I pulled the covers back and I just kept trying to talk to him and get him to talk to me. . . . I just shook him and kept saying, Stan! Stan!"

As she listened to her own description of that morning, Joyce began to cry again, tears running down her cheeks in streams. She removed her glasses and wiped her face with her bare hands. Her lawyers, sitting at her side, seemed oblivious.

The first week of the trial ground to a close, and so far, the evidence seemed to play out just the way the prosecutors had hoped. But they knew the tough witnesses were yet to come: Officer Catherine Carter, who belatedly recalled Joyce Cohen's incriminating (but admittedly ambiguous) statement: "I shouldn't have done it." And Frank Zuccarello, a cross-examiner's dream with his self-serving motive, conflicting stories, and violent criminal acts. Would the jury believe a man like that?

There was more to worry about. Dr. Charles Wetli, Deputy Chief Medical Examiner, had just dropped a bombshell. He had changed his mind, he told DiGregory, about the probable time of Stan Cohen's death. For three and a half years, Wetli had stuck by his original statement that death could have occurred at any time from midnight to 6 A.M. But now he believed that the time of death was between 2 and 3 A.M.—just as Frank Zuccarello said.

DiGregory was elated. But he knew Dr. Wetli's last-minute switch would infuriate Ross. He was right. When he told Ross about Wetli's new opinion, Ross went off like a rocket. DiGregory knew Ross would move heaven and earth to discredit Wetli and keep his new opinion out of evidence. It would be up to DiGregory to protect Wetli and get his testimony before the jury. It wouldn't be easy.

There was yet another witness whose testimony the jury might find hard to believe: Bernard Ahouse, the man from New York who had been visiting friends in the Grove and who remembered hearing something unusual the night of Stan's murder. Who was he, and how accurate could his recollections be after three and a half years? Moreover, if his testimony supported the prosecution's case against Joyce, wouldn't it seem a little suspect that he had never come forward earlier, that no one had even heard of his existence until just one week before Joyce's trial? In fact, Ahouse had refused to come to Miami to testify. Kastrenakes and Amsel would travel to New York on Saturday, October 28, to videotape his testimony for presentation to a jury that would have every right to be skeptical.

In short, the crux of the prosecution's case against Joyce Cohen seemed to rest on the testimony of a police officer with belated recall, a jailhouse rat, a medical examiner who had changed his mind after three years, and a mystery man from New York.

# Twenty-One

•

**P**romptly at 9 A.M. on Monday, October 23, DiGregory called the state's next witness: Miami police officer Catherine Carter. On the witness stand, Carter told her story without embellishment. She had been the first officer to arrive at the Cohen house on March 7, 1986. There she found Joyce Cohen, distraught and hysterical. Upstairs lay the body of Stan Cohen, face down on the bed, bleeding from head wounds.

Carter said that as she listened to Joyce Cohen's account of the crime that morning, she had been puzzled about why the alarm didn't go off and the Doberman pinscher didn't stop the intruders. She had turned off the home's alarm system, Mrs. Cohen had told Carter, so she wouldn't accidentally set it off and awaken her husband. And she kept the Doberman pinscher with her for the same reason.

The jury was intent.

As Mrs. Cohen sat cross-legged on a cushion, staring off into space, Carter continued, she began to talk as if she was thinking out loud. Then she said: "I shouldn't have done it." Carter had heard it clearly. Just then a detective walked up. The phone rang.

Alan Ross's cross-examination lasted nearly an hour. He took Carter back through her own sworn statement about that morning, probing for inconsistencies. Finally he came to the point. If Carter had heard Mrs. Cohen say, "I shouldn't have done it," wouldn't it have been important to ask what she meant? "You never asked Mrs. Cohen what it was she shouldn't have done?" Ross demanded incredulously.

"That's correct," Carter answered.

Did you tell anyone? Ross queried. Like Sergeant Tom Waterson, who was right there at the scene? Or Detective Jon Spear, lead investigator on the case? Or your supervisor, Detective O'Connor?

"I thought I had told Detective O'Connor," Carter replied.

Then why isn't it in your sworn statement to Detective O'Connor? Alan Ross slammed the statement on the podium. "Read the last question in that statement: 'Is there anything else that you can tell us that might assist us in this investigation?' Your answer: 'No.' "

"I told [Detective O'Connor] what he wanted me to say. He didn't want me to add any information," Carter told the jury. The explanation sounded weak. Officer Carter was excused. Alan Ross hadn't budged her. But what impression had she made on the jury? Would they think she was lying? Or honest but careless? It was impossible to read the jurors' faces.


Next John Kastrenakes called Frank Zuccarello, the state's star witness, to the stand. Now twenty-five years old, Zuccarello still looked young. But he had acquired an air of experience during the three and a half years since his arrest. He looked at ease as he settled himself in the witness box, and in fact, he was. He had already testified against his old pals in several other trials.

Zuccarello made a good appearance. With his neatly trimmed dark hair and small mustache, he looked, as one spectator commented, "like a waiter in an Italian restaurant. All he needs is a bow tie and a jacket." Indeed, he described himself to the jury as a part-time waiter putting himself through business school.

Then John Kastrenakes led his witness into his dark past. He had been a professional home invasion robber, Zuccarello told the jurors, in a gang with pals Anthony Caracciolo, Tommy Lamberti, and brothers Jay and Scott Richitelli. In the first three months of 1986, they had robbed ten or eleven homes in Dade and Broward counties.

To get inside, they posed as police officers, mailmen, delivery men. They carried revolvers, semiautomatic pistols, machine guns. They tied people up. And their robberies were always inside jobs. Why did he do it? "Money got the best of me," he explained nonchalantly. "I took the easy road."

He had already pled guilty to a total of twenty-three felonies, Zuccarello told the jury. He could have pulled twenty-three life sentences. But the state gave him a plea bargain that was a real bargain. He was sentenced to just five years in prison, and he actually served less than half that time. He was already out on parole. And he would never be charged in the crime he was going to tell the jury about: the murder of Stanley Cohen.

Zuccarello launched into his story. It started out as another inside job, he said, a home invasion robbery a dark-haired woman hired the gang to pull on her own home. "The victim," gang leader Caracciolo had told Zuccarello, "would be Stanley."

Then in February 1986, the plan changed to murder. "She wanted her husband dead. She didn't love him anymore. She couldn't file for a divorce, she wouldn't get anything," Zuccarello explained. The woman called Caracciolo's apartment several times. She planned to pay them for the job when she got her husband's life insurance money. But Zuccarello got his pay up-front from Caracciolo: $2,500 cash and a black El Camino.

He had first seen Joyce Cohen, Zuccarello continued, when she drove her white Jaguar to a 7-Eleven store in North Miami Beach to meet Anthony Caracciolo. There was a man in the car with her. When she got out of the car, she gave Caracciolo a hug and a kiss on the cheek. Zuccarello got a good look at her. Her companion shook Caracciolo's hand. Then he handed Caracciolo a map of the house where the murder would take place—a detailed sketch of the house, the bedroom, the alarm system with panic buttons, even the Cohens' Doberman pinscher.

The murder was supposed to look like a botched burglary, as if Stan had awakened and been shot during a struggle, Zuccarello told the jurors. The best time to do it, they decided, was from 1 to 3 A.M. "Joyce was supposed to supply Anthony [Caracciolo] with a gun when we got to the house. Anthony wanted to know about the dog. Is it turnable? Could we handle it or would we have to kill it?" For

$155, he said, they bought a dart gun to take along in case they had to kill the Cohens' Doberman pinscher.

"Do you recognize this?" Kastrenakes waved a contraption that looked like a large, heavy crossbow which could be armed with a thick steel arrow. The jurors eyed it intently. Several of them owned dogs. Juror Dr. Catherine Poole had a Doberman pinscher. The mental picture of an enormous "dart" skewering a dog, even a large dog like a Doberman pinscher, was horrifying.

"That's the dart gun," Zuccarello confirmed, nodding.

The dart gun was admitted into evidence. The jurors settled uneasily back in their seats.

On the morning of the murder, March 7, 1986, Zuccarello had worn jeans, sneakers, and a shirt; Tommy Lamberti was dressed in black; and Anthony Caracciolo had worn fatigues. Each carried a gun in his pants. And around 2 A.M., they drove in the black El Camino to the Cohen house in Coconut Grove. He recalled the time because he saw it on the digital clock on the dashboard. Joyce Cohen met them at the front door. She let them in. "Hurry up," she said. "Get it over with." He saw the woman clearly. She was wearing a light-colored robe.

"Can you identify the person here today?" Kastrenakes asked.

"Yes," Zuccarello replied. "The lady sitting at the table in the black and white." He pointed straight at Joyce, who stared back at him from the defense table.

Tommy Lamberti went to the rear of the house with the lady to show her how to fake a break-in. Anthony Caracciolo went upstairs, Zuccarello said, and he was supposed to stay by the front door. But he got nervous. "I kept thinking, Here I am going to do a murder!" He dashed upstairs to see what was going on. He heard a couple of shots, he wasn't sure how many. He saw Caracciolo with the gun in his hand. Then they both ran down the stairs and dashed out the front door. Lamberti met them at the car and they drove away.

In the car, Caracciolo blew up. "He started yelling at me," Zuccarello recounted petulantly. "He told me I made him panic. He thought he missed him one time. He ran out of the house so quick— he was just running, he was tripping over himself, he doesn't know what he did with the gun."

Joyce glared at Zuccarello, frequently shaking her head in disgust. She scribbled furiously on the yellow legal pad she kept before her throughout the trial. She whispered urgently to Alan Ross.

Three days later, on March 10, Zuccarello said, they pulled another home invasion robbery. He was arrested the next day. And a few months after his arrest, he decided to tell the cops about the Cohen homicide. He identified Joyce Cohen from photographs. And he picked out a photo of her companion at the 7-Eleven store. The name on the back of the photo: Lynn Barkley.

Finally it was Alan Ross's turn to cross-examine Zuccarello. He could hardly wait to get started. He began by hammering away at Zuccarello's career as a violent home invasion robber, and his use of cocaine. But soon he zeroed in on his major attack: Zuccarello's constantly changing stories about the murder.

Didn't Zuccarello first claim that he saw Joyce Cohen and Lynn Barkley at the Wind & Sails Surf Shop in Coconut Grove, not at the 7-Eleven in North Miami Beach? And didn't he claim the meeting took place in January 1986—when Joyce was actually in Steamboat Springs, Colorado? No, Zuccarello replied serenely, the detectives just confused his story.

Did Zuccarello tell the cops that his pay for the crime was $2,500 and the El Camino? Or $10,000? Or $150,000 in cocaine? Or three kilos of coke that the gang took with them in a pillow case from the Cohen house? In fact, he had given all those versions at different times.

And what about the convenient digital clock on the dashboard of the El Camino? Ross produced photos of the El Camino dash. The only clock visible was the standard type with hands, and it was broken.

One more thing: While you were in jail, and giving detectives all this information about Mrs. Cohen's involvement in the crime, didn't Detective Jon Spear sign you out of jail, take you for haircuts at your favorite salon, drive you to your girlfriend Gina's house and *wait outside in the squad car while you had sex with her*? Didn't all this special treatment *buy* testimony from you that the state wanted against Joyce Cohen?

Zuccarello flatly denied it. And he defended the cops. Detective

Spear didn't know about the sex. He had thought Gina's parents were chaperoning the visit.

Over two days, Ross battered Frank Zuccarello for nearly seven hours, frequently provoking nasty exchanges. Zuccarello claimed he had been harassed by defense lawyers during his pretrial deposition, which had lasted a grueling five days. "I was called lots of names," he complained. "I was a piece of garbage. I was an asshole. I was nothing without a gun and a mask."

Ross let that hang in the air. He hoped the jury would agree with that character assessment. And he was certain that Zuccarello came across as a lying, conniving, manipulative creep with a violent past. But would the jury believe he was lying about *this* crime? The answer might depend upon whether they also believed the evidence the state came up with to corroborate Zuccarello's story about the Cohen murder.

During Ross's blistering cross-examination, John Kastrenakes objected repeatedly. Most of his objections were denied perfunctorily by Judge Smith, with occasional flashes of annoyance at the prosecutor's demeanor. When Zuccarello was finally excused from the stand, he confronted Kastrenakes in the corridor outside the courtroom. "You're a fucking wimp, John! You let that judge push you all over the courtroom!" he snarled.

But Kastrenakes just smiled. Zuccarello had stood up pretty well to Ross's pounding, he thought. And the best was yet to come.

At nearly 5:30 that afternoon, after the jury had been excused for the day, DiGregory requested a hearing. He had been advised, he told Judge Smith, that Dr. Charles V. Wetli, Deputy Chief Medical Examiner, had changed his mind about the probable time of Stan Cohen's death. Although he had previously stated that Cohen died sometime between midnight and 6 A.M., Dr. Wetli now believed that the time was probably between 2 and 3 A.M.—just as the state (and Frank Zuccarello) had contended all along. Dr. Wetli had changed his mind after he read the deposition testimony of the defendant's own medical expert, Dr. Michael Baden.

Ross had been furious about Wetli's new opinion ever since Di-

Gregory informed him of it a few days earlier. He was determined to prevent the jury from hearing Wetli's revised testimony. His entire trial strategy, he insisted to the judge, had been predicated on what he believed was the scientific evidence. Now Dr. Wetli wanted to change that evidence. He was no longer a neutral expert. Now he was coming to the aid of the state in this prosecution, Ross raged. "The reason Dr. Poole is on the jury is because we believed we were on solid ground on the scientific tests, on Dr. Baden and Dr. Wetli," he complained angrily to Judge Smith.

This could have just come out at trial with no prior notice. It happens frequently. Experts see each other's depositions. Wetli reads Baden's deposition, the judge replied noncommittally. "Isn't that what happened? That's what I understood them to be saying."

"Your Honor would like to look at it that way," Ross shot back. It was a rare fit of pique for the usually courteous lawyer. The intense pressure was beginning to tell.

"I really don't have any way I am looking at it." The judge bristled. "That's what I understood the state to say."

"It's just an excuse to say Dr. Baden's deposition prompts this," Ross went on angrily.

But Judge Smith wanted to hear what Dr. Wetli had to say. She set the matter for evidentiary hearing at 9:00 the next morning, Friday, October 17.

Ross sighed loudly. It was going to be a grueling day. The deposition of Sharon Johnnides was already scheduled for 8:00 that morning. After the Wetli hearing, the judge planned a full day of trial. And the following day, Saturday, Kastrenakes and Amsel would be videotaping the deposition of Bernard Ahouse in New York at a town called Waterloo. The irony of the name did not escape the lawyers.


Alan Ross was under siege, and he knew it. He was the first one in the courtroom the next morning, still seething. There was no banter among the lawyers as they arrived for the hearing. Judge Smith appeared promptly at 9:00. Dr. Wetli took the witness stand, was sworn, and began to testify.

Wetli told the judge that it was the deposition testimony of the defense's medical expert, Dr. Michael Baden, that had led him to his new conclusion. He had reviewed a copy of that deposition transcript in preparation for his own trial testimony. In that deposition, Dr. Baden stated that if Cohen had died at 2 or 3 A.M., lividity (the blood's pooling and staining of body tissues after death) should have been visible on Cohen's body in the slides Dr. Wetli took at 3 P.M. the next day. Dr. Baden reviewed copies of Dr. Wetli's slides and saw no lividity. Therefore he concluded that death occurred shortly before 5:30 A.M., as Joyce Cohen had said.

After reading Baden's opinion, Dr. Wetli said he took another look at his own slides. This time he used the originals, not copies, and he projected them in total darkness, in the windowless conference room in the basement of the new medical examiner's building. Then he saw it—faint but recognizable, just as Dr. Baden said it should be—a pattern of faded, mottled reddish color on the right side of Cohen's body. Lividity. He had called Kevin DiGregory immediately.

Despite Dr. Wetli's unemotional recitation, Ross refused to give up. He complained to the judge that DiGregory had pressured Dr. Wetli to change his mind and give the state the evidence it needed on the time of Cohen's death.

"Did Kevin DiGregory have anything to do with the change in your opinion?" the judge asked Dr. Wetli directly.

"Nothing whatsoever," he replied.

I see no basis for your allegations, Judge Smith told Ross evenly.

But Ross was not mollified. Because of the unreliability and prejudice of Dr. Wetli's new opinion, that evidence shouldn't come before the jury, he argued angrily. Judge Smith ruled that Dr. Wetli could testify in accordance with his new opinion. Ross promptly moved for mistrial, and the motion was denied. But in response to his outraged cries, the judge permitted the defense to use an additional medical expert to corroborate Dr. Baden's opinion that Cohen had died shortly before 5:30 A.M. as the defendant claimed. Ross already had someone in mind: Dr. Werner Spitz, former medical examiner in Detroit, Michigan.

It had been a bad day for the defense. As pieces of the state's case seemed to fall into place almost miraculously, so Ross's carefully constructed defense was being sabotaged. Ross looked exhausted, embattled. And his client was beginning to show the strain. Joyce complained of a headache at lunchtime, and by the end of the day her face was flushed and her eyes teary.

For the first time, the prosecution team cautiously scented victory. "Now we've got two ways to win this," Paul Mendelson said excitedly. "Frank Zuccarello's testimony and the physical evidence. If the jury doesn't believe Zuccarello, no problem. We have the experts and the physical evidence against her."

Shortly before 9 A.M. on Monday, October 30, Ross, Amsel, and Joyce Cohen walked down the hallway from their encampment on the fourth floor, a large room provided as a courtesy to counsel and defendants in lengthy criminal cases. The room, which Florida Supreme Court Justice Gerald Kogan used when he was in town, was stocked with dozens of file cabinets, files, legal pads, books, all the paraphernalia of the case. It was where Joyce Cohen and her attorneys had lunch every day, a brief respite from the media and the courtroom spectators. It was also where Ross kept witnesses on ice awaiting their turn in the box.

The defense team arrived in court shortly before the scheduled starting time. But the prosecutors were late—again. They showed up about 9:12, DiGregory pushing an ungainly, heavily loaded evidence cart ahead of him into the crowded courtroom. He couldn't get an elevator down from his sixth-floor office, he apologized.

Judge Smith was not impressed. "This is the last day an apology is going to work," she warned. It's only twelve or thirteen minutes, but it all adds up. From now on, be on time or I'll hold you in contempt.

The bailiff led the jurors out of the tiny, cramped jury room where they had been waiting, and they settled themselves in the jury box. DiGregory called the state's next witness: Gopinath Rao. A small, neat man with graying dark hair, Rao had been a criminalist on the Metro-Dade staff for eight years, and he spoke with a lilting Indian accent. His job, he said, was to analyze gunshot residue particles, the tiny bits that collect on the hands of the shooter, on the weapon, and on the target—the gunshot victim. These particles—lead, barium, and antimony—eject from the primer and gunpowder of a bullet as it is fired.

Kevin DiGregory handed Rao Stan Cohen's .38-caliber Smith & Wesson, the gun that killed him, to illustrate. The particles, Rao explained to the jury, spew from the breech of the gun in a fine cascade called "breech blast." They also shower out of the muzzle, with particles from the bullet itself, in "muzzle blast." Some of the muzzle blast blows back toward the shooter, "blowback." By analyzing the number and type of gunshot residue particles found, experts can determine whether the particles are breech blast or muzzle blast. The particles that collect on the shooter's own hands are mostly breech blast.

DiGregory led his expert witness methodically through the technical testimony. These particles are very tiny, Rao continued, nearly invisible. Ninety percent of them can't be seen with the naked eye. The particles are collected from hands, weapons, and targets by swabbing with alcohol, and then the swabs are sent to the laboratory for analysis.

Finally Rao turned to his analysis of evidence in this case. He had examined a paper facial tissue with a blue-and-white print on it, he said. The tissue had been collected at the Cohen home, found under an empty tissue box in Joyce Cohen's private bath. There was a dark stain on the tissue. The evidence tag on the plastic sleeve holding the tissue indicated that it had previously been tested by a serologist, Kathy Nelson, who determined the presence of nasal mucus from a person with type B blood.

Rao had isolated the area of the dark stain on the tissue and flooded it with alcohol to put any particles in suspension. Then he poured the alcohol through a polycarbonate filter to trap the particles. After the filter was dried in an oven and specially coated, he examined the filter under a scanning electron microscope: state-of-the-art technique in gunshot residue analysis. He found fifteen bismuth particles, common in ladies' cosmetics, and twelve pure lead particles that could only have come, Rao said, from a bullet. The conclusion was obvious. The tissue had come into contact with muzzle blast. But how?

Next DiGregory handed Rao State's Exhibit #147, the gunshot residue handswab kit. Rao identified four alcohol swabs taken of

Joyce Cohen's hands on that long-ago morning at the Miami Police Department. The swabs were labeled right web (the area between the thumb and first finger, where a pencil—or a gun—would lie), left web, right palm, left palm, plus a control swab to be analyzed for inadvertent contamination.

Rao had prepared a filter as he had before, and then examined the filter and trapped particles on each swab under the electron microscope. He found five gunshot residue particles on the swab from the left hand, and twenty-six from the right, a total of thirty-one particles. His conclusion: Joyce Cohen's hands had been covered with muzzle blast.

"Did Joyce Cohen fire the weapon?" DiGregory asked his expert witness. The jury strained forward intently.

"No," Rao replied. Based upon the number and type of particles that he found, he said, this person couldn't have fired the weapon.

"What other ways are there to get this gunshot residue?" DiGregory asked. Could she have been between the gun and the target?

Yes, Rao answered.

Standing next to the shooter?

Yes.

Touching the wound?

Yes.

"Did you find any blood on [Joyce Cohen's] handswabs?"

"No, sir," Rao replied.

"Based upon the number of particles that you found on the defendant's handswabs, are the results that you got consistent with this defendant having handled a recently fired gun that was fired four times?"

"Yes, sir," said Rao.

DiGregory moved in for the kill. He handed Rao State's Exhibit #135, the soiled blue-and-white tissue. Based upon the number of particles you found, he asked, are the results consistent with this tissue having touched a recently fired gun?

"Yes, sir," Rao answered.

"Are they consistent with the defendant having taken the gun in her hands and having wiped it down with this tissue that is State's Exhibit Number 135?"

"It is consistent, sir."

It was, of course, evidence supporting the prosecutors' basic theory, the solution to the problem of putting the murder weapon in Joyce Cohen's hands. This was the strategy that DiGregory and Kastranakes had worked out so painstakingly, over long hours with the physical evidence scattered like jigsaw puzzle pieces across DiGregory's battered wooden conference table.

Alan Ross leaped to his feet for cross. Aren't your results also consistent with her having touched the victim's pillows, or the victim, and then touching the tissue? he asked.

"Yes," Rao agreed readily.

At Ross's urging, Rao described how Joyce Cohen could have gotten gunshot residue on her hands by touching her husband's bedding or his shoulders and then could have transferred residue particles to a tissue that she used to wipe her nose.

But DiGregory had one more question on redirect. If the defendant touched the victim or his bedding and then blew her nose and transferred gunshot residue to the tissue, would you expect to find the *number* of particles that you found on her hands to still be there?

"Not likely, sir," Rao answered. "First of all, there are too many particles to contend with to come on the tissue and secondly, by going through that kind of activity, you wouldn't have that kind of residue present."

If the jury had followed DiGregory through the maze of technical jargon and abstruse legal phraseology, they would conclude that Joyce Cohen had used that tissue to wipe down the gun that killed her husband. But that was a big if. And Ross had handed the jury a plausible, innocent explanation for the defendant's soiled hands and tissue. Would this be one of the "reasonable doubts" Ross had promised the jury?

The state's next witness was Anthony Middleton, a tall young man whose long blond hair was pulled back in a ponytail. A diamond earring glittered in his right ear. He wore a loose white shirt and tight black pants. Middleton was the former floor manager at Biscayne Baby, he told the jury in a clipped British accent. He recognized Joyce Cohen. She used to come in to the Champagne Room at Biscayne Baby about twice a week, he said. He saw her there occasionally with Myra Wenig or Geri Carroll. Once he noticed Joyce with her husband, Stan, and once she was with Lynn Barkley.

Middleton recognized photos of two other Champagne Room customers: Anthony Caracciolo and Tommy Lamberti. He told the jury about one busy evening in February 1986. He was delivering liquor to the Champagne Room when he tripped and knocked over the drinks of two customers, Caracciolo and Lamberti. As he regained his balance, he looked up and recognized Joyce Cohen standing right in front of him. "Are you all right?" she had asked him. Middleton didn't see any conversation between Joyce Cohen and Caracciolo and Lamberti, and he wasn't sure she was with them. But it was a very small room.

During the lunch break, television monitors were installed in the courtroom. The videotaped testimony of Bernard Ahouse, taken by John Kastrenakes and Bob Amsel the weekend before, would be shown at 1 P.M.

When the jury assembled in the courtroom after lunch, Kastrenakes rose dramatically. "The state," he intoned, "calls as its next witness Bernard Ahouse, who will testify by videotape."

There he was, finally, the mystery witness from Lodi, New York, who had been a guest in a condominium not far from the Cohens' house in the Grove the night Stan was shot. An older man with a weathered face and a full head of white hair, Ahouse was dressed for the occasion in a blue suit and tie. His expression was solemn, even dour, his voice rough-edged. He was, he told the video camera, a grain farmer, had been one for over forty-four years.

In response to Kastrenakes's questions, Ahouse told his story. In March 1986, he said, he went to Florida with his wife, Eileen, to visit her mother in Lake Worth. On March 6, he flew to Miami alone to meet with Frank Miller. He had some business with Miller, whom he had known for several years.

He arrived in Miami about ten o'clock that night, Ahouse continued, and Miller picked him up at the airport. They drove to Miller's condominium in Coconut Grove where he spent the night with Miller, whose wife, Charlotte, was out of town. It was an elaborate apartment, he recalled, up on the fourth or fifth floor.

That night, Ahouse said, he went to bed around eleven. He slept in a bedroom facing South Bayshore Drive. There were sliding glass doors overlooking the street, and he left them slightly open when he went to bed.

During the night Ahouse was awakened by gunshots. "Bang. A slight pause. Then, bang-bang-bang." A total of four shots.

He got up, walked across the bedroom, and looked out the sliding glass doors. He saw nothing.

"Then I heard a sound like backing into a garage door," Ahouse said. The sounds came from the left and toward the front of the building. It was very quiet, a still night. "I happened to look at the digital clock in the bedroom. It said three o'clock. I went back to sleep afterwards."

There it was, the last piece of the puzzle the prosecutors had assembled so patiently. Ahouse had heard exactly four shots at three o'clock in the morning.

"Do you know what kind of gun it was?" Kastrenakes prodded.

"A small-caliber handgun," Ahouse replied. "My opinion, based on what I heard, it was a .38-caliber weapon."

He was familiar with firearms, Ahouse explained to Kastrenakes. He owned ten rifles and six shotguns. He had handled handguns in the army during World War II, and he had friends who owned handguns. "I can distinguish between rifle shots, shotgun, and handgun fire," he said.

When Ahouse had awakened at seven the following morning, Frank Miller called him to the television in the kitchen. There was a crime scene that looked like something out of "Miami Vice." Then Miller told him, "Look out the window." He saw the same scene—yellow tape, police officers, squad cars—about 200–300 yards down the street in the direction from which the noises had come the night before. He told Miller about the shots he had heard.

After breakfast they left to drive to Lake Worth, where Ahouse's wife was staying. But first Miller drove him past the crime scene on South Bayshore Drive. As they turned the corner, a police officer leaned toward the car and told them to keep moving. He never heard anything about the case again until Kastrenakes called from Miami.

As Amsel watched the videotape on the courtroom television, he relived his frustration. Ahouse's testimony seemed tailor-made for the prosecution. And Amsel had had precious little to go on for cross-examination. But he had been determined to give it his best.

"Where was the clock?" Amsel asked Ahouse.

"To the left on a dresser nearby the bed," Ahouse replied. "It was a digital clock with a light that showed up in the dark."

Are you certain about the time?

"I recall it was three o'clock. It could have been a half hour either way," Ahouse answered. Could it have been as late as 5:30? Amsel asked. No, Ahouse replied.

Amsel plodded on doggedly. How long before you heard the crunching sound? What time did you fall back asleep? Did you hear anything else out of the ordinary that night? An alarm? Sirens?

But despite his best efforts, Amsel couldn't budge Ahouse. For the life of him, he couldn't figure out how Ahouse might be connected with the case or what motive he could have to lie. The old man must be simply mistaken, Amsel concluded. But how could he prove it to the jury?

The videotape concluded abruptly, and Judge Smith excused the jury for the day. As they filed out of the courtroom, the jurors seemed unaware of the high drama that had played out before them. After years of fruitless searching for a witness, the one man who heard shots that morning had finally corroborated the story that Frank Zuccarello—lying, conniving, scheming Zuccarello, as Alan Ross described him—had told Detective Jon Spear more than three years before: the shots were fired between 2 and 3 A.M. Apparently Bernard Ahouse was unaware of the significance of what he had heard. But given all the publicity that had surrounded the murder, it was surprising that Frank and Charlotte Miller hadn't grasped the importance of what he told them. At least Charlotte Miller had remembered, but it was just plain dumb luck that she had mentioned it to Kastrenakes and that he had found Ahouse.

But Ahouse was bad news for the defense. Ross's shoulders slumped with exhaustion as he stood up to pack his briefcase. Tomorrow would be another long day. The state planned to call Dr. Charles Wetli, and Ross had to be ready.

# Twenty-Two

•

A huge viewing screen was erected opposite the jury box. Everyone knew what would be projected upon it: the medical examiner's slides of Stan Cohen's nude corpse. The courtroom filled to capacity, and many frustrated onlookers were turned away. Several tried to peer into the courtroom through small glass panes in the door. Judge Fredricka Smith dispatched her bailiff, Alex Bosque, to keep order in the corridor outside.

That Thursday morning, November 2, Joyce Cohen looked grim. Her face was swollen, as if she had cried all night. "The defendant does not wish to be present during Dr. Wetli's testimony and slide presentation," Alan Ross told the judge solemnly.

"Mrs. Cohen does not have to remain, but she must waive her presence," Judge Smith replied.

Joyce Cohen rose from her seat. "Please," she addressed the judge. She was excused.

But Gary Cohen and Gerri Helfman remained in the gallery with the other spectators. Gerri had never seen the grisly photographs that would soon dominate the courtroom, and she had no intention of looking at them now. But she was determined to hear Dr. Wetli's testimony, to know how it went. It was something she had to do.

A hush descended over the courtroom as the lights were extinguished, leaving only dim illumination over the witness box. The first slide was projected on the screen and brought into sharp focus.

There, nearly life-size, was Stan Cohen, lying supine on the floor of his bedroom, nude, arms and legs spread-eagled, genitals clearly visible. The eyes were closed, the right eye purplish and swollen, the nose bloodied, the small mouth slack. A heavy gold chain encircled his thick neck. Round cardiac monitor patches, "pasties," still clung to his chest. Blood pooled on the floor beneath his head.

As he stepped into the witness box, Dr. Wetli looked neat and composed in his conservative gray suit, white shirt, and navy tie. He knew Alan Ross was still seething over his change of opinion about the time of Stan Cohen's death. His cross-examination would be brutal. The two men had dueled before, and Ross was an excellent attorney, one of the best in the city.

Yet in a strange way, Wetli was actually looking forward to the contest. The Cohen case was a marvelous professional opportunity for him—an important, high-profile case in which the medical examiner's testimony would be controversial and maybe decisive. Such cases were rare, and Wetli had reserved an entire row of seats so the residents in his training program could observe his testimony. Residents had to learn how to testify at trial, he believed, especially under the kind of blistering cross Alan Ross was sure to deliver. It was going to be some show. But Dr. Wetli would start out easy, with DiGregory leading him through his background and qualifications, then the autopsy of Stan Cohen, and finally his conclusions about the time of Cohen's death.

Ignoring the awful picture on the screen, Wetli told the jury that he had been with the Dade County Medical Examiner's Office for twelve years, nine of those as deputy chief medical examiner. He was the author of *Practical Forensic Pathology*, as well as fifty-five book chapters and publications on the subject. He had performed over 5,000 autopsies, about 20 percent of which involved gunshot wounds.

Turning to the autopsy in the Cohen case, Wetli used a diagram to illustrate the four gunshot wounds he found on Stan Cohen's head. Three were penetrating wounds, one a graze that didn't enter the cranium. He showed the jury the stippling pattern of red dots he found around one wound. "Unburned gunpowder," he commented matter-of-factly. One shot had been fired from intermediate range.

Kevin DiGregory wanted to make sure the jury knew just how devastating those gunshots had been. What was the cause of Stan Cohen's death? he asked Dr. Wetli.

"Gunshot wounds to the head," he replied. "In this case, large portions of the brain were destroyed. There was destruction of vital centers of the brain. The bullets caused this, by what they struck, and the energy."

Wetli showed the jury the bullet fragments he had removed from Stan Cohen's brain. One fragment was compressed and rounded off. "Bullets are designed to expand after they hit a target like bone," he explained. Despite the dry, scientific delivery, the mental image brought shudders to the courtroom.

He was called to the Cohen home about 3 P.M. on March 7, 1986, Dr. Wetli told the jury, to examine Stan Cohen's body. He took numerous slides of the crime scene and of the corpse. The detectives at the scene had told him that the victim was killed around 5:30 that morning. Months later, the investigators changed their minds. They suspected that Cohen had died between 2 and 3 A.M., not 5:30, they said.

But he found nothing to confirm 2 to 3 A.M. as the time of death, Wetli continued, until he reviewed the deposition of Dr. Michael Baden. In that deposition, Dr. Baden stated that *if* Cohen had been killed between 2 and 3 A.M., and *if* he had lain face down on the bed until nearly 6 A.M., when paramedics rolled him onto the bedroom floor, there should be visible lividity on the front of his body—a broken pattern of reddish discoloration and pale areas, "contact pallor," where the body had pressed down on the rumpled bedsheets after death.

According to Dr. Baden, that pattern would have been sufficiently "fixed" during the three or four hours that Cohen's dead body had lain face down on the bed so that it should still be visible in Dr. Wetli's slides taken around 3 P.M. that afternoon.

When he took another look at his original slides, Wetli told the rapt jury, he saw just such a pattern.

Dr. Wetli turned to the life-size slide projection of Stan Cohen's corpse. Using a pointer, he outlined the right side of the body. "There are stripes on the right side of the chest and thigh," he said. "Typical of lying on the right side. There is contact pallor on the right knee. . . . The body was lying on the right side on sheets for a couple of hours after death."

The jurors and courtroom spectators saw *something* in the area Dr. Wetli indicated. But was it lividity, as he claimed? How could the jury decide?

Watching Dr. Wetli, waiting for his chance to cross-examine, Alan Ross could only hope that his high-powered experts, Dr. Michael Baden and Dr. Werner Spitz, could convince the jury that what they saw on the slide of Cohen's body wasn't a pattern of fixed lividity at all. Ross watched juror Dr. Catherine Poole and pondered her inscrutable face. What was she thinking? Now that there would be direct contradiction between the medical experts, would Dr. Poole become, in effect, the jury's expert on the medical evidence?

Based upon the slides, Dr. Wetli concluded, I can now narrow the time of death. Because of the fixed lividity, which takes several hours to appear and become fixed, the body was on its right side for two to four hours before the body was moved.

"Is this consistent with the time of death at 5:28 A.M.?" Kevin DiGregory asked.

"Inconsistent," Wetli replied firmly.

"Is this consistent with death between 1:30 and 3:30 A.M.?"

"Consistent with that time frame."

At last Ross took center stage for his cross-examination of his nemesis. "On what date," he began, "Did you get to reviewing the slides and come to a new opinion regarding the fixed lividity?"

"On October 20, 1989," Dr. Wetli answered. That was, of course, after the trial had begun.

"Your 'cursory' examination of the body at the scene," Ross continued, sarcasm beginning to tinge his voice. "Is that offered as an excuse as to why you didn't see lividity at the scene?"

"No," Wetli replied. On the day of the murder, he said, he simply had no reason to make any observation related to the time of death. And in response to Ross's questions, he admitted that the scene observation report he prepared contained nothing about lividity. "To an extent," he said, "I relied upon a summation of what the investigators told me about the case at that time."

"Everything now is 'to an extent,' right?" Ross's tone turned hostile. "Just 'to an extent,' right, Dr. Wetli?"

Wetli knew that worse was coming.

"Isn't it true that your testimony is tailored to fit—"

"No," Wetli shot back while Ross was still talking. "I do not draw a conclusion and then make the facts fit the conclusion."

"So, the sole reason for your change of opinion about the time of death is lividity, is that correct?" Ross asked.

"Yes," Dr. Wetli replied.

"Did you note residual lividity during the autopsy, Dr. Wetli?"

"No," he replied. "I may have seen it, but I didn't notice it or make note of it."

Ross took the witness through a series of meetings with homicide detectives regarding the time of Cohen's death. "You offered absolutely nothing inconsistent with Joyce Cohen's statement about the time of his death, did you, Dr. Wetli?" he commented belligerently.

"That's correct." Wetli appeared unruffled.

"In preparation for your deposition on September 18, 1989, did you review your slides, Dr. Wetli?"

"Yes, I looked at the slides, but I didn't project them."

"Did you see any lividity, Dr. Wetli?" Ross's voice rose.

"No, I didn't."

"Are you *blind,* Dr. Wetli?" Ross bellowed. At least Wetli and others in the courtroom thought that's what they heard. His face flushed bright pink, but Ross couldn't shake him. He steadfastly maintained that Stanley Cohen had probably died between 2 and 3 A.M. on March 7, 1986, rather than at 5:30 A.M. as Joyce Cohen claimed. But what would the jury make of Dr. Wetli's sudden discovery of lividity on Stan Cohen's body more than three years after his death? Was it simple error? Or was it simply convenient?

At 3:30 that afternoon, the state of Florida rested its case against Joyce Lemay Cohen, and it was Alan Ross's turn to lay out the defendant's case for the jury.

He began by calling witnesses from the Cohens' neighborhood, like Hal and Layne Kendall, who recalled being awakened early on the morning of the murder. There was a strange man knocking on doors and ringing bells, they told the jury. He wanted money, and he told a tale about needing cash to have his car towed or to take his sick father to the hospital. He was a dark man, with a Latin-sounding name. After the stranger left, Layne Kendall sat up nervously watching the front door, a loaded revolver in her lap, as her young children slept nearby. But none of the neighborhood witnesses had heard gunshots or alarms or sirens that morning.

Next Ross paraded experienced police officers and paramedics across the witness stand to testify that they believed Stan Cohen had died only moments before they arrived at the Cohen house about 5:30 A.M. on March 7. His body was still warm when they found him, they said. They saw no lividity, no rigor mortis. The blood was wet, not dry. And Joyce Cohen was hysterical, crying, a grieving widow.

Former Miami homicide detective Steve Vinson had noticed something else: "I saw a tissue on the front doorstep, on the front porch," he told the jury. It was clearly visible in police photos taken at the crime scene. "The tissue paper was white," Vinson recalled. The same color as the two tiny bits of tissue that clung to the grip of the murder weapon. But by the time ID Technician Sylvia Romans went back to the Cohen home to collect tissue samples, the white tissue had disappeared from the front step.

After a long weekend break, the trial resumed on Monday, November 6. With the jury ensconced in the tiny, airless jury room, the lawyers argued motions to the judge. Ross wanted to ask the Miami homicide detectives why they didn't follow up on leads pointing to fugitive Miami attorney Frankie Diaz as a suspect in the case—the "third-party culpability" issue. But he wanted to make sure the detectives wouldn't be allowed to answer, "We already knew Mrs. Cohen was our prime suspect because she refused to let us search the house on the morning of the murder and made us get a warrant." Judge Smith had already ruled that that couldn't come before the jury, and Ross didn't want to open the door to it now.

While the lawyers debated, an attractive, stylishly dressed blond woman entered the courtroom and settled herself in a choice seat in the press section—the seat that Gerri Helfman had occupied every day since the trial started nearly a month earlier. No sooner was the woman seated than Gerri came into the courtroom. She approached the older woman and asked her to move. "I'm Alan Ross's mother," the woman replied with a trace of hauteur. She had a theatrical air.

"Well, I'm Stan Cohen's daughter, and I've been sitting here every single day." Ever her father's daughter, Gerri Helfman was not about to be dispossessed.

Alan Ross's mother moved.

The jury returned to the jury box. Toni Pollack, Joyce Cohen's business partner in SAC Interiors, took the witness stand. She was a small, pretty, dark-haired woman who spoke rapidly in a heavy Latin accent. In an animated voice, she told the jury how she met Joyce Cohen in interior design classes at Miami-Dade Community College, and how they decided to go into business together in 1980. "We wanted to use all the available sources that [Stan] had. . . . We wanted to have our company perceived as an extension of the construction company," she explained.

After a lengthy description of their decorating projects, Pollack turned to the last week of Stan Cohen's life. She said that on Wednesday, March 5, she and Joyce had worked all day collecting fabric and floor covering samples for a warehouse that SAC Construction was building for Morris Feudernick in Tampa. At 5:30 or 6:00 that afternoon, they went to the SAC Construction office to put together a proposal for interior design of the project. Joyce planned to take the proposal and samples to Tampa for presentation the following day. Stan remained at the SAC office until around 8:30 P.M.

"Joyce and Stan said good-bye, kissed at the door. After he left we locked the door— made sure the door was locked. . . . I saw [Stan] leave . . . in Joyce's Jag," Pollack told the jury. Stan left his tan Bronco for Joyce to drive.

"Did you do anything different that night?" Ross prompted.

Yes, we double-checked the door to be sure it was locked, she said. I was concerned to be working alone there. The phone rang at least three times. It was Stan. Stan never called like that before while I was there. I got in my car and left around 11:30 P.M. Joyce locked the door behind me.

If the jurors were left wondering what Pollack's testimony was all about, the answer was provided by Metro-Dade police officer Silvia, who testified that he was called to the SAC Construction Company office that night around midnight. When he arrived, Silvia said, he found Mrs. Cohen alone in the office. She told him that two Latin men had come to the door of the office, but she didn't let them in. She was frightened, so she called the police.

It was Ross's predicate for the third-party culpability argument: Stan Cohen had been involved with some very bad men, including Frankie Diaz. These men were threatening Cohen, and he was frightened. They—not his widow—murdered Stan Cohen.

Ross moved on to the next issue: the state of the Cohens' marriage. On his witness list were several of the Cohens' friends, beginning with Stan's pal Edward G. Smith. Smith had a ruddy face, thinning gray hair, and a self-confident air. His blue suit was well tailored to his rather portly frame.

"I met Stan Cohen in 1968 or '69," Smith began in a loud voice. "We became very good friends—skiing together, boating, drinking. We saw each other constantly. We were very, very close friends. I met Joyce when Stan brought her into the Grove, into our crowd, as his date, girlfriend, future wife. She was a little overpowered with our group."

Smith filled the jury in on the group's elaborate social life: long weekend parties at his vacation retreat at the exclusive Ocean Reef Resort on Key Largo; ski vacations and more parties at the Cohens' ranch in Steamboat Springs; the annual Good Friends Christmas Party, and still more parties in Miami in each other's homes.

"And it's a very enjoyable lifestyle that you and your wife live?" DiGregory later asked Smith at one point during his cross-examination.

"Yes, I'm very happy and proud of that," he responded.

Ross led his witness through his recollections of the Cohens. I last saw Stan and Joyce together on February 1 through 8, 1986, in Steamboat Springs, Colorado, Smith continued. I saw Stan and Joyce at least five days—skiing, après-ski, or dinner. I went to Stan and Joyce's party, a large dinner-dancing party for the entire ski club. "Joyce and Stan just were Mr. and Mrs. wonderful host and hostess to a gathering of eighty to a hundred people. They were lively. They were fun. They danced together. They were just perfect host and hostess."

I skied with Joyce and Stan many times that week, Smith went on. I never saw either of them consuming any drugs.

"Did the conduct of Mrs. Cohen cause you to suspect that she was using drugs?" Ross asked.

"There were times that Joyce acted a little hyper or more outgoing

than normal. I didn't really know why, what, or if anything was causing that, and I just don't know. I'd say no."

Sitting in the gallery, Gary and Gerri listened intently to the testimony. They wondered whether Ed Smith was giving a watered-down
version of his observations of their stepmother. How could he not
have suspected that Joyce was doing coke? Had Smith's strong-
willed wife, Sam, convinced him that Joyce didn't do drugs?

My wife and I went skiing in Europe at the beginning of March to
mid-March, Smith continued. We were skiing in Gstaad when we
learned of Stan's death. I first saw Joyce five or six weeks after Stan's
death. Joyce came to live with me and my wife. She stayed two or
two and a half weeks. I don't think Joyce slept for those two weeks
except when she was physically exhausted.

"What were your observations of the emotions and demeanor of
Joyce Cohen when she lived in your home for these two and a half
weeks, please?" Ross asked.

"It's very difficult to describe. Excuse me, it's very emotional to
see what she was going through." Smith broke down, his flushed face
streaming with tears, his voice cracking. "She would sit on the floor
for hours, rocking back and forth, crying, sobbing incoherently—
just a minute." Now Smith broke into sobs: "—talking to herself as
to why something like this should happen, who would do something
like this to Stan, and just go on for hours and hours and hours.

"You couldn't have a coherent conversation with her, and I would
get up in the morning and she would be doing these things. I would
come home from work and she would be crying. I would go to bed at
night and she would be acting the same way. I don't know how a body
can produce so many tears. She could not have been involved . . ."

When Smith had finished his testimony, Joyce was crying, too.

Time for cross. At the prosecutors' table, there was a hurried conference. Kastrenakes was taken aback by Smith's performance on
the stand. Although he had prepared for the cross-examination, he
hadn't anticipated this: a distraught, sobbing witness, a grown man
blubbering like a baby, huge tears running down his ruddy cheeks.
Kastrenakes was completely nonplussed.

DiGregory wasn't impressed by Smith's tears. "Let me take him,"
he whispered to Kastrenakes. "I owe you one anyway." He marched
to the podium. "In fact, though your very close and dear friend was

murdered, you didn't get back to Miami until he was already dead a week?" he began.

"That's correct," Smith replied, struggling to compose himself.

"And, as a matter of fact, during that week's time that you were in Switzerland you were still skiing, you were still going to these après-ski parties while your friend lay dead, correct?" DiGregory was aggressive, sarcastic.

"Mostly because we couldn't get a flight back in time."

"You are telling us that you couldn't get a flight back even to comfort Mrs. Cohen? Is that what you are telling us?"

"I had a prepaid trip to Switzerland. We tried to make airplane arrangements to get back, and we could not make them." Smith sounded defensive.

Next Smith's wife, Sam, took the stand. She wore a purple suit and high heels. With her short, spiked, white-blond hair and dark eye makeup, she bore a faint resemblance to actress Joey Heatherton. Her voice was husky.

Sam Smith had been outside the courtroom while her husband was on the stand. But her testimony echoed his. The Cohens' marriage seemed very good. In December 1985, Stan had given his wife a beautiful diamond ring for their wedding anniversary. Joyce was very excited about it. Sam never saw either of them doing drugs. After Stan's death, Joyce was distraught.

The prosecutors were more interested in Sam's recollections about the European ski trip that kept the Smiths from Stan's funeral. You extended your trip so that you could do some sightseeing? DiGregory asked her.

"I said I may or may not have. I don't remember," she responded.

"And my final question of you is, you are a travel agent, aren't you?"

"Part-time travel agent," she replied, nodding agreeably.

An unspoken question hung in the air. Couldn't a travel agent have arranged a quick flight home for a dear, close friend's funeral?

Next Ross called Patty Bartell, a longtime Cohen friend and houseguest at Wolf Run Ranch in Steamboat Springs. "Did you observe any conduct on the part of either that made you believe there was any problem in the marriage?" Alan Ross asked.

"Absolutely not at all," Bartell replied firmly.

"Did you ever observe Joyce Cohen or Stan Cohen ever use cocaine?"
"Never."

Bartell described a blissful ski vacation that she and her husband and two sons spent with the Cohens in Steamboat Springs at Christmas, 1984. "Some days I would go skiing and come home . . . and [Joyce] would have dinner ready, and she would have my clothes all washed and ironed, which was embarrassing for me that she would do all this for me, but she did."

The last time we saw the Cohens, she continued, was the Sunday before his death. "We met them at the art show in South Miami. Well, we walked around, started looking at the different art, and ate a lot. Joyce was very excited about [Gerri's] wedding."

Gerri Helfman groaned aloud from her seat in the gallery.

Alan Ross flew to his feet. "Your Honor, may we come to side for a moment?" Judge Smith sent the jury back to the jury room.

"Your Honor, I renew my motion to exclude Mrs. Helfman," Ross began.

Judge Smith addressed Gerri, still sitting in the gallery. "Mrs. Helfman, I think the reason the motion is being made is because you made an audible sound, which I heard as well, when the witness just testified. And I know that the wedding that was referred to was your wedding. You can only remain in this court if you don't do that."

"I understand," Gerri replied. She didn't seem embarrassed at being singled out in the courtroom.

The jury returned, and Bartell resumed her testimony.

"We were very excited about [the wedding]," she said. "That's all we [could] talk about." Gerri was silent.

I saw Joyce right after Stan's death, Bartell went on. "She was just what you would expect. She was very—she was very upset. She couldn't believe it. She just sat in one chair. . . . She had his jacket over her . . . she was like hugging the jacket and I guess it had a scent."

Joyce, watching from the defense table, sobbed softly and twisted a tissue in her hands.

On cross, Kastrenakes pursued a comment Bartell had made in her deposition. "You feel this prosecution is ridiculous?" he asked.

"Yes," she replied.

Ross saw an opening and he seized it. He knew that Patty Bartell believed in Joyce Cohen's innocence partly because she knew Joyce had taken and passed two polygraphs. Since polygraphs are inadmissible in Florida, Ross had no way to get his client's test results before the jury. But maybe Bartell would do it for him—in response to the state's own question.

Ross had one question on redirect: Please tell the jury why you feel this prosecution is ridiculous.

Before the witness could answer, Kastrenakes was on his feet. "Objection, Judge!" He guessed what Ross had in mind.

"Overruled," the judge responded.

"Judge, excuse me. I would object and ask for a sidebar for one specific area!" Kastrenakes was adamant.

Judge Smith sighed. "You may come to sidebar."

The lawyers approached the bench on the side away from the jury, and Judge Smith leaned over to hear them. Although neither spectators nor jurors could hear their words, there was no mistaking the waving arms, the agitated features. Abruptly the lawyers returned to their places.

The jury is excused until one-thirty this afternoon, Judge Smith said.

After the jury filed out of the courtroom, Ross turned back to the witness, still seated in the witness box. "Mrs. Bartell," he asked, "tell us in your own words why you think this prosecution in this case is ridiculous." He held his breath. Would she mention Joyce's polygraph results? He willed the words to come out of her mouth. Kastrenakes stood by, ready to pounce with an objection at any mention of the polygraph tests.

"Well," Bartell began, "I've been talking to the main people since the beginning and I know what everyone else knows and I don't see it the way they see it. . . . I don't understand what has happened to these people and I'm only doing what I think is right in being a compassionate person!" She clutched the edge of the jury box. "They are basing their decision on love and hate and jealousy and I just think it's terrible!"

Ross could bear it no longer. "Did the fact that Mrs. Cohen passed a polygraph examination—" he blurted.

Objection! Kastrenakes angrily cut him off.

"Sustained." Judge Smith was the calmest person in the courtroom.

Those two hours I spent with Joyce on March 2 could not have been a fake. I just don't see it the way the prosecution sees it, Bartell concluded. The witness was excused.

Judge Smith ruled: She can give her original answer, but not include the polygraph results.

But it shouldn't be excluded just because the witness didn't say it first as a reason, Ross argued, because I told all the witnesses not to mention polygraphs.

I gave her a further opportunity to say why, and she didn't mention the polygraph, Judge Smith said. So she can answer with her original and unprompted answer, but no mention of the polygraph. Judge Smith was firm. Court recessed for lunch.

Ross was undeterred. "You don't see many chances like this," he confided over lunch. "I haven't given up yet!"

When trial resumed after lunch, Ross tried again. The only reason Mrs. Bartell didn't mention the polygraph in response to the Court's question is because I told her not to, he reiterated to Judge Smith.

The problem is, this gets into areas not otherwise admissible, Judge Smith explained. If she can't answer honestly without the polygraph, Mr. Ross can't ask the question. If she can answer honestly without the polygraph, you can ask her: Tell us why you think the prosecution is ridiculous.

The bailiff brought the jury back into the jury box and Ross repeated the question to the witness.

Bartell launched into another impassioned defense, minus the polygraph results. "She was a normal person, married to a normal man, living a normal life, and they took pieces out of it and twisted it. . . . She had a great marriage. She had everything she wanted in the marriage. There'd be no advantage in a divorce. . . . I have never seen anything to tell me that she's guilty, so—"

Mercifully, Judge Smith excused the witness from any further attempts to explain her personal convictions. Alan Ross returned to counsel table with a rueful smile, conceding defeat gracefully. The jurors had no idea what had transpired—or what they had almost learned about Joyce Cohen.

The trial was an emotional roller coaster for Joyce. Some days she seemed composed and confident; on others she looked harried, exhausted, depressed. Every day, jurors tried to make eye contact with her, hoping to read the truth in the dark eyes behind the school-marmish black-rimmed glasses. But when she returned their gaze, Joyce's face remained a mask that the jurors couldn't penetrate. The effect was disquieting. To some she appeared defiant, hard; to others, simply inscrutable.

During her ordeal, Joyce stayed with Ed and Shu Sampson. Robert Dietrich and Shawn had remained behind in Chesapeake, Virginia. Neither one wanted to be available in Miami for a last-minute prosecution subpoena to testify at the trial. One night Joyce called Terry Jacobs, the makeup artist who used to do her face for parties and special events when she was a Grove socialite. It seemed so long ago. Would Terry be willing to do her makeup now? Of course, she responded, come to the studio. She could see that Joyce needed her help. She didn't look so good on the nightly television news, Terry thought. But Joyce never showed up for her makeup session. The next day she called and said she had had car trouble. Terry never heard from her again.


Joyce was excused from the courtroom again on Wednesday, November 8. Another slide show was scheduled, and this time it would be conducted by Alan Ross's forensic pathologist, Dr. Michael Baden. A middle-aged, professorial type with thinning gray hair and a small mustache, Dr. Baden summarized his impressive professional credentials for the jury: board certified in anatomic pathology, clinical pathology, and forensic pathology; chief investigator of the 1971 Attica Prison deaths; chief forensic pathologist for the U.S. House of Representatives Select Committee on the Assassinations of Dr. Martin Luther King, Jr., and President John F. Kennedy; former chief medical examiner for New York City (demoted, Dr. Baden commented wryly, in a political dispute with Mayor Edward Koch); presently director of forensic sciences for the New York State Police. He had performed over 20,000 medico-legal autopsies, he said, mostly in New York. Kevin DiGregory cut the impressive recitation short by stipulating to Dr. Baden's expertise in forensic pathology.

At Ross's request, Dr. Baden launched into an explanation of lividity, rigor mortis, and algor mortis (the cooling of the body after death), and how those features help a forensic pathologist establish time of death. He made an excellent witness—articulate, pleasant. Speaking directly to the jury, gesturing and illustrating as he went along, he held them effortlessly.

Turning to the Cohen case, Dr. Baden described the information he had reviewed—witness statements, depositions, autopsy report, and photographs. All, he declared, supported his conclusion: Stan Cohen died shortly before 5:30 A.M.

Ross projected the now-familiar slide of Stan Cohen's nude body lying supine on the bedroom floor. He directed Dr. Baden's attention to the area where Dr. Wetli had seen an interrupted pattern of lividity. "Do you see lividity on the right side of the body?" Ross asked.

Several jurors leaned forward intently.

"No," Baden replied. "This is an area of paleness of the photograph, not pallor of the skin. I say that on the basis of thousands of bodies and photographs I've seen. This is an artifact of the photograph." He was firm, confident.

"Is this pressure pallor on the right kneecap?"

"No," Baden said again. "There is some slight discoloration in the middle but it doesn't have the appearance of pressure pallor. . . . It was caused by the flashbulb."

"Dr. Baden," Ross asked in conclusion, "do you have an opinion to a reasonable degree of medical certainty as to when Stan Cohen was killed?"

"Yes, I do."

"When?"

"Within less than an hour before 5:30 A.M. Close to 5:30 A.M. This opinion takes into account all factors discussed today."

DiGregory waited patiently through Ross's direct examination of his second medical expert, Dr. Werner Spitz, a tall, stoop-shouldered, shambling man with crew-cut white hair, dark-rimmed glasses, and a baggy gray suit. Dr. Spitz spoke with a guttural accent that sounded like actor Mel Brooks playing a German scientist.

He had trained in Geneva, Dr. Spitz told the jury, and he had thirty-six years' experience as a forensic pathologist. Before he retired in 1988, he had been chief medical examiner of Wayne County, Michigan. His practice now was mainly consulting on cases such as this. Like Dr. Baden, Spitz saw no lividity in the photographs of Stan

Cohen's body. The dusky look of the skin was due to cyanosis, not lividity, he explained. His opinion as to the time of Cohen's death: "No reason to believe he died at any other time than 5 or 5:15 A.M."

On cross, DiGregory took the witness back through the slides and his own deposition testimony, probing for inconsistencies. The exchanges grew loud and angry.

In a final effort to cast doubt on Spitz's expertise, DiGregory said, "You left Wayne County in October 1988. You retired. The county supervisors thought you spent too much time on outside consulting work rather than time at Wayne County; correct?"

"Well, there was a little bit of a story preceding that." The witness looked uncomfortable for the first time.

"Did it have anything to do with your dismissal that you allowed police officers to use bodies for gunshot experiments?" DiGregory was loud, aggressive.

"Wait a minute. No, no, no, no, wait a minute!" Dr. Spitz trembled with anger.

"Objection!" Alan Ross was on his feet. "Your Honor, I would like to go to sidebar."

The lawyers huddled near the judicial bench on the side farthest from the jury, and Judge Smith leaned down to hear them. In an urgent whisper, Ross objected vehemently to DiGregory's attempt to impeach Spitz with the inflammatory charge.

"Do you have a good faith basis to ask it?" the judge asked DiGregory. He handed her a copy of a June 29, 1989, article from *The Chicago Tribune* reporting on Spitz's testimony in another trial. In that case, according to the article, "Spitz acknowledged that he had allowed 'two or three' bodies in the county morgue to be used for 'gunshot experiments.' "

"It's horrible-sounding," the judge agreed, "but why does it have anything to do with his credibility as a witness?"

"Judge, it has everything to do with his competency as a human being, let alone as a medical examiner. This is just outrageous conduct," DiGregory whispered back. But in the end Judge Smith agreed with Ross that the information was not proper impeachment material.

While the lawyers argued at the bench, the jurors chuckled openly. Finally Judge Smith sustained Ross's objection. "I'm going to ask the jury to disregard that last question," she announced.

In the jury room later, the jurors joked about the episode. Hyperbole, they laughed. They couldn't imagine there was any truth to the outrageous allegation.


There was one more witness the courtroom spectators were anxious to see: Lynn Barkley, Joyce Cohen's onetime lover and alleged (but uncharged) accomplice in the murder of her husband. He was tall, with longish, graying blond hair. Even in his suit and tie, he looked slightly rumpled. Still, he was good-looking in a raffish way. It was easy to imagine that Joyce might once have found him attractive.

Ross brought up the alleged murder conspiracy soon after Lynn Barkley took the stand. "Did you ever, ever have anything to do with a conspiracy to murder Stan Cohen?" he asked.

"Absolutely not," Barkley replied confidently.

"Ever see this person before?" Ross showed the witness a photograph of Frank Zuccarello. Barkley put on horn-rimmed glasses to examine the picture. Then he removed them. "Absolutely not."

"Ever see this person?" A photograph of Tommy Lamberti.

"Absolutely not."

Nor, Barkley stated, had he ever seen Anthony Caracciolo or had any meeting at a 7-Eleven.

Barkley described his relationship with defendant Joyce Cohen: "Socially friends."

"Did you ever have a sexual encounter?" Ross asked.

"Yes, only one time." It was after a dinner at the Cohens' home, Barkley recalled. They had sat on the couch, talking and drinking wine—and, as Barkley admitted on cross, snorting a little cocaine.

"Did you ever have a conversation about killing Stan? Ever give a sketch of the house to anyone?"

"Absolutely not. It's all hogwash." Barkley sounded bored. He told the jury that he had run into Joyce unexpectedly the day before Stan was murdered. They had had a drink, talked over a prospective business venture. Then the conversation turned personal. Joyce had told Barkley that she wanted a divorce. Stan was having an affair, she said. And she hadn't had sex with her husband for the past two years.

The next morning Barkley had seen police cars at the Cohens' home. I stopped to see if there was anything I could do—see what happened, he told the jury.

"Did you say to a police officer, 'Did she finally kill him?' " Ross asked his witness.

"Absolutely not. That's just nonsense." Barkley was disgusted.

The police had grilled him for an entire day, Barkley related, accusing him of being Joyce Cohen's lover. "If one physical encounter constitutes a lover, then there's a lot of us in trouble," he said with a smirk, gazing around the courtroom. There were no answering smiles in the jury box. No expression crossed Judge Smith's face.

"They asked me to take a lie detector test, which I agreed to do, and did and have had to pay for," Barkley went on.

"Objection!" Kastrenakes yelled, leaping to his feet.

"Ask your next question," Judge Smith told Ross. The spectators who had sat through the Patty Bartell episode knew what the problem was: Testimony about polygraph tests was off limits.

With the jury and the witness excused from the courtroom again, Kastrenakes moved to exclude any testimony about Barkley's interview with Warren Holmes, the polygraphist who tested Barkley—and passed him.

It's already before the jury, Ross argued. On redirect, I should be allowed to inquire as to the circumstances under which the statements were made.

"[Barkley's] a loose cannon," Kastrenakes fumed to the judge. He *wants* to tell the jury about the polygraph!

"It is already before the jury," Judge Smith commented. If he only says that, it's before the jury already. Mr. Ross, on redirect ask leading questions in this area. I will admonish the witness to listen carefully and answer only what he's asked.

Ross called Barkley back to the witness stand.

Mr. Barkley, please answer only the question being asked, Judge Smith instructed.

"Yes, ma'am," he replied.

The jurors filed back into the jury box and after a few preliminary questions, Ross asked, Who was present when you made the statements to Warren Holmes?

"There were two detectives and an attorney," Barkley replied. "[But] not when I was taking the polygraph test." There it was again. Judge Smith looked stern. Kastrenakes was on the edge of his seat.

Was the statement recorded? Ross continued.

Make it clear, Judge Smith warned. When the witness and Warren Holmes were alone?

"Yes," Ross agreed. How was the statement recorded?

"I was on the polygraph machine—" Barkley began.

"Objection! Objection!" Kastrenakes was furious. The attorneys moved to the bench for sidebar.

Lynn Barkley slouched in his seat. He yawned. He gazed about the courtroom.

Gary Cohen, who had sat stoically through the long weeks of trial, finally lost his temper. He bolted from his seat in the gallery and stalked out of the courtroom. The door slammed angrily behind him. Outside in the corridor, Gary fumed. "That was so predictable!" Judge Smith was letting Alan Ross and Lynn Barkley get away with murder in there, he complained. Although he was a lawyer himself, he had now lost all faith in the criminal justice system. It seemed the victim had no rights here, only the defendant. It was a mockery of justice. And he was deeply disgusted by the antics of the attorneys. "Makes you proud to be a lawyer, doesn't it?" he asked sarcastically.

Inside the courtroom, Lynn Barkley's testimony wound to a close. "You may be excused," Judge Smith announced.

"Thank you so much!" Barkley stepped jauntily from the witness box. Ed Smith and a few of Joyce Cohen's supporters chuckled. There was no mirth on the bench or in the jury box.

As Barkley walked by the defense table, he turned to face Joyce and mouthed what looked like "See you later." She smiled slightly as he passed.

The trial was recessed for lunch. For the first time in weeks, Joyce looked relaxed, even happy. Things were going well. She chatted with the friends who stopped to speak to her. "See you after lunch!" she said gaily.

There were awkward moments when everyone trooped down to the Pickle Barrel on the first floor of the Metropolitan Justice Building, the only place to get a quick lunch. The trial spotlighted the deep division among Stanley Cohen's friends, many of whom were witnesses or spectators. The gallery of the courtroom resembled the seating at a shotgun wedding. Joyce's friends sat behind the defense table, while Gerri Helfman and her supporters occupied the opposite side of the gallery near the press section. Gary Cohen and Uncle Artie, Stan's wheelchair-bound brother, staked out neutral territory at the center of the courtroom.

That night, Gerri was deeply depressed. She felt the tide turning against the prosecution. Joyce, her hated stepmother, might actually get away with it after all. For Gerri, the trial had rekindled all the old pain, the unresolved feelings about her father. She was seeing a psychiatrist to help her through this difficult time.

Most nights when she came home from the trial, Gerri clung to her baby son, Douglas, as the one glimmer of hope in her life. I'll get through this, she told herself. The trial will end, and when it's all over, I'll still have Douglas, no matter what.

But the stress of the trial—and the long years leading up to it—was taking its toll on her. Gerri had a bad cold, and that night she couldn't even hold her son. She cried herself into a troubled sleep.


Judge Fredricka Smith was alone in her chambers at night, working late on the Cohen trial. She recalled that she had left an important document on the trial bench that afternoon. When she walked into the deserted, shadowy courtroom to retrieve it, she was suddenly overcome by a sense of wrenching human emotion. It seemed the very walls of the courtroom had absorbed the violence, the anguish, the misery that played out there during the day. She could almost hear the voices of all the people who had passed before her, echoes thrown back by those walls at night, when no one else was there.

Judge Smith shivered and hurried back to her chambers.


After an exhausting day of trial, DiGregory and Kastrenakes worked far into the night on the state's closing argument. They had to consolidate the lengthy trial for the jury, to lead them to the inescapable conclusion that Joyce was guilty. What should they emphasize? She had lied about what happened, they were certain, and perhaps the most demonstrable lie was about the time the murder took place. But had they proved beyond every reasonable doubt that Cohen died between 2 and 3 A.M. rather than 5:30 A.M.?

In Kastrenakes's mind, Bernard Ahouse was the key to the case, the linchpin, the link they had sought for more than two years. Here was a witness, he argued, whose credibility should be unassailable. He was completely disinterested. He knew none of the participants and had nothing to gain. Surely the jury would recognize the value of Ahouse's testimony that he heard shots at 3 A.M.. Together with Dr. Wetli and Jerry Mandina, who had heard only the sound of breaking glass around 5 A.M., Ahouse supported Frank Zuccarello's story. If the jury believed these witnesses, they knew Joyce had lied. And if she had lied, of course she was guilty.

DiGregory played devil's advocate. Ahouse, he reminded Kastrenakes, hadn't even come to court to testify, so the jury couldn't look into his eyes and evaluate him as they had the other witnesses. They had to rely on a videotape, which was much less compelling than in-person testimony. What would the jury make of the fact that Ahouse hadn't showed up? And Dr. Wetli himself was vulnerable. What if Dr. Poole was disturbed by his change of professional opinion? For that matter, what if Poole, a radiologist, didn't see any lividity on the slides? Jerry Mandina seemed solid, but what about Zuccarello? They had discussed his shortcomings as a witness a hundred times.

What it came down to, DiGregory said, was that Ross had an answer for everything. There was so much conflicting testimony. If the jury made even one wrong determination, the case could be lost. How could they guide the jury through that maze? All it took was a single reasonable doubt and Joyce would walk. They had to fight for every fact and every inference. Nothing could be conceded. But could they come up with something else, Kastrenakes wondered? A shortcut, a single fail-safe sequence of events that could be proved beyond a reasonable doubt and that would let the jury escape the morass of conflicting evidence?

After a while Kastrenakes said, I think I've got it.

# Twenty-Three

•

After more than a month of trial, one question remained. Would Joyce Cohen take the stand in her own defense? Out of the jury's earshot, Kevin DiGregory asked Alan Ross directly.

I won't say right now, he replied.

"You know, this isn't really a game," Judge Smith said brusquely. "If you call Mrs. Cohen, would you be calling her today?"

"Yes."

Then Ross laid his final cards on the table: His client would testify if, and only if, she would be permitted to tell the jury about the two polygraph tests she had passed. DiGregory objected vehemently. Polygraph tests are inadmissible in Florida courts. But Ross pointed to a new federal court decision admitting test results under some circumstances. He offered to permit Joyce to take an additional polygraph by a state examiner immediately. But DiGregory promptly refused.

Judge Smith denied Ross's request to admit the test results, and Joyce did not testify. Although Ross stood firmly behind his decision not to put her on the stand, others disagreed. They felt Joyce needed to be "humanized" for the jury. She had a hard look, which even Ross recognized. He knew she was afraid, and the only way she could cope with the ordeal facing her was to put up a wall around her. He could only hope that the jury would see it that way.

Closing arguments were scheduled for November 14. When the jurors arrived in court that day, many brought homemade snacks— cakes, cookies, coffee cakes—in anticipation of long hours of deliberation. All brought their overnight bags. They knew they'd be sequestered until they reached a verdict.

The State of Florida presented its closing argument first. DiGregory strode to the podium and addressed the Court in formal manner. "May it please the Court. Counsel, members of the jury, good morning." He gestured toward the gilded motto above Judge Smith's head. WE WHO LABOR HERE SEEK ONLY TRUTH. It has been said, he told the jurors, that a jury trial is the ultimate search for truth. And you have become searchers. You have a compass to aid your search. You had it before you came here: your common sense.

Use your common sense, he urged the jury, your "built-in compasses," to test the two opposing theories in this case. Either Stan Cohen was murdered by two shadowy figures or he was murdered by Joyce Lemay Cohen, his wife, to inherit his money.

To believe Joyce Cohen's story about the two shadowy figures, Di-Gregory continued, you must accept an unbroken string of coincidences and dumb luck that defy logic. Two mysterious strangers arrive; the alarm system happens to be turned off; they break in without alerting Joyce Cohen or her Doberman pinscher; they run upstairs to Stan's bedroom and find his loaded gun on the nightstand; they kill him with his own gun; and then they run out of the house before Mrs. Cohen can get a good look at them. The dog didn't even chase them out the door, DiGregory commented wryly, shaking his head. "How lucky can you get?"

Before you consider the state's evidence in this case, DiGregory told the jurors, set your built-in compasses on the defendant's own story, her sworn statement to the police. She told them that she heard a noise in the yard that night and ran upstairs to get her husband. Stan took a loaded gun, and the two of them looked around the yard, then returned to their bedroom, where he left the loaded gun on the nightstand. Later Joyce went downstairs alone, turned off the alarm system, and locked up the dog with her in her son's room. Then, while she was on the phone with a person in Colorado, she heard a noise. She hung up the phone and followed the dog into the dark kitchen. She didn't call upstairs to her husband with the loaded gun.

She didn't call police or even stay on the telephone line.

"What does she do?" DiGregory asked. "This woman, who sought her husband when danger was outside in the yard, now follows the dog into apparent danger. So far, in your search for truth, you're finding only lies."

Using a prepared chart, DiGregory reviewed the phone calls to and from the Cohen home on the morning of March 7, beginning with the first call from Steamboat Springs at 5:18 A.M. Joyce said that call was from Kimberly Carroll, he reminded the jury, but Kimberly told the police she had handed the phone to Kathy Dickett. A follow-up call from Colorado at 5:20 found Joyce hysterical, screaming that Stan had been shot. According to Joyce, she must have found her husband's bloody, murdered body about 5:19 A.M. But records showed she didn't trip the alarm that called the 911 emergency operator until 5:25 A.M., more than five full minutes later.

"While Stan lay bleeding, within reach of the panic button which *she* wanted installed and *she* could activate with one push!" DiGregory thundered at the jury. "Would an innocent woman wait *five minutes* to sound the alarm, to call 911? What does your common sense tell you?

"Do you know how long five minutes is?" With that, DiGregory turned on his heel and strode back to counsel table. He sat down and folded his arms across his chest, staring straight ahead. There was dead silence in the courtroom.

All the jurors intently watched the prosecutor, except one. Dr. Catherine Poole stared straight at Joyce Cohen.

As he sat beside DiGregory, Kastrenakes fought his own frustration. He doubted that Joyce had killed her husband. She had hired someone else to do that and had planned the alibi phone calls. His scenario fit neatly into the evidence that the murder had occurred at 2 to 3 A.M. It also jibed with Joyce's insistence in her sworn statement that the calls had come at three o'clock. She had even invited Detective Spear to check the time with Kimberly Carroll and the phone records. But Kastrenakes had reluctantly agreed with DiGregory that proof of that scenario was conjectural at best. And raising such conjectures with the jury might be confusing or, worse, damaging to their credibility.

Kastrenakes gazed at Joyce sitting at the defense table and wondered again. What had she been doing for two or three hours while she waited desperately for the phone to ring? He was pretty sure she wasn't staging the break-in. Neighbor Jerry Mandina had heard that around 5 A.M. And she probably wasn't upstairs with the body. He guessed she had saved that part for last—and then panicked when she discovered the gun where Caracciolo had apparently dropped it. So what *was* she doing while her husband lay upstairs, murdered in his bed? Kastrenakes was haunted by the scenes he imagined.

After the interminable silence, DiGregory rose and returned to the podium. "That's how long five minutes is," he said softly. In the courtroom, it had seemed like an hour. "That's how long she waited to call 911. What was she doing? Now it's time to consider the physical evidence. It will convince you she used that time to wipe down the gun that had been used by her hired assassin, Anthony Caracciolo, to kill Stanley Cohen."

Sometimes shouting, sometimes whispering so that jurors had to lean forward to hear his words, DiGregory summarized the physical evidence against Joyce Cohen: the gunshot residue on her hands and on the blue-and-white tissue hidden in her private bathroom; the two tiny bits of white tissue on the murder weapon, found in the Cohens' front yard. Gopinath Rao testified that he found similar gunshot residue particles on Joyce's hands and the soiled tissue. His results were consistent with her having handled a recently fired weapon—or having touched a gunshot wound. Rao was limited to his tests, DiGregory reminded the jury, but you know that there were tiny pieces of white tissue on the murder weapon. "That tells you conclusively how the gunshot residue got on the tissue."

That blue-and-white tissue, with mucus from a person with Joyce's blood type, was hidden beneath an empty tissue box in Joyce's bathroom wastebasket. The only tissues adjacent to the bedroom were blue. Perhaps, DiGregory suggested sarcastically, a mysterious stranger had found Joyce's used tissue and wiped down the gun. And then took it to her bathroom to hide in a wastebasket? No, the only reasonable explanation, DiGregory continued, was that Joyce used that tissue to wipe down the gun. Then she hid the tissue in her wastebasket and threw the gun off the terrace outside.

It's really very simple, DiGregory told the jury. If Joyce Cohen wiped down the murder weapon, she's guilty. And you know it. It was Kastrenakes's shortcut through the myriad conflicting testimonies, the single issue on which Ross had produced no witness. But would the jury focus on it?

When she was giving her sworn statement to the police, DiGregory continued, the wheels in her mind were turning. What if she didn't get all her prints off the gun and the cops found it? So she invented a story. She told them she picked up the gun earlier that night and said, Stan, why are you leaving this here? Too convenient.

And what about Joyce's hysteria when the cops arrived? Phony? "Most certainly. Stan Cohen had been dead since 3 A.M.," DiGregory said. "You can rely on Jerry Mandina and Bernie Ahouse. Ahouse had no favors to play. There was nothing uncertain about his testimony. He was positive. He heard gunshots at 3 A.M. Because of his experience, he identified the shots fired as from a .38-caliber revolver. And that's what we have here—a .38-caliber revolver. And Jerry Mandina, directly across the street from 3:30 till 5:30, heard no shots, just glass breaking shortly after 5 A.M.

"The only living person at the Cohen house at 5 A.M. was the defendant herself. And the defendant is the person who had the most to gain from Stan's death." Just coincidence, DiGregory asked? Do you believe the defendant is the victim of unlucky coincidences? He shook his head.

You don't have to find that Joyce pulled the trigger, DiGregory reminded the jury. If she intended for it to happen and participated, she's as guilty as the one who pulled the trigger. This was a planned killing. "Let your verdict speak the truth."

Then it was Alan Ross's turn. As one, the jurors turned to him expectantly. When I was getting dressed to come to court today, he began dramatically, I wondered, what could I say? What could one person say? In defense of this person, he gestured toward Joyce, on trial for her life, against the forces of the state, the police, these well-trained prosecutors. And I thought for the first time how much doctors deserve our respect (he glanced at juror Dr. Catherine Poole), because they undertake responsibility for another person's *life*. And that's the responsibility I've undertaken here.

What's Mrs. Cohen's defense? Ross continued. She didn't do it.

She's not guilty. It's as simple as that. A few weeks ago, I asked you to look across at her and say, "Mrs. Cohen, I absolutely presume you innocent." That was your promise, your oath. Now *you* have her life in *your* hands. The issue, Ross said, is whether the state has proved the defendant's guilt beyond every reasonable doubt. That means where the hand fits the glove, he explained. Is the state's case like that? No.

Warming to his task, Ross thundered that he had a list of 175 reasonable doubts about the evidence against his client, any one of which required the jury to find her not guilty. If Joyce Cohen had wanted her husband killed, did it make any sense to have it done while she was in the house? And would she really have been stupid enough to wipe down the murder gun, throw it into her own front yard, and then hide the tissue in her own wastebasket? Wouldn't she at least have flushed the tissue down the toilet?

Ross's explanation for the tissue was simple and innocent. He described for the jury how Joyce got gunshot residue on her hands by touching her husband's wounded head when she found him unconscious. Then, sobbing, she blew her nose and wiped her soiled hands on the tissue, thereby transferring some gunpowder residue from her hands to the tissue. The state's own witness, Gopinath Rao, had testified that it could have happened that way. Then Joyce simply threw the tissue into the wastebasket out of habit. Why was she in her bathroom? She went there because it had the only window from which she could watch for the police pulling into her driveway on Southwest 17th Avenue. Of course this was argument, not evidence. But Ross was most persuasive. Would the jury discern the difference? Or care?

It was the intruders who shot Stan Cohen who wiped off the murder gun with white toilet tissue on their way out the front door, Ross continued. That tissue was found on the front steps of the Cohen home on the morning of March 7. It was clearly visible in ID Technician Sylvia Romans's photographs of the crime scene. But it vanished before it could be examined—another instance of inept investigation leading to wrong conclusions about the crime. Ross shook his head sadly.

As for the state's star witness, Frank Zuccarello, he was a garden-variety liar, primed by the cops. "He knew whatever they wanted him to know. He bought his way out of jail with false testimony!" Ross growled. "It's as obvious as the nose on his face!"

Despite Zuccarello's testimony that Anthony Caracciolo and Joyce Cohen had exchanged several phone calls, the detectives couldn't find any record of them, Ross continued. For one simple reason. They never happened. And neither did any of the other events that Zuccarello told them about in such detail. How about Lynn Barkley? If they were so sure Frank Zuccarello was telling the truth, why wasn't Barkley charged? He was never arrested or charged for one reason: Zuccarello is a liar.

"Frank Zuccarello lied to you. . . . And every time Zuccarello lies, that's a reasonable doubt," Ross intoned.

And as for the dramatic "missing five minutes"? There was no missing five minutes, Ross declared. "It was just the state attorney's guess! And with that five minutes, he puts Joyce Cohen in the electric chair!"

It was nothing more than a slight variation in the time reported by the Southern Bell telephone records, by the Dictagraph alarm system, and by the 911 emergency operator. "My watch," Ross looked down as he spoke, "says one-twelve. The clock [above the door] says one-oh-nine. If each of you looks at your watch, you'll have various times." But the jurors didn't look at their watches. They gazed intently at Ross.

What about Bernie Ahouse? He couldn't have heard any shots, Ross said, because he was so far away from the Cohens' house, he was practically in another city. Yet he claimed he heard a .38. "If we had asked him a few more questions, he would have told us the serial number." And Ahouse heard those "sounds" forty-five minutes *after* the time Zuccarello gave for the shooting. "The glove doesn't fit. It's got four fingers, not five. And that's a reasonable doubt."

"The next area will convince you to a certainty," Ross continued. "The time of Stan Cohen's death. It's not the defendant's responsibility to prove to you that Stan died at 5:18 A.M. It's the state's burden to prove that he died between 2:15 and 2:18 A.M." Do you have a doubt? How about the paramedics who testified that Stan's body was still warm? There was no lividity, no rigor mortis. And Dr.

Baden—how qualified must you be to chair a committee investigating the deaths of Martin Luther King, Jr., and John F. Kennedy? But the best witness was Dr. Wetli, who for more than three years consistently agreed with Joyce Cohen's statement about the time of Stan's death—until he changed his mind during this trial.

Every inconsistency in the evidence, every gap, every guess the prosecutors made about what might have happened—each one is a reasonable doubt, Ross continued. "If you waiver or vacillate, stop right there," he instructed the jury. "There's reasonable doubt. I outlined one hundred seventy-five reasonable doubts. You need to have but one. And then your verdict has to be 'not guilty.'

"This is the most important decision you'll ever be asked to make," Ross concluded. "The life of this woman is in your hands. That's not an exaggeration. . . . Only one verdict. One that you should be proud of. The only verdict an innocent woman deserves: *not guilty.*"

Bob Amsel watched his partner return to his seat at counsel table. After that great closing, he thought, I would be shocked at a guilty verdict. No way that Joyce Cohen is going to be convicted of killing her husband.


The case went to the jury late in the afternoon on November 14, still too close to call. After a few hours' deliberation in the tiny jury room behind the courtroom, the jurors were escorted to the aging Holiday Inn down the street from the Metropolitan Justice Building, where they would reside until Joyce Cohen's fate was decided. To shield them from news about the case, they were given rooms with no telephones or televisions.

When a jury is out, a peculiar atmosphere envelops a trial's participants and spectators. There is anticipation mixed with dread, hope mixed with despair. But mostly there is just—waiting. The lawyers and their clients and family and friends roam the corridors, unable to leave until the jury returns. A strange sort of bonding takes place. They chatter nervously, joke, try to read, make phone calls. But mostly they just wait.

The jury was led back into the jury room at 9 A.M. the following day, Wednesday, November 15, to continue their deliberations. A note was delivered to the judge. The news flew down the hall. The lawyers, the defendant, and spectators hurriedly assembled in the courtroom to hear Judge Smith read the note aloud. The jury wanted to hear criminalist Gopinath Rao's testimony about the gunshot residue again. Judge Smith granted the request. It was considered a favorable sign for the prosecution. The jury, it seemed, was following Kastrenakes's shortcut through the maze of conflicting testimony to a single issue. If they believed Joyce Cohen had handled the recently fired murder weapon, she *had* to be guilty.

The jury returned to the jury box. Rao's lengthy, technical testimony was read aloud by the court reporter, who never missed a word of the difficult transcript. When the reporter finished, the jury filed back into the tiny, cramped jury room.

In public, Alan Ross seemed unconcerned. He even laughed that he should have worn his favorite pin on his lapel during closing argument: "2" (meaning two words—"not guilty"). But privately he feared the worst for his client. "It doesn't look good," he told Joyce with a frown.

Without a word to his partner—or their client—Bob Amsel began work in earnest on the penalty phase of the case.

A rumor flashed through the courthouse. At Joe's Stone Crab Restaurant on the beach, someone claimed to have sat at a lunch table next to Ross's law partner and secretaries from his office. They were discussing plans for his victory party in the Cohen case. The champagne, it was said, was already on ice. Gary Cohen and Gerri Helfman, who had taken six-week leaves of absence from their jobs to attend every day of the trial, heard the rumor. They steeled themselves against their worst nightmare: that their stepmother would walk out of the courtroom a free woman.

In the silence of her chambers, Judge Fredricka Smith still thought the verdict could go either way. There were so many factual issues, so much conflicting testimony and evidence. Was there reasonable doubt? Or was there anything else? The judge couldn't predict.

Kevin DiGregory joked nervously that if he lost this case, at least he would be in good company—with Florida Supreme Court Justice Gerald Kogan. As a young prosecutor in Dade County in 1965, Kogan had lost his case against accused husband killer Candace Mossler and her nephew, the same case that had fascinated Stan Cohen. Passing the time in his office, DiGregory mentioned to colleagues that his wife had just learned she was pregnant with the couple's fourth child. Counting backwards, some calculated that the child must have been conceived literally on the eve of the Cohen trial.

More rumors. The wife of a prominent Miami attorney commented that if Joyce Cohen was acquitted, she would line up luncheon speaking engagements for Joyce all over town. There were plenty of women who would want to know how she got away with killing her husband—and would pay the price of an expensive lunch to find out.

The day ended without a verdict. The jury went back to the Holiday Inn for a second night.

The next morning, November 16, they returned to continue deliberating. Then, suddenly, it was over. About 9:30 that morning, after a total of eight hours of deliberation, the jury foreperson advised Judge Smith's bailiff that they had a verdict.

The news swept down the fourth-floor corridor like a strong gust of wind. As DiGregory rushed to the courtroom, he thought of Kastrenakes. He had stayed home that morning with a high fever.

Judge Smith entered the packed courtroom and silenced the spectators. She gave a stern warning. No matter what the jury's verdict was, it was to be respected by all those present. She would not tolerate any emotional outbursts of any kind. Having made that clear, she sent the bailiff to bring the jury in.

The jurors filed into the courtroom. The jury foreperson, Dr. Catherine Poole, handed the verdict up to the judge. *Well, at least I called that right,* Ross thought nervously. He had predicted Dr. Poole would be selected foreperson.

Judge Smith glanced at the verdict form. Ross was certain he could read her fleeting expression—surprise. Without comment the judge passed the verdict to her clerk to read aloud. Joyce Cohen and her attorneys rose and faced the jury.

"As to the first count, murder in the first degree—guilty." Alan Ross exhaled sharply. His shoulders slumped.

But Joyce continued to stare at the jury, dry-eyed, expressionless.

"As to the second count, conspiracy to commit murder—guilty. As to the third count, display of a firearm in the commission of a felony—guilty."

The courtroom surged with shock, anguish, and jubilation.

A loud, low moan escaped Gerri Helfman. She sobbed with relief as her husband, Steve, held her. "It's all over now," he soothed. "It's really all over."

Tears coursed down Gary Cohen's cheeks as he clutched his nine-month-old son to his chest.

Across the courtroom, Joyce Cohen's friends sat silently, stunned. Sam Smith burst into tears.

Judge Smith solemnly thanked the jury for its long service in the case. Then she dismissed them, with instructions to return on November 20 for the penalty phase of the trial.

When the jury was gone, Judge Smith called the defendant to the bench for adjudication, the formal pronouncement that made Joyce Cohen a murderess in the eyes of the law.

Joyce was wooden, nearly immobile, barely able to walk the short distance to the bench. Standing beside her, Ross and Amsel towered over her. She suddenly seemed vulnerable, childlike. She didn't even glance at her lawyers. Neither one spoke to her.

No one had noticed the uniformed corrections officer, Ben Moreno, waiting quietly near the back door of the courtroom. Now Officer Moreno came to meet Joyce at the bench. Methodically he inked her fingers and rolled them onto fingerprint cards as Judge Smith spoke. "Pursuant to the jury's verdict, I adjudicate you guilty . . ."

As she listened, Joyce absently wiped her dirty fingers on a tissue that the officer handed her.

Then it was over. Officer Moreno led Joyce out the back door for the first time, into the small holding cell. She never looked back. But once inside the tiny cell, she collapsed. Moreno held the sobbing woman in his arms and rocked her like a baby.

Outside, television cameras and reporters waited down the hall near the escalators and elevators, in the zone where they were confined to work. Lights flashed on and reporters scrambled for interviews. Gerri Helfman walked by, now smiling but still refusing to break her public silence about the case.

But Gary Cohen spoke briefly. "Nobody thought this case was a winner," he said quietly. "Everybody always believed she was guilty, but no one thought she'd be convicted. This was not a neat, tidy case."

Every radio and television station in Miami broke into programming with the news of the verdict. John Kastrenakes, home with the flu that morning, heard the verdict on the radio before DiGregory could even get upstairs to his office to call him. Sick as he was, Kastrenakes couldn't stay in bed. He dressed hurriedly and rushed to work.

Although Detective Jon Spear thought this was the most important case of his seventeen-year career, he took no real pleasure in the conviction. He commented somberly that he was sorry for everyone, even Mrs. Cohen. "All things equal out," he sighed. "I'm a firm believer in what goes around, comes around."

Alan Ross was devastated by the verdict. It showed in his sagging shoulders and on his face, which suddenly looked haggard. He had lost thirty-five pounds during the grueling trial, and his well-tailored suit hung in loose folds on the last day. While spectators surged around the prosecutors and Gary and Gerri with congratulations, he stayed behind in the courtroom, struggling to maintain his composure. "What do I say?" he mumbled absently, eyes red, voice raspy. "What do I say now?"

Ross managed to maintain his professional demeanor for the television cameras waiting in the corridor. But his comments to the press rambled. "As a criminal defense lawyer, you always know if your client did it or not," he began. "I've always known. All these years, through all these cases, I've always known. I'm in the best position to know. But even I, this time, still really don't know if she did it. So it makes it awfully tough to say there was no reasonable doubt."

It wasn't exactly what he meant to say. What Ross wanted to emphasize was his disbelief that the jury hadn't found even one reasonable doubt. But it sounded more like a lawyer whose faith in his client's innocence was faltering. When Kastrenakes heard Ross's remarks, he thought, We did it. We put some reasonable doubt about her innocence in Ross's mind, just like I said.

On the sixth floor of the Metropolitan Justice Building, an impromptu victory party was assembling. Dade County State Attorney Janet Reno stopped by to congratulate her prosecutors and hear their excited comments. Someone sent out for champagne. In a large office, Gary and Carol Cohen, Gerri and Steve Helfman, and Artie Cohen and his wife, Mary, sat on sofas and chairs and leaned against bookcases, giddy with relief, laughing at the prosecutors' jokes and war stories about the Cohen case. Kastrenakes imitated Ed Smith on the witness stand, tears rolling down his face. Everyone howled with laughter.

Kastrenakes's father, a Miami real estate attorney, came by to offer congratulations on the verdict. He also had some advice for his son. It was time to stop celebrating and start preparing for the next phase of the case: the hearing on the penalty to be imposed against Joyce Cohen—life in prison or death in Florida's electric chair, "Old Sparky."

Ross and Amsel made the long, sad trip downstairs to visit their client in her cell. They found Joyce alone in a locked room, tucked into a fetal position in a corner. And she was—*howling*. There was no other word for it. Amsel was shaken. I've never heard a human being make those sounds, he thought. For Ross, it was the worst professional experience of his life. She trusted me, he thought as he gazed down at her. She gave her life over to me, here it is, don't damage it.

Ross worried that Joyce might even try to kill herself. He was overwhelmed by her tragedy and by his own sense of failure. In his mind, he had already gone over every decision, every judgment he had made in the case, back to the first day, March 7, 1986, when he told Joyce Cohen not to consent to a search of the house. Endless second-guessing, chastising. But he always came back to the same point. He had done his very best for his client. And he would make the very same decisions again.

Finally Ross drove back to his office. When he was alone, he sat down at his desk and cried.

Amsel didn't have the luxury of surrendering to his emotions. His task lay ahead—the penalty phase. Joyce Cohen's life was now truly in his hands. It would be his first capital penalty hearing—and he had just three short days to prepare.

He didn't really even know his client, Amsel worried. Despite the countless hours he had spent with her—traveling, working, endlessly discussing her case—Joyce remained an enigma. She was very, very emotionally closed to people, Amsel thought. She never opened up. Even when he had tried to discuss her past life with her, she refused.

"Look. I'm innocent," she would reply. "Absolutely innocent." There would never be a penalty phase, she was certain. So there was no need to discuss her life. Amsel could see why some people thought she was cold. It was just the way she looked.

But he had to have her help now. Her life literally depended on it. Amsel had to probe his client's past for mitigating factors to invoke the jury's sympathy for the penalty phase of the trial. Who was Joyce Lemay Cohen? Where had she come from, this beautiful young woman who had so mysteriously appeared in Stan Cohen's life? He had loved her, had given her everything she wanted: houses, clothes, jewelry. He had given her a life. What could possibly explain why she had killed him—and destroyed herself?

# Twenty-Four

•

*C*arpentersville, Illinois, is one of the northern suburbs of Chicago, a working-class community in Kane County, about thirty miles from the city via the grimy Northwest Tollway. Beatrice Wojtanek lived in Carpentersville in a modest three-bedroom, one-bath frame house with a breezeway and a garage, in a neighborhood of aging families and thirty-year-old maples, oaks, and sycamores. It was the house where Joyce Cohen had grown up. But when the phone rang that November day and Beatrice Wojtanek reached for it, her thoughts were far from her niece Joyce. As far as she knew, Joyce was still in Virginia with that new boyfriend of hers. Besides, Aunt Bea, as nearly everyone called her, had her own problems. She had just come home from a hospital stay. Five children and decades of hard factory work—shipping clerk, janitor, bench press operator, forklift driver—had destroyed her health. She was diabetic, and her kidneys had failed. Daily dialysis treatments were keeping her alive.

Bea answered the phone. She had no premonition.

Alan Ross was calling from Miami, the voice on the phone said. The name meant nothing to her. Ross was Joyce Cohen's lawyer, the voice explained. Joyce had just been convicted of murdering her husband, and they needed Aunt Bea's help to keep her out of the electric chair. Would she be willing to testify before a jury on Joyce's behalf?

Bea sat, stunned, unable to speak. Finally she said yes, and the voice on the other end of the phone said someone would be in touch with her in the next few days.

After she hung up the phone, Bea began to sort out her memories of Joyce. What could she say about her niece? She recalled the first time she had seen the baby born to her sister-in-law, Eileen, and her husband, Bonnie Lemay, on July 18, 1950. They named her Joyce Annette Lemay. She was a beautiful, happy baby who had her father's American Indian features—dark, slightly almond eyes and black hair—rather than the delicate blond coloring of her mother's family, the Polish Wojtaneks. Eileen Lemay adored her baby daughter. When Bea saw the baby, she fell in love with her, too. Joyce looked like a little pixie, Bea thought, and she was such a good baby. Eileen asked her brother, Ed Wojtanek, Bea's husband, to be the baby's godfather, and he agreed. Joyce was christened in her mother's Catholic faith.

But soon there was trouble. Eileen wasn't well, and she couldn't seem to take care of Joyce. When Bea and Ed went to visit Eileen, they were worried. Bea suspected that Bonnie beat his wife and that she didn't eat well. They decided to take Joyce home with them. Bea had no children of her own yet, and she was delighted to take care of Joyce. When Eileen recovered enough to take Joyce back home, Bea and Ed were sorry to see the baby leave.

Then one day, without warning, Bonnie Lemay took Eileen and Joyce to Arkansas. Bea never knew why they left, and she missed them very much. She heard that they were living in a shack and working as sharecroppers in the fields. Bea hated to think of her pretty little niece in a shack.

Years passed, and the Wojtaneks lost track of Eileen and Joyce. They heard that Eileen had had another child, a son she named Terry. Then someone told Bea that Eileen had left Arkansas, but no one seemed to know where she had gone or why. In fact, Eileen was drifting from one place to another, from one man to another, sometimes marrying, sometimes not. For a while she left Joyce and little Terry at St. Vincent's Catholic Orphanage in Freeport, Illinois. Whenever Eileen got together with a new man, she would take her children to live with her. But something always seemed to go wrong, and soon Joyce and Terry would be sent back to St. Vincent's.

Finally Eileen took Joyce and Terry out of the orphanage for good, but when she decided to move on, Eileen simply deposited her children with some neighbors and disappeared. It was the last time Joyce and Terry ever saw their mother. When she failed to return, the neighbors found some Lemay relatives to take the children in.

Then one day someone called Bea Wojtanek from Chicago to say that Eileen had died there, all alone—of unknown causes, they said. Ed and Bea were shocked and saddened. When they went to claim Eileen's body, the Wojtaneks were told that she had been managing what was euphemistically called a transient hotel, where she had lived in one small room. The Wojtaneks contacted some Lemay relatives in Sycamore, Illinois, about the funeral. The Lemays arrived in Chicago on the day of the funeral, bringing Joyce and Terry with them. Bonnie didn't come.

Bea was surprised to see Joyce. She had no idea her niece was back in Sycamore with the Lemays. Joyce was about ten years old then, neatly dressed and still pretty with her long, dark hair. But Bea was struck by Joyce's solemn little face—the laughter had gone from her dark eyes. Joyce didn't remember her Wojtanek relatives, and she wasn't friendly to them. Bea thought Joyce and Terry seemed almost frightened. After the funeral, the children disappeared again.

For the next few years they passed from relative to relative, from one dreary place to the next, always outcasts, never part of a family. Joyce and little Terry were put to work in the fields, chopping cotton and doing chores. With no one to protect them, they were always at the mercy of anyone bigger or stronger who happened to be around. Even relatives treated them harshly. By the time Joyce was twelve years old, she had been physically and sexually abused by her own father, among others.

One spring day in 1964, Bea received a phone call from a Mrs. Barthol of Kane County Family Services. "Do you know a Joyce Lemay?" she asked.

"Of course," Bea replied, "That's my niece. Where is she?"

"Joyce is a ward of the state. We have her placed as a foster child."

"You what?" Bea was stunned.

Mrs. Barthol told Bea that Joyce had been living with some Lemay relatives who turned her over to Kane County Family Services and made her a ward of the state of Illinois. The Lemays claimed that Joyce stole from them and that they couldn't control her. But Bea doubted that. She thought the Lemays probably just wanted to get rid of Joyce, didn't want to be bothered with her anymore. Bea asked about little Terry, but he wasn't with Joyce.

Mrs. Barthol told Bea that Joyce had lived at the Kane County Youth Home in Geneva for a while, but about two years before she had been placed with a foster family, the Clanceys. The Clanceys were rich; they lived in a beautiful big house in nearby Geneva. But the family was leaving Illinois, and although they wanted to take Joyce with them, Family Services wouldn't permit it because Joyce was a ward of the state. Mrs. Barthol wanted to find a blood relative to take Joyce, and she suggested that Bea and her husband consider bringing their niece into their home. She thought it would be a good idea to invite Joyce for a weekend visit with them first. Bea agreed to speak to her husband about it.

Bea and Ed and their children piled into their old car for the drive to Geneva to pick up Joyce for her visit. When they arrived, the Wojtaneks were struck by the magnificence of the Clanceys' large Georgian brick home with pillars at the entrance. Inside, an elegant white grand piano was the centerpiece of the large formal living room. Bea thought the furniture was all French Provincial. Over the piano hung a gilt-framed reproduction of the famous Blue Boy, by Gainsborough. Bea was overcome by the grandeur of it all. Years later she could still describe that room in vivid detail.

Mrs. Clancey was a small, very pretty woman, perfectly groomed and fashionably dressed. She was polite to the Wojtaneks but not really friendly. Even though she made a fuss over Joyce, Bea still thought she was cold. "Oh, look at Joyce. Doesn't she look beautiful, isn't she just lovely? I've taken in other foster children and she's the best one we've ever had," Mrs. Clancey gushed.

Joyce was fourteen years old, and indeed she was lovely, very short, like her mother, with long, straight black hair and big, dark eyes. She was wearing a pretty pants set, and her clothes for the weekend were packed in a little suitcase at her feet.

Outside in the car, when Joyce wasn't listening, Ed summed up Mrs. Clancey: "What a phony." But they could see that Joyce absolutely idolized Mrs. Clancey, who had been a foster child herself. Mrs. Clancey had married a rich man—the Wojtaneks never did meet him—and hers was a life of luxury by their standards. They couldn't really blame Joyce for being smitten by the Clanceys, who had far more than the deprived, abandoned child had ever seen before. Bea and Ed supposed their niece was dazzled simply to be living in such a fine place.

In fact, Joyce didn't want to leave with her Wojtanek relatives. She longed to stay with the Clanceys and move with them to Oklahoma, where Mr. Clancey had been transferred. But now, once again, she was being sent away. It had been the pattern of her life. But perhaps she had glimpsed another possibility. Mrs. Clancey had been a foster child like Joyce, shuttled from place to place, yet she had managed to get this wonderful life for herself. And if Mrs. Clancey could do it, maybe Joyce could, too—a rich husband, a beautiful home, nice clothes, jewelry, travel—all the good things.

But it seemed to Bea Wojtanek that, in a way, the Clanceys' beautiful home was a terrible place for Joyce. She thought Mrs. Clancey put all kinds of ideas into Joyce's head—bad ideas and false values. Bea feared that material things were too important to Joyce and that only the best was good enough for her, just like Mrs. Clancey. Bea worried, and years later she would still blame Mrs. Clancey's influence on Joyce.

In Carpentersville for a visit, Joyce looked around the Wojtaneks' modest home on Topeka Drive and remarked, "It's little, isn't it?"

"Well, it's all we can afford," Bea replied defensively. "We just can't afford a house like those other people can."

When the school year ended that June, the Wojtaneks went back to the Clanceys' fine home to pick Joyce up again. Joyce looked resigned. She had only one request for Bea. Could she go to visit the Clanceys once they were settled in Oklahoma? Of course, Bea replied, if you're invited. Secretly Bea doubted that invitation would ever come.

Reluctantly, Joyce Lemay moved into the Wojtaneks' crowded little house. Bea and Ed gave up their bedroom and moved out to the breezeway to sleep, so Joyce could have a room of her own. "You're going to live here now," Bea told her. "And you've got to live by our rules."

"What are those?" Joyce asked warily.

"Well, you have to go to school. We have a curfew at night. And you have to let me know where you are. Now, are those so bad?"

"No," Joyce replied hesitantly.

Bea was pleased when she saw Joyce making friends with other teenage girls in the neighborhood. But even though she seemed reasonably content, Bea knew that Joyce still yearned for the Clanceys, who had moved to Oklahoma as planned. She wrote to them several times, hoping to be invited to their new home for a visit. Mrs. Clancey wrote back once—and then Joyce never heard from her again. Bea knew that she was hurt, but she never mentioned it. So often, it seemed, Joyce simply withdrew behind an impenetrable blank wall. Bea could only guess at the feelings hidden behind her impassive face.

Once Joyce asked Bea if she had any pictures of her as a child. But Bea had none. Joyce's childhood had not been chronicled by family photographs lovingly pasted into pretty albums. There was so little Bea could offer Joyce about her family, her history. She resolved to take plenty of pictures of her niece in the future.

As the months passed, Bea worried that Joyce still seemed so quiet, reserved, withdrawn. She thought her niece might need psychiatric help, and she discussed her concerns with Mrs. Barthol. Joyce just didn't warm up to the family, Bea tried to explain. It seemed that she wanted love but was afraid. When Bea put her arms around her, Joyce would pull back. But Mrs. Barthol didn't seem to understand Bea's concerns, and she refused to get counseling for Joyce. Reluctantly, Bea let the matter drop.

Still, Bea and Joyce shared some good times. Bea knew that Joyce was very particular about her appearance. She wore her dark hair very long, and she always wanted it completely straight. Bea would set up the ironing board in the kitchen, and Joyce would kneel next to it so her long hair lay along the board. Then Bea would iron Joyce's hair between sheets of waxed paper. One day Bea's neighbor dropped in and found them like that. "My God, Bea, what are you doing?" she shrieked. Bea and Joyce howled with laughter.

The following summer Bea decided to give a party for Joyce's sixteenth birthday, on July 18. Joyce seemed pleased and invited several friends. The party was to be an evening cookout in the Wojtaneks' backyard, with floodlights and records on a record player set up on a card table. But Joyce objected to the floodlights—too bright, she said. So Bea and the children strung multicolored Christmas lights through the picket fence around the backyard and in the trees. Joyce and her friends wore jeans and shirts to the party. They drank Cokes, ate the hotdogs and hamburgers that Ed and Bea cooked on the charcoal grill, danced on the grass, and cuddled on lawn chairs in the shadows.

Bea asked a friend to put an article about the party in the local newspaper. Joyce was pleased. She really enjoyed the publicity. That girl wants to be somebody, Bea mused.

That summer Joyce told her aunt and uncle that she wanted a car of her own. "Well, you'll have to work," Bea replied. "We just don't have the money to put out, so you're going to have to work for it if you want it."

They worked out the finances. Joyce would have to earn about $600 total: $500 to buy the car and pay for maintenance, gas, and oil, plus a $100 deposit in the bank to defray the $100 deductible on the Wojtaneks' auto insurance policy, in case she had an accident.

Joyce got a job at the Thom McAn shoe store in Meadowbrook Shopping Center a few blocks away. She worked all summer, and when school started in the fall, she worked after school and weekends. Her boss at Thom McAn liked Joyce and thought she was a hard worker. She saved her money and dreamed of the day when she would get her car.

As she had promised Mrs. Barthol, Bea saw to it that Joyce went to school regularly at Irving Crown High School in Carpentersville. She took secretarial classes and was an average student. But some of her teachers thought perhaps she had more ability. If she would apply herself, they told Bea, maybe she could attend nearby Elgin Community College after graduation. Bea was enthusiastic and promised to help Joyce with expenses if she wanted to go. That evening, Bea discussed the idea with Joyce. Joyce was pleased and decided that Elgin Community College would be her goal. Maybe she could become a nurse. At age sixteen, in her junior year of high school, Joyce finally seemed to be headed in the right direction, for the first time in her life.

The major event in the teenage lives of Joyce and her friends was the weekly trip to The New Place, a converted barn north of Carpentersville on Route 31, near Crystal Lake. It was a teen hangout serving up Cokes and chips and live music—even big groups out of Chicago occasionally played The New Place. Crowds of teens came from the northern suburbs of Chicago—Elgin, Carpentersville, Dundee, Crystal Lake, Cary, Algonquin, all the way up to the Wisconsin state line. There was some beer drinking and pot smoking in the dark parking lot, especially near the motorcycles. But most of all there was dancing to the pounding music.

Joyce met George McDillon at The New Place. He was a year older than she was, a wrestler and football player at affluent Cary Grove High School in nearby Cary, Illinois. Joyce thought George was sexy. He had curly, blondish hair and blue eyes and even, handsome features. George considered himself a ladies' man, and he was captivated by Joyce the first time he saw her. She was dancing with a girlfriend, and she was surrounded by a crowd of admiring guys. They all wanted to dance with her—she looked so good in her tight jeans. But she only wanted to dance with George.

One afternoon George came to the Wojtaneks' house to meet Aunt Bea. He told her that he lived in Cary with his older sister, Sandy, and her husband and three children. His father died when he was very young and his mother had recently passed away. An older brother, Bill, was in military service, and George also intended to enlist after high school. Bea thought George was very handsome. He made a good impression on her, and she liked him well enough.

George began stopping by the Wojtaneks' house to pick Joyce up and take her to McDonald's, the local teen hangout, or to the shopping center. Sometimes Joyce went out with George when she knew she was supposed to stay home and do homework or baby-sit the younger Wojtanek children while Bea worked. Once Mrs. Barthol brought Joyce home after she found her necking with George at the Meadowbrook Shopping Center. "You're not going to be doing that, Joyce," Mrs. Barthol admonished her snappishly. Joyce said nothing.

Bea began to worry that George might be a bad influence on her niece. He seemed to have complete freedom, no restrictions or supervision at home. She suspected that George was encouraging Joyce to evade the Wojtaneks' rules. And she didn't need much encouragement. But for Joyce and George, it was a fantasy teenage romance—riding off together on George's motorcycle, dancing at The New Place, secret meetings, and passionate kisses.

Finally Joyce saved enough money to get her own car. That January, in 1967, Bea and Ed took her to look at a car that a friend had for sale. It was a little red Opel. It looked like a shoebox on wheels, and Joyce loved it. They bought it on the spot.

At first Joyce abided by the restrictions Ed and Bea put on the car. She had to tell them where she was going, couldn't stay out too late, and was allowed to go to The New Place only one night a week. But soon she found ways to evade their strict rules. She would tell them she was going to spend the night with her friend Fran and then sneak off with George to The New Place. Sometimes she spent the night with people who lived at Lake of the Hills, a tiny community near Cary. She told them that Bea and Ed were foster parents who treated her badly.

Although she didn't know about the clandestine trips to The New Place or Lake of the Hills, Bea was growing uneasy. Occasionally Joyce's friends would let slip that she hadn't been at their homes when she said she was. Finally guilt got the better of Joyce's friend Fran, and she told Bea the truth about the nights when Joyce had supposedly been staying at her house. Bea and Ed were angry and upset. They decided they would have to take the car keys away from Joyce.

Joyce was furious. "I need the car! I have to have the car! I want the car!" she screamed.

"I'm sorry, Joyce," Bea said. "These are the rules, and you don't want to live by them. That's it."

Joyce ran to her room and started throwing things. She smashed a ceramic chess set against the wall, piece by piece. It was a beautiful set that Joyce had made herself in the workshop at the Kane County Youth Home. Bea and Ed were dismayed by her rage.

After that, life in the Wojtanek household became a constant battle between Joyce and her aunt over the car keys. Sometimes she would go to her uncle Ed and try to persuade him to let her have her way. But Ed always replied, go talk to your aunt. Bea began to feel that Joyce was disrupting the entire household. The fights, the tantrums, the slamming doors. When their other children started acting up, too, Bea and Ed finally decided they had had enough. Joyce would have to go back to Family Services.

Joyce was sent back to the Kane County Youth Home, a dreary, single-story brick building in a rural area near Geneva. But soon Mrs. Barthol placed her with another foster family, the Tovars, in Dundee, a small town just down the road from Carpentersville. Joyce enrolled at Dundee High School to continue her junior year. The Tovars had several foster children and were very strict. Joyce liked living with them even less than with Bea and Ed.

One day Mrs. Barthol called Bea and said she would have to move Joyce again. There had been some sort of altercation at the Tovars' house—some accusation that Joyce had stolen something, which Joyce vehemently denied. Joyce had pushed Mrs. Tovar down the stairs, they said. She couldn't stay there anymore. Would Bea give her another chance?

"Well, all right, we'll try it," Bea agreed reluctantly.

Joyce came back to the Wojtaneks, promising to turn over a new leaf. She managed to finish her junior year in high school, and for a while everything went well. But eventually the same problems reappeared—lying, sneaking off with George McDillon. This time Ed decided to sell the little red Opel.

After that, Joyce was determined to get out of the Wojtaneks' house for good. But she wouldn't be going to the Kane County Youth Home or another foster home. She would have a home and a family all her own—she would marry George McDillon. George had graduated from Cary Grove High School in June 1967, and signed up for the army as he had planned. He expected to be sent to Vietnam and wanted to marry Joyce before he left. His sister, Sandy, was in favor of the plan. The newlyweds could live with her, she said.

Joyce was seventeen years old, beginning her senior year at Irving Crown High School, and Bea did her best to dissuade her. "Joyce, don't get married," she pleaded. "Don't let this push you into marriage because it might be worse than what you've got now. Think about it. Just to say I'm getting married so I can live on my own—it isn't that easy."

But Joyce was determined to go through with it. She never really felt she belonged with the Wojtaneks. If she had any doubts about George McDillon, she pushed them aside. They were really in love. And anyway, it was too late to turn back.

Since Joyce was only seventeen, she needed consent to be married. Bea flatly refused, but somehow Joyce talked Mrs. Barthol into giving the county's consent. Joyce and George planned to be married by a justice of the peace on November 10, 1967. George's sister, Sandy, would host the wedding reception at her house in Cary. Bea and Ed were not invited to the wedding or the reception.

Bea was heartsick. On Joyce's wedding day, when girlfriends came to the Wojtaneks' house to help the bride dress, Bea took her baby daughter, Amy, and fled. She couldn't bear to watch Joyce leave. The afternoon turned cloudy, dreary. With only George's sister in attendance, Joyce and George were married in a brief, perfunctory ceremony in the little town of Woodstock, Illinois. On her wedding day, Joyce briefly wondered whether she was doing the right thing. But she was determined to get on with her life.

Soon after the wedding, George was posted overseas to Germany, and Joyce remained behind with Sandy and her husband and three children. Joyce transferred to Cary Grove High School to complete her senior year. And she discovered that she was pregnant.

By the time she graduated from high school in June 1968, Joyce was seven or eight months pregnant, somewhat scandalous in a small midwestern town, even though she was married. She felt awkward and uncomfortable, and she hardly knew anyone at Cary Grove High. By then, Joyce's only educational goal was simply to graduate from high school. She joined no clubs, took part in no extracurricular activities. Neither teachers nor counselors remembered her later. Her name and face were not in the Cary Grove High School yearbook for 1968, nor in the Irving Crown High School yearbooks for 1966 and 1967. She passed through her high school years leaving little trace, almost as if she had never been there.

Shawn William McDillon was born in Sherman Hospital in Elgin on August 4, 1968. Joyce was barely eighteen years old. Shawn was a beautiful baby, as his mother had been. He had Joyce's dark, slightly almond eyes.

Joyce called her aunt Bea from the hospital and asked her to come see the baby. It was the first time she had called Bea in months. Nobody would come and see her, Joyce complained. George was still overseas, and she had had a spat with her sister-in-law, Sandy. She asked Bea to buy some clothes for the baby. She had nothing for him to wear home from the hospital. One more thing, Joyce said. I need some clothes, too. And get me a girdle! I've got to have a girdle!

Bea took time off from her job, shopped for the new baby, and then went to Sherman Hospital. She thought little Shawn was beautiful. She brought him a kimono, a receiving blanket, booties, shirts. She told Joyce she couldn't afford to buy new clothes for her, too, but she did bring her a girdle.

Then Joyce told Bea about her troubles with her sister-in-law. "Can I come and live with you?" she pleaded.

"You can't, Joyce," Bea said flatly. "We have no room for you and the baby. We just put the house all back together, and Ed and I have our own bedroom now. I can't disrupt everybody again."

"Well, what am I going to do?" Joyce wailed. "Sandy won't let me back in the house."

"Are you sure? Why don't you call Sandy and talk to her?"

Bea never knew how Joyce managed it, but Sandy finally went to the hospital to pick up Joyce and Shawn. Bea was pleased when Joyce called and asked her to be the baby's godmother. George came home in time for the christening, which was held at Cary's only Catholic church. Sandy had a party at her house after the christening, and this time Ed and Bea were invited. Bea began to hope the marriage might turn out better than she had anticipated.

After George was discharged from the service, he came home and went to work as a drywall carpenter. George and Joyce and Shawn lived in an apartment in Carpentersville for a while. Later they bought a small house in Lake of the Hills. George's brother, Bill, also returned to Cary and married his girlfriend, Beckie. Bill was a drywall carpenter, too, and he and George worked on construction jobs together. Life seemed settled and comfortable for the McDillon brothers and their families.

Bill and Beckie McDillon were a friendly, outgoing couple, and they liked Joyce right away. They thought she looked like an Indian with her long, straight dark hair, but she told them she was part Hawaiian. Bill and Beckie adored Shawn, and they could see Joyce was a very good mother. Soon Bill and Beckie had a child of their own, a son named Todd. And when Todd and Shawn were toddlers, Beckie would play her guitar and sing country songs while the little boys danced.

Sometimes Beckie took care of Shawn while Joyce worked. Joyce tried several jobs, off and on—secretarial jobs, telephone sales. Finally she got her real estate license and decided to try her hand at selling homes. But the market was slow, and she managed to earn only one small commission.

George and Joyce loved each other passionately, but soon the arguments and fights began. It seemed that most of their problems started with money. George complained to his brother that if he made $600, Joyce spent $800; if he made $800, she spent $1,000. One day George came to work fuming. Joyce had spent $165 on peacock feathers. What were the feathers for? Bill asked curiously. Just for decoration—to set next to the living room couch. Bill was mystified.

Beckie knew Joyce had really good taste and always wanted the best of everything—clothes, perfume, jewelry, whatever the best brands were from year to year. And she always shopped at the best stores in town, at full price. This surprised Beckie a little, because she had heard that Joyce was raised in poverty. Where did she pick up these habits? Joyce told Beckie about the Clanceys, the wealthy foster family she had lived with, in a big, beautiful house. There was a daughter in the family, and Joyce always felt inferior to her, coming from the background she did. But now Joyce wanted to be just like that girl.

For entertainment, Beckie and Joyce sometimes went to garage sales together. Joyce always looked for big, fancy homes where they might find something really fine that rich people were selling. It seemed to Beckie that she went to see the homes more than to shop at the sales. She could just imagine Joyce dreaming of living in one of those big homes and having that kind of garage sale herself. And that kind of life.

Joyce decided she had to get out of Illinois. She hated the cold, dreary weather, and she complained that George was spending too much time drinking in the bars with his friends. Maybe they would get along better if she could get George away from there, she explained to Beckie. She was ambitious. Why shouldn't she try to better herself? No one would want to live the way she had as a child. Joyce didn't intend to end up like her mother, Eileen, dying a sad, lonely death in a pitiful flophouse.

Joyce had an idea where she might find the life she wanted: Florida. The weather was sunny and warm, and Florida had a certain glamorous aura that appealed to her. She made up her mind to go. "We have nothing here," she told George. "Let's go and try it."

Finally George agreed. He got a job as a drywall carpenter on a condominium project in Coral Springs, Florida, just north of Fort Lauderdale. They sold their furniture and the house in Lake of the Hills and prepared to move.

Before they left, Joyce went to say good-bye to Bea. "Aunt Bea, we're moving to Florida," she announced, "because George wants to."

"But, Joyce, you'll be so far away from everybody." Aunt Bea was dismayed.

"That's better," Joyce replied.

In 1973, George, Joyce, and Shawn McDillon moved to Florida in search of a better life. But a year later, George McDillon was back in Illinois—alone.

It was years before Bea saw her niece again. Then one Saturday afternoon she returned from grocery shopping to find a neighbor boy on his bicycle waiting for her in the driveway. "You'll never guess who was here!" the boy shouted. "You'll never guess in a million years! I couldn't believe it when I saw her. Joyce!"

"Oh, you're kidding," Bea replied. "What would she be doing here?"

"She's coming back. She said she'll be back later."

Bea could hardly believe Joyce would turn up in her old Carpentersville neighborhood without any warning. But a few hours later, she pulled up in front of the Wojtaneks' house on Topeka Drive, driving a sleek, expensive rental car. Bea was thrilled to see her and awestruck by how beautiful she looked—so nicely dressed in obviously expensive clothes, purse, and shoes.

Joyce told her aunt all about her wonderful marriage to her fabulously wealthy new husband, Stan Cohen—how much he loved her, how rich he was, what a wonderful life they had together. She didn't mention that her divorce from George McDillon was final only ten days before her second wedding. But where was Joyce's new husband? Aunt Bea expected to meet him. Stan couldn't come this time, Joyce replied. He was too busy—and Shawn couldn't come, either. Aunt Bea assumed Joyce would be staying the night with her, but she had a reservation at Chateau Louise, the only really fancy motel in the area. Bea was impressed that Joyce could afford to stay there.

Joyce called her former sister-in-law, Beckie McDillon, who still lived in nearby Cary, Illinois. They hadn't kept in touch, and Beckie, who was still happily married to Bill McDillon, was surprised to hear from her. Beckie promptly invited Joyce to come for a visit. She looked great, Beckie thought—so thin and tanned, with her shiny, dark hair perfectly coiffed. And she was beautifully dressed in pants and a matching top, with lots of necklaces, bracelets, and diamonds. Joyce said she was on her way home to Miami from Colorado, where she had been vacationing. Beckie was impressed.

"You must be doing fine, Joyce," Beckie remarked admiringly. She had heard that Joyce was married again, but she didn't know who her new husband was. Joyce didn't mention him.

Then Joyce asked Beckie where she could find her ex-husband, George McDillon. Beckie was surprised. Well, she thought, maybe Joyce isn't so happy after all. Beckie named a little Mexican restaurant, La Tinita, just outside the nearby town of Woodstock, Illinois. George was playing softball with his buddies, and they often stopped there for a beer after the game. Beckie heard later that Joyce had found George there.

After that, Joyce made regular trips back to northern Illinois, often in August during Cary Days, a sort of fair in Cary. She usually found time to visit her aunt Bea, but she always refused invitations to spend the night with the Wojtaneks. Only once would Joyce stay for dinner, and only once did she bring Shawn along. Stan never came.

Between visits, Joyce bought lavish, impractical gifts for her aunt Bea. She always sent something for Mother's Day, usually a big bouquet of flowers. It seemed to Bea that her niece was trying to repay her, and she was touched by the gesture. Once Joyce sent a huge, decorative Christmas basket—far too large for any space in Bea's living room. Another time Bea came home from the grocery store and noticed what appeared to be a large bush next to the garage door. When she got close, she could see that the bush was a gigantic tropical potted plant. It was from Joyce.

Bea and Ed Wojtanek's son Roy planned to be married on June 16, 1984, in Carpentersville, and Bea asked Joyce to come. It would be a big wedding, with all the Wojtanek relatives in attendance. When Joyce arrived, alone as usual, she looked absolutely stunning—thinner than ever, tan, beautifully dressed. She wore her hair in a chic, straight french bob with bangs, and her makeup looked professional. Years later Bea still marveled at the beautiful white lace dress Joyce wore to the wedding. She was positively glamorous.

Bea kept an album of photographs of Roy's wedding. In the pictures the Wojtanek relatives strongly resembled one another—all fair-haired, blue-eyed, hardworking, plain. Next to them, Joyce Cohen looked like a beautiful, exotic creature—shiny black hair and dark almond eyes, perfect makeup and manicure, exquisite lace dress, and elegant jewelry. Those were the only pictures Bea had of Joyce. The teenage snapshots had vanished. And there never were any baby pictures.

Stan Cohen still hadn't come to Carpentersville. Bea always thought this was odd. Didn't Stan mind his wife traveling so often without him? No, Joyce replied, it's all right with him. Everything is fine. Bea was happy for Joyce. She had a loving husband and all the beautiful things she had always wanted.

After the wedding, Beatrice Wojtanek didn't hear from Joyce again until she called to say that her husband had been killed. Bea had been very sorry to hear it. And now there was this call from a lawyer in Miami who said that Joyce had been convicted of murdering her husband and might go to the electric chair. Why would she do that? Bea wondered. And what could she say about Joyce to explain it when she didn't understand it herself?

# *Twenty-Five*

•

*O*n November 20, the Monday before Thanksgiving, the court reconvened to hear evidence bearing on the sentence to be imposed on Joyce Cohen for the contract murder of her husband. Under Florida law, the jury in a capital case must hear and weigh evidence of aggravating factors and mitigating factors in the commission of the crime. Then the jury deliberates and votes on the two statutory penalties for first-degree murder: life in prison without the possibility of parole for twenty-five years; or death in the electric chair. The jury's vote is termed "advisory" since the judge bears the ultimate responsibility for imposing sentence.

Courtroom 4-2 was jammed as usual, but this time there were some new faces. Shawn was there with his pretty blond wife and infant son. He looked just like his mother—dark, slightly almond eyes, long, dark hair caught in a ponytail at the back. He was twenty-one, and his young, soft face looked somber and vulnerable. His son—Joyce's grandson—sat on his mother's lap, sucking occasionally on a pacifier.

Robert Dietrich was there, handsome in a neat dark suit but teary-eyed. And Joyce's friends turned out in force—Shu Sampson, Sam and Ed Smith, Toni Pollack, and others.

Joyce Cohen entered Courtroom 4-2 through the holding cell. Her appearance was shocking. She wore baggy jeans and a rumpled pink shirt. Her hair was pulled back severely in a french braid, with her gray roots showing and her ears protruding; her face was pale and bloated, her eyes swollen almost shut, no makeup softening the effect. It was Alan Ross's idea. "Let them see how she's going to have to live now," he had said bitterly.

Joyce Cohen looked not like a killer but a victim. She crossed the courtroom and sat between her lawyers at the defense table. Ross rested his arm lightly on the rail behind her chair. "How are you?" he asked quietly. She nodded slightly, looking down, hands clasped in her lap. Ross laid a comforting hand on her arm.

Assistant State Attorney Paul Mendelson addressed the Court. He wanted Joyce Cohen's friends and family excluded from the courtroom if they planned to testify before the jury on her behalf. Then he added, "The state moves to exclude evidence regarding death by electrocution as cruel and unusual punishment."

"We may argue how a person dies in an electric chair—what happens—but we won't go into graphic details," Bob Amsel replied.

It was too much for Joyce. She gulped, swallowed, and started to sob. Ross talked softly to her and she calmed down.

The Cohen family entered the courtroom: Artie Cohen in his motorized wheelchair, and his wife, Mary; Gary Cohen with his wife, Carol; Gerri and Steve Helfman.

The bailiff brought the jury into the jury box, and Judge Smith explained their task. They would hear evidence bearing upon aggravating and mitigating circumstances in the commission of the crime, and they would weigh these factors. Then, after deliberating, they would render an advisory opinion to the Court regarding the sentence to be imposed upon Joyce Cohen. The final decision as to sentencing, Judge Smith emphasized, lay solely with her.

John Kastrenakes rose. "The state relies upon the evidence presented at trial," he announced. He would call no new witnesses.

Bob Amsel called his first witness: Dr. Lawrence Cohn, a Miami psychiatrist, entered the courtroom. He was a small, graying man with glasses, neatly dressed in a dark suit and striped tie. He carried an accordion file bulging with papers. He had first treated Joyce Cohen, Dr. Cohn told the jury, on May 6, 1985, when first she was hospitalized for an overdose of Tylenol and Halcion, a powerful sleep medication. An apparent suicide attempt.

Across the courtroom, Joyce began to sob.

Dr. Cohn read from his notes. Acute and chronic depression—considerable suicidal potential. He had prescribed Mellaril, a tranquilizer, and recommended transfer to a psychiatric hospital. But the patient had refused.

Most of Joyce's friends in the courtroom had no idea she had attempted suicide, and they were shocked and saddened. Even Shawn knew nothing about the episode. But Sam Smith knew. She was the one Joyce had called for help.

After she recovered from her drug overdose, Dr. Cohn continued, Joyce had agreed to see him as an outpatient, and she kept her appointments sporadically for several weeks. She told Dr. Cohn she had been taking Dalmane, a potent sleeping pill, in addition to Halcion. She had great difficulty sleeping, she said.

In her sessions with him, Dr. Cohn testified, Joyce had discussed her relationship with her husband, which was miserable, and her own childhood, which had been even worse. She told him that her mother was a prostitute who had died when she was young, and that she was raised in multiple foster homes. Joyce said that she never knew her father. But she also told Dr. Cohn that her father and some uncles had molested her—"episodes of sexual touching," Dr. Cohn read from his notes. All her life, Joyce told her psychiatrist, she had hated sex.

Shawn, sitting behind his mother, was startled to hear about her unhappy childhood. Whenever he had asked her about her family, she replied only that her parents were dead. He had no idea of how his mother had suffered.

Throughout her childhood, Joyce had told Dr. Cohn, she was desperate to find a family to take care of her. She married Stan Cohen, she said, to have a financially secure father figure for her son and herself. But then she developed terrible fears of losing this "father," and of being poor. Joyce would be anxious about anybody or anything that would be a threat, a rival for Stan's attention, Dr. Cohn explained to the jury. Including Stan's daughter, Gerri. Although Joyce was very dependent and even clinging, she also resented her neediness and the power others, especially Stan, had over her. Eventually she came to hate him. When she took all those pills that landed her in the hospital, Joyce had told Dr. Cohn that she wasn't really trying to kill herself. She just wanted to hurt Stan the way he hurt her. "Spiteful suicide wish," he had written in his notes.

When Joyce stopped seeing Dr. Cohn after a few sessions, he wasn't surprised. Although she was still very depressed, she wasn't ready for serious therapy. She just wasn't willing—or, perhaps, able—to put forth the effort. Instead, Joyce took shortcuts: alcohol (she confessed to "at least four or five drinks a day") and cocaine. She used coke PRN, he explained, as needed when she felt inadequate or insecure.

In November 1985, Dr. Cohn took a panicky phone call from Stan Cohen at 3 A.M. Joyce hadn't slept for a week, and now she felt pain, like electricity going up and down her body. She couldn't even walk. He thought it might be an allergic reaction to the Mellaril he had prescribed for her, Dr. Cohn told the jury. Or she might be having a nervous breakdown. He had suggested that she go to Baptist Hospital, but she refused. Call me tomorrow morning, Dr. Cohn had instructed, but Joyce never called. He phoned her home, and the woman who answered said Joyce was resting.

The next time Dr. Cohn saw Joyce was right after Stan's murder. She appeared to be shocked, disorganized, forgetful, and she was very depressed. She had a lost, childlike quality, he thought.

Dr. Cohn summarized his final diagnosis: borderline personality disorder; dependent personality; severe depression. But this was not a psychotic depression, Dr. Cohn clarified. He saw no evidence of delusions or psychotic thinking. Joyce Cohen was not insane.

Didn't Joyce lie to you about her chronic drug abuse? Kastrenakes asked Dr. Cohn on cross.

She never described chronic drug abuse to me, Dr. Cohn replied. She could have lied to me about some things.

And she told you she wasn't involved in the murder of her husband, Kastrenakes persisted. She didn't admit that she was involved, did she?

She implied that she didn't do it, Cohn answered. She told me she felt guilty about leaving the alarm turned off that night.

Did Joyce's condition lead her to blame her husband for all her problems?

Yes, Cohn replied.

One final question, Kastrenakes said. Can Joyce Cohen be cured?

I have trouble with the word "cured," Dr. Cohn replied. No, one can't be cured in the sense of having no further evidence of problems. Can some people get much better with skillful therapy? Lead a normal life? It's possible. But with this mixture it would take years and years and years. It would require Joyce's active participation.

And she wasn't really committed to treatment, was she? Kastrenakes asked. She just wanted to feel better.

Next Bob Amsel called Sam Smith. By the time she reached the witness stand, she was already teary. Her friend Joyce was often depressed, Sam told the jury, because she suspected Stan of having affairs. One of those affairs drove her to overdose on sleeping pills. Sam sobbed openly, wiping her streaming eyes with a tissue as she described Joyce sitting on the asphalt parking lot at Doctor's Hospital, crying hysterically. She had had to carry her friend into the hospital, Sam said.

At the defense table, Joyce wept.

On cross, John Kastrenakes had one question. "Didn't you tell this jury before that the Cohens' marriage was good?"

"I said it had its ups and downs," Sam replied with a flash of anger. "Just like mine!"

Robert Dietrich took the witness stand and, with tears in his eyes, described the sweet, quiet, gentle woman he had fallen in love with. He looked longingly at Joyce across the courtroom as he said his only regret was that they hadn't married before the trial. In anticipation of her acquittal, he told the jury in his soft voice, they had decided to delay their wedding until after the trial. Now it was too late.

Shawn watched without expression as Dietrich told the jury about his love for Joyce. His words didn't change Shawn's opinion that his mother would have dumped Dietrich if she had been acquitted.

Joyce's aunt Beatrice Wojtanek testified via a telephone hookup broadcast into the courtroom. Her voice shook with sobs as she described her niece's childhood. They lived in a helper's shack, she said, and they all chopped cotton in the fields. Joyce's first marriage had been a mistake, and Aunt Bea had lost touch with her niece after she moved to Florida.

Then, when Joyce married Stan Cohen, Aunt Bea thought she had turned her life around. But "Joyce knew how to cover things up," she sighed. "She'd mask it so you wouldn't know anything was wrong." Still, even if there had been problems in the marriage, she would never believe Joyce had murdered her husband. "I don't think they should take her life," Aunt Bea said, weeping over the long-distance line. "I don't think she deserves it. She had a rough life, very rough. I wouldn't want any of my kids to live life like that." The line went dead.

"Good afternoon." John Kastrenakes addressed the jury in his final argument. "It's been a long one and a half months. Now you are coming to the end of your duties. You must decide what to recommend this murderer," he paused to gesture at Joyce, "should get for the contract murder of her husband. . . .

"You have clear definitions of aggravating and mitigating circumstances. You must weigh them and decide which is heavier. If the aggravating circumstances are heavier, she should get the death penalty. If the mitigating are heavier, life in prison without possibility of parole for twenty-five years.

"You are not responsible for the decision you're about to make," Kastrenakes reminded the intent jury. "*She* put herself in that chair, in that predicament. You played no role in her decision to end her marriage with a .38-caliber revolver. . . . She carefully considered and weighed her options. And she chose an illegal option."

Kastrenakes argued that two aggravating factors warranted the death penalty for Joyce Cohen. She killed her husband for financial gain; and she planned the crime in a cold, calculated manner, inviting hired killers in to murder her sleeping, defenseless husband "in his castle" and calmly waiting downstairs while they finished the job.

"Look at the pictures of the Good Friends Party. You know she was putting the best face on it. The marriage was horrible. He held her hand, they smiled for the picture. What's she thinking? 'How am

I going to have him killed? How's he going to die so no one will know about it?' That's cold. . . .

"She's a great actress, folks. And why was this murder committed? It's for money. The most evil of all reasons to commit a crime. A murder that's committed for the love of money—avarice, greed—knows no equal.

"Are you troubled by her early childhood? Where is the nexus between her childhood and this crime? There is none. From the time Joyce was ten, she was in loving families. She was taught the difference between right and wrong. She knew the difference. Here's what Joyce Cohen's childhood has to do with this case: She didn't want to go back to being poor. If she had to take out her husband to do it, so be it.

"This is evil," Kastrenakes concluded. "The only just recommendation—the only one that speaks the truth—is a recommendation to Judge Smith that this defendant be put to death for her crime. Follow your oaths."

With Alan Ross sitting silently at the front of the courtroom, Bob Amsel strode to the podium. "By your verdict," he began, his eyes searching the jurors' faces, "you have ensured that Joyce Cohen will spend the rest of her life in jail. That is no longer an issue. You've worked hard. I respect your decision, although I'm disappointed. So the issue is not whether Joyce Cohen will get a break. She will not get a break. The issue is whether the state has proved, beyond every reasonable doubt, that there's only one sentence for this case: to kill this woman.

"It's easy to say, 'Kill this woman because *she* killed *him*,' " Amsel continued. "But this isn't a Roman amphitheater where we throw her to the lions. This is a court of law. You have two concerns: punishment and protecting society. Killing Joyce Cohen is not necessary to accomplish these things. Keeping Joyce Cohen in jail for the rest of her life will accomplish those things without taking another life. Joyce won't commit any more crimes.

"Look at the disparity between Joyce Cohen and Frank Zuccarello. I don't know what you thought of Zuccarello. But that man is everyone's nightmare. That man, who's loose on the streets now. How is Frank Zuccarello, who's still on the street, punished? This prosecution asks you to kill Joyce Cohen while it lets Frank Zuccarello go free.

"You're considering whether to have Joyce Cohen wiped off the face of the earth," Amsel continued solemnly. "You should know what kind of person she is. She is *not* a rich lady with a rosy life and no problems. . . . Her marriage wasn't a bed of roses. The marriage had major problems. Stan Cohen had affairs, not once but twice. Joyce knew. And she tried to kill herself over it.

"Some of you have dogs. I'm sure you treat your dogs better than Joyce Cohen was treated as a child. Joyce was moved from home to home. She was abused. And that does something to you. It's like a child who does something bad. If we see no reason for it, we punish the child more. But if we see the child is troubled, maybe we understand a little more. So the law recognizes this mitigating factor.

"Joyce Cohen is not a monster. Joyce Cohen is not a cold-blooded killer. A serial killer who goes on killing people—that's why we have the death penalty.

"Think about Joyce Cohen's life in jail. She will be sleeping in a small room with a toilet in the middle of it, sharing it with someone else. For the rest of her life, Joyce Cohen will not have a home-cooked meal, hold loved ones, be able to walk in a field, see the stars. She'll be told when to get up, eat, sleep. December 31, 1999, when we're toasting the new century—she'll be in jail. In 2009, Joyce Cohen will still be in jail. Is that not punishment? It may be a fate worse than death.

"Stan Cohen is dead. He died instantaneously. He didn't suffer. Killing Joyce Cohen doesn't bring Stan Cohen back. What is accomplished by it? Nothing.

"I stand here," Amsel said as he gripped the podium with both hands, "more scared than I've ever been in my life. Maybe I've missed something or not said the right words. I ask each of you to make the argument for life to the other jurors, in case I've missed something. I ask you, ladies and gentlemen of the jury, in the name of justice and in the name of mercy—come back with a verdict which says, 'We believe in the sanctity of life. Joyce Cohen, we're going to let you live—but never among us again.' Thank you."

• • •

Throughout the hearing, Joyce sat quietly sobbing, her small feet encased in shapeless prison slippers, dangling short of the floor.

At 5:40 P.M., the jury returned to the cramped jury room for the last time. Robert Dietrich reached over the rail to touch Joyce Cohen's shoulder. The bailiff noticed, frowned, and shook his head. Dietrich hastily withdrew his hand. Joyce returned to the holding cell to await the jury's recommendation.

While the jury deliberated, Alan Ross worried about his young partner, Bob Amsel. He was afraid that if the worst happened, if the jury recommended the death penalty, Amsel would take it all on his own shoulders and be crushed by the burden. "Bob," Ross told him. "If the jury recommends life, I just want you to know that this lady owes you her life for the fine job you did here."

Amsel did not reply.

At 6:15—only thirty-five minutes later—the jury sent a note to the judge. Joyce Cohen was led back into the courtroom. She looked composed but exhausted, drained. She sat down carefully, as if she were suddenly very old. The jurors filed to their seats. They did not look at the defendant.

Jury foreperson Dr. Catherine Poole handed the form to Judge Smith's clerk, who passed it to the bench. Judge Smith read aloud, "The jury's advisory sentence is for life imprisonment."

A majority of the jurors felt that Joyce Cohen should be spared the death penalty because of one mitigating factor: Frank Zuccarello would never even be charged with the crime. It seemed unfair that Joyce should die for her part, while Zuccarello walked the streets a free man.

But four jurors had voted for the death penalty.

There was silence, solemn faces. Judge Smith discharged the jury with her thanks for their long and difficult service.

The jurors were glad to leave. It had been a wrenching experience. Outside the Metropolitan Justice Building, some reporters pursued the departing jurors with minicams, tracking them to their cars in the dark parking lot across the street. But none of them wanted to talk about their ordeal. They had made a pact not to discuss it.

Judge Smith would review the jury's recommendation overnight and sentence Joyce Cohen the following day. But first she would hear from the victim's family.

• • •

That night Gerri Helfman pondered once more whether to speak out after her long years of silence. Finally she decided she should address the Court. It was the last thing she could do for her father. Gerri knew her brother and her uncle Artie intended to ask Judge Smith to impose the death penalty on her stepmother. But Gerri wasn't so sure. She had always been squeamish about the death penalty. Besides, she reasoned, Joyce would probably suffer more living in prison for the next twenty-five years or so.

Gerri called Gary. What should she say about the penalty? she asked. Gary told her he felt that the family should be united. If Gerri wasn't comfortable advocating the death penalty for their stepmother, perhaps she shouldn't mention punishment at all. Just tell Judge Smith what was on her mind without asking for a particular penalty.

Finally Gerri reached her decision. As she had throughout the long years of their ordeal, she would follow her brother's lead. She sat down to make notes on what she would tell Judge Smith.

On Tuesday, November 21, two days before Thanksgiving, Judge Smith reconvened the Joyce Cohen case for the last time. The defendant entered the courtroom from the holding cell, dressed in a shapeless black sweater, white blouse, and baggy jeans. Her hair was plaited in another french braid.

John Kastrenakes rose and addressed the Court. "Your Honor, we do wish to call a few witnesses to make comments to the Court concerning sentencing. We will first call Mr. Gary Cohen, the son of the victim, to come forward and address the Court."

Gary strode quickly to the podium, carrying his notes. He was deadly calm. "Judge, I'm here before you to request on behalf of myself, my father, and my family that you impose the death penalty in this case. I think the death penalty is fair and correct for all the reasons pointed out by Mr. Kastrenakes in his closing argument yesterday.

"With respect to the mitigating factors the defense talked about yesterday, I think certainly one of those factors did exist. I think it's clear that the marriage was over, notwithstanding what the defense character witnesses said in the guilt/innocence phase of the trial. Those people who either didn't know my father and Joyce well enough to realize that there were problems in the marriage, or chose to ignore them and testified differently during the trial, now come up during the sentencing portion of the trial and tell you, 'Yes, there were problems.' And that this should be a valid mitigating factor in not imposing the death penalty. I don't understand that."

Gary seethed with anger, especially at his father's old friend Ed Smith. He found it difficult to believe that Smith had not known about Joyce's coke habit and the Cohens' severe marital problems. In Gary's view, Ed had betrayed his father, and Gary could never forgive, would never forget.

"Defense pled for mercy yesterday in this case," Gary continued. "They argued that she wasn't a Bundy and she wasn't a Manson, and those are the kind of people that deserve the death penalty. I'd agree she's not that type of person, because those people were defective and they didn't know what they were doing. What she did was worse. She knew exactly what she was doing. She knew it was wrong to kill our father. She knew how heinous it was. And she went ahead and did it anyway. . . .

"I don't think she deserves to live after she deprived him of his life. . . . If you can't find it in you to impose the death penalty, I would say at the absolute minimum that you should maximize the jail time so she doesn't ever have to live among us again. Thank you."

Artie Cohen, Stan's brother, maneuvered his motorized wheelchair to the well of the court to address Judge Smith. "On March 7, I was the one that had to tell my mother that her son was dead. She said, 'The children have to bury parents, not the parents bury the children.' My mother went downhill after that. I watched her for ten days in a coma at Baptist Hospital, going in and out, saying, 'I want to die.'

"When Stan died, she died. It took a year.

"Stan was the focal point of the family. He took care of my mother. He said, 'Artie, I'll always be there for you.' Obviously, I have problems. They are never going to get better, only worse. I don't have my brother anymore to take care of me. Joyce took care of that."

Finally it was Gerri Helfman's turn. Stark and elegant in a simple black suit, she walked briskly to the podium. "Nearly four years ago," she began in a strong, clear voice, "I was awakened in the early morning hours and told that my father had been murdered. Since that day I have avoided making any public comments about my father's murder. . . . But I think it's appropriate today to share some of my thoughts with you as you decide the punishment that Joyce deserves for murdering my father.

"Yesterday the defense begged for mercy for Joyce. She had no mercy for my father when she murdered him, no mercy at all. The defense said that Joyce's life should be spared because of the sanctity of life. Where was the sanctity of life when she killed my father? My father's life has to mean something in this process. Otherwise I just won't understand it. . . .

"What's offensive is Mr. Amsel's suggestion that because my father died instantaneously and somehow didn't suffer, that she shouldn't suffer with the death penalty. I would suggest that death by the electric chair is also instantaneous and an appropriate penalty."

Her harsh words hung in the air.

"Three days after my father was murdered, I got a call from Kings Bay Travel," Gerri continued. The travel agent had told her that her father had purchased a travel voucher as a surprise wedding present. When her father was killed the agent called Joyce, thinking she would want to pass the gift along to Gerri. "The agent told me that Joyce told her to cancel it and not tell me about it. That's the kind of caring, loving person Joyce is," Gerri said bitterly. "My father had just been murdered, and *she* would prefer for me to spend the rest of my life not knowing that he cared enough to buy me a wedding present, to go out and surprise me with a wedding present.

"She killed my father three weeks before I got married," Gerri's voice began to quaver, "depriving me, more importantly depriving my father of walking me down the aisle, of giving me, his only daughter, away. She prevented my father from enjoying life. He never met his grandchildren. I have a five-month-old baby at home, and he'll never know his grandfather. My brother has a nine-month-old baby, and he'll never know his grandfather because *she* killed him. He'll never enjoy his grandchildren, and they'll never enjoy him.

"Why should she enjoy one day left of her life? She deserves to spend the rest of her life in prison, and she deserves to die in prison. Thank you."

Gerri turned and walked back to her seat beside her husband. She passed within three feet of Joyce, sitting at counsel table between her lawyers. But she never glanced her way.

Finally Judge Smith was ready to address the courtroom. As she took out her prepared notes, Gerri was dismayed. She had hoped the family's remarks might have some impact on the judge's decision. Now she felt the whole process was a sham. Victims and their families really had no rights, she thought bitterly.

But Judge Smith was bound by law to follow the jury's recommendation for mercy unless there were legal grounds for a "jury override," as it is called. And even the prosecutors agreed that no such grounds existed.

"I'd like you to come forward, please," Judge Smith said to Joyce Cohen. As before, Joyce stood between her lawyers in front of the judge's high bench.

"The jury has found you guilty of first-degree murder beyond a reasonable doubt," Judge Smith began. "They have recommended that you be sentenced to life in prison without parole for twenty-five years. . . . Unless I can say that the facts suggesting a death sentence are so clear and convincing that no reasonable person could disagree, I am bound to follow the jury's recommendation. That is the law.

"The law is no longer an eye for an eye, a tooth for a tooth, a wound for a wound," said the judge, searching the faces of Stan Cohen's family in the gallery. "Although such a law may comfort the victim's family, and satisfy a primitive and really human need for retribution, it is not the law of the state of Florida.

"I agree with the jury that the mitigating circumstances outweigh the aggravating circumstances," Judge Smith concluded.

For first-degree murder, the contract murder of Stan Cohen, the judge sentenced Joyce to life in prison without possibility of parole for twenty-five years. On the conspiracy count, she imposed a sentence of fifteen years in state prison to be served consecutively to the life sentence. For the display of a firearm during the commission of a felony, the sentence was fifteen years to run concurrently with the other sentences.

Joyce will be at least sixty-four years old before she is eligible for consideration for parole.

• • •

Outside the courtroom, Gary and Gerri collided with Ed Smith. "We don't appreciate it that you lied on the stand," Gary growled, still fuming over Smith's favorable testimony on behalf of Joyce.

Smith bristled. He believed he had testified truthfully.

"Well, you got what you wanted—the money," he retorted.

"Forget it, Gary." Gerri laid a restraining hand on her brother's arm. "He's just an asshole."

Smith brushed past them, headed toward the escalator. Then suddenly he turned on Gerri. "Nice talk for a TV girl!" he shouted, red-faced. "You cunt!"

Steve Helfman rushed over and grabbed Smith by the lapels. A bailiff standing nearby pinned Steve's arms and hustled him off down the hall. Ed Smith fled.

The confrontation took place just beyond the boundary line for the television news crews. They could see it, but they couldn't quite hear it—and they couldn't throw enough light down the hall to film it.

The nightly news miniseries of the Joyce Cohen murder trial was finally over.


Ross and Amsel drove back to their office in separate cars. They arrived at the same time and parked their cars side by side in the lot.

Ross was still devastated, exhausted. But he thought his young partner needed some reassurance about the case. "Bob, I just want you to know something," he began. "Thank God for the job you did. If you hadn't done such a spectacular job on the penalty phase, I'm sure that this jury, as cold-hearted as they were, would have recommended death."

Amsel gazed at him a moment. "Well, if you had held up your end, we wouldn't have gotten that far," he replied coolly.

Ross stared at Amsel. Then both erupted in hysterical laughter, the first moment of relief they had had in weeks.


Thanksgiving was a real holiday for Gary and Gerri and their families. After nearly four years of anguish, they had achieved their objective. Their stepmother was in prison for their father's murder. But now came the hardest part—the day-to-day living without him, knowing that past wounds had left permanent scars.

In the weeks that followed Joyce's trial, Gerri often visited her father's grave. She had things to tell him, things she didn't get to say before he died. She hoped her father knew how much she loved him. And she understood how much he loved her, despite the gulf between them. But the chance to tell him face-to-face that she knew all along, that she understood, was gone forever.

At her father's grave, Gerri spoke to him aloud. And she waited and watched for an answer, a sign.

But there was none.

A year later Gerri was watching her young son, Douglas, striding around the room. His sandy brown hair and bright eyes were a blend of the features of his parents. He didn't really look much like his grandfather Stanley, but people told Gerri that he reminded them of him somehow. Maybe it was the way Douglas walked, she thought, his tough-guy swagger, his take-on-the-world stance. For Gerri, it was some solace.

It would have to be enough.

# Epilogue

Alan Ross filed an appeal of Joyce Cohen's criminal conviction in Miami's Third District Court of Appeal, the courthouse that Stan Cohen built. Shawn had agreed to give Ross $120,000 out of his inheritance from his stepfather to pay for the appeal. He later reneged, and Ross eventually settled for $40,000.

In the civil case filed against Joyce Cohen by Gary Cohen and Gerri Cohen Helfman, the Third District Court of Appeal upheld the trial court's ruling that under a Florida statute, Joyce's murder conviction stripped her of any right to her husband's estate and life insurance proceeds. His heirs, Gary Cohen, Gerri Cohen Helfman, Michael Cohen, Shawn Cohen, and Arthur Cohen, each received $85,000 from Stan's life insurance proceeds. Shawn paid Alan Ross the $40,000 out of his share.

When Stan Cohen's estate was settled, there was not enough cash to fund the specific cash bequests that he had made to his heirs in his will. Gary and Gerri each received $60,000 in cash and property valued at $145,000. Arthur and Michael Cohen each received $30,000 in cash and $72,500 in property. Shawn had already renounced his interest under the will in exchange for a quick cash settlement. He needed the money.

Ross calculated that he was owed nearly $1.5 million in fees for the criminal case. He predicted that Joyce's conviction would be overturned on appeal and that she would be acquitted on retrial. Then he would get paid. If necessary, Ross said, he would pursue Gary and Gerri for their inheritance to pay his attorney's fees.

Anthony Caracciolo and Tommy Lamberti finally cut a deal with the state. They pleaded "no contest" to reduced charges of second-degree murder. Caracciolo was sentenced to forty-one years, and Lamberti got thirty-nine. The sentences were concurrent to the already lengthy terms both men were presently serving for numerous home invasion robberies.

Caracciolo and Lamberti insisted that they pleaded "no contest" only as a matter of convenience, to avoid the possibility of the death penalty if they were convicted at trial. Both still claim that they had nothing to do with Stan Cohen's murder. They never even met Joyce Cohen, they say.

At his sentencing hearing, Tommy Lamberti was granted permission to address the Court. Gary, who had been following the case, was sitting in the gallery, his long vigil about to end. Wearing wrist and ankle shackles, his full-color Donald Duck tattoo decorating his right forearm, Lamberti stood and spoke. "I wish to address Mr. Gary Cohen and Your Honor. I feel bad about your father, and I know what it is like to lose a family member. I lost mine.

"I assure you I am the wrong man in this courtroom. I am just taking this plea because it is in my best interest. I don't care what they think, I am innocent. . . . I offered, since the day I have been arrested, to take a polygraph test and they have refused me. . . . I maintain my innocence on this, and I am still willing to take a polygraph test just to prove my innocence. All I want is for someone to believe me."

Outside in the corridor, the prosecutors shook their heads in disgust at Lamberti's performance. But someone was listening to Lamberti. Special Agent Steve Emerson, the detective from the Florida Department of Law Enforcement, still wondered whether Lamberti was really involved. "I had a good relationship with him," Emerson said. "I think he would have copped out to me if he did it."

The case still haunted Bob Amsel. And his client remained an enigma. "I'm sure there are things about Joyce Cohen that we will never know, that she never told anyone. Her deepest, darkest secret. . . . I will never know to the day I die whether she did it or not."

In the aftermath of the trial, Len Levenstein no longer had any doubt that Joyce had engineered her husband's murder. And he thought he understood why. "I think she panicked," he said. "It wasn't a split-second reaction. I think she panicked over a period of months over a situation she was losing control of." She was afraid of losing the money—and the Jaguar, the fancy homes, the clothes and jewelry it bought. But more fundamentally she was afraid of losing herself—her identity, which was so closely bound up with the Miami lifestyle Stan provided and then threatened to take away. She could never go back to her old life, to being that Joyce. "I'm not a psychiatrist," Len concluded, "but I've got to believe that somewhere, sometime, subconsciously a decision was made. It's him or me." Either she would have that life or he would. And she chose herself.

Joyce Cohen lives at the women's maximum-security prison, the Broward Correctional Institution, north of Miami on the Dade-Broward county line. The prison is a series of connected two-story cement buildings painted battleship gray, with surprising pink trim around the doorways. The buildings surround a large grassy square. Cement benches line cement walkways criss-crossing the yard. A few small shrubs and spindly palms break the monotony.

On a hot May afternoon in 1991, inmates—mostly young black women—were gathered on the cement benches, chatting and blinking in the bright sunshine. Their prison uniforms resembled a surrealistic 1950s party—short-sleeved, shapeless chemise-style dresses in pastel green or yellow, white tennis shoes and socks. Some of the dresses bulged over pregnant bellies. There were elaborate hairstyles: french braids and cornrows.

Inside, the prison cafeteria served as an interview room. Green stripes bordered the peach walls. Fast-food restaurant–style tables and booths in butcher block Formica were scattered about the large room. A few straggly plants hung from the ceiling.

There were posters: JUST SAY NO TO DRUGS. "If you're torn apart by stress, anxiety or depression, call toll-free." On a plaque decorated with bluebirds and pink blossoms: "This new dining booth is dedicated to Mrs. Kathy Hartog, a woman who committed herself to the tireless pursuit of making your dining area a pleasurable experience."

It could have been a high school cafeteria. Except for its clientele.

Joyce Cohen wore a yellow prison dress and espadrilles. Her hair was clean, full, soft, curly—a noticeably lighter shade of brown than before, lightly streaked with gray. (Hair coloring is not permitted in prison.) She seemed fit, rested, self-assured. She was very tan, with a fine sprinkling of freckles across her nose.

"Not much to do here on weekends except sit in the sun—and keep an eye on your laundry!" she said with a laugh.

Joyce looked great. She smiled that big smile, those white, even teeth, eyes crinkling up at the corners, reliving her romance with Stan Cohen. "I remember seeing him on the construction job, by the sales office. And of course people would say, 'That's the new general contractor,' or whatever. He was really nice, he was funny to talk to. Very enthusiastic. He was always real tan. He had a boat at the time and I guess he spent a lot of time out there. And his hair was real long, real full. Yeah, it was real long.

"I think it was his personality and his charisma [that attracted me]. He really was very charismatic. There was kind of an aura about him, I always thought, that kind of attracted people to him. . . . Well, we would just talk, right? And he asked me to lunch, and we went to lunch several times and just got to know each other. He was excellent with Shawn.

"We went to the Down Under in Fort Lauderdale for dinner. It was real nice. That was our first date. . . . We were seeing each other. . . . And then he went on a motorcycle trip in Europe and he was gone for several weeks. And then he returned. I had missed him a lot and he missed me. And we just started talking. . . . And we talked about getting married and things. And we decided to get married. . . .

"I loved him and I think it's— There are a lot of things. He was older than me, and a lot of people thought that was strange and things. But I think, in a lot of ways, I think I saw the security. And please, I'm not meaning financial security at this point, although that does enter into it. What I mean is just someone stable, someone that would really be there. And someone that cared about my son and I.

"And that was a big thing to me, the way I grew up. Someone that would love my son, and Shawn would also have a safe, secure, stable home. And that played a big part in it, because I may not have married as quickly if it were just me to think about. Although, like I said, I really did love Stan. . . .

"Stan was so much of a protector for me. Like he sheltered me so much from anything that could have hurt me or anything. So he didn't just thrust me into these people and leave me. He was there, for me to lean on and things. . . . He was a very giving man to the people he cared about and loved. . . . He would buy me one fabulous present a year. I mean, I bought all the things I wanted. . . . During the year, he didn't like to shop, so it was just kind of like, this was our thing. Rather than him going out and getting things that really didn't mean anything, he'd rather just get something. . . . I mean, he was very generous and things. One year he gave me a full-length red fox coat. He gave me diamond studs. A Rolex.

"When he got me my diamond studs, I didn't know what he got me. When he got me a necklace with diamonds, I didn't know what it was going to be. He was good about that. Our last anniversary. He got me a beautiful ring. I really couldn't describe it. It was just real, real pretty. I had seen a picture of it and he ordered it for me. It was more than enough. It was a wonderful gift. I was surprised, really. He was very generous and things, but that was an exceptionally nice present. . . .

"A funny thing with the ring. When the ring came, he called me from his office and said . . . to meet him at Burdine's, he was picking up some clothers. I'd drag him over to Burdine's or Baron's a couple of times a year to shop. He hated to shop! So he said he had to go over there, so I met him there. And we were sitting there in the men's section, and he just tossed this box on my lap and said, 'Oh, here, by the way. I've got something [for you].' I opened it and there it was!" Joyce laughed heartily at the memory."

[December 1985] was our last anniversary. I think it was our twelfth. We would have been married thirteen years."

[But you were married in 1974, right?]

"Yeah. I don't know why, all these dates and things, it's very confusing. And time in here has no meaning."

The interview concluded, and Joyce began to chat happily with Alan Ross about her pending appeal.

Her conviction was just a horrible mistake. "I'll be out of here by Christmas!" she said. "And I'll need a job. Maybe I'll come to work for you, Alan, as your secretary. You need a new one!"

• • •

On June 11, 1991, the Third District Court of Appeal affirmed Joyce Cohen's convictions and sentences for first-degree murder, conspiracy to commit murder, and display of a firearm during the commission of a felony. Her attorneys filed a petition for review with the Florida Supreme Court.

On December 5, 1991, the Florida Supreme Court denied Joyce Cohen's petition for review.

# *Acknowledgments*

•

I embarked on this project three years ago with no idea how difficult it would be—or even whether it was possible. It was possible, I discovered, but only because of the assistance, encouragement, and support of many fine people. I wish to thank them here.

First the professionals: To Herman Klurfeld, my good friend and a fine writer, my deepest thanks for years of advice and encouragement. And to John Boswell, my agent and a terrifically successful writer and book packager, who bravely agreed to take on my first project. Through his efforts, I gained the invaluable assistance and inspiration of Fred W. Hills, brilliant senior editor at Simon & Schuster, and his excellent professional team, especially Burton Beals. I'm very grateful to all of you for your encouragement and boundless patience as well as your professional expertise.

There were many others, talented professionals in their respective fields, who gave unstintingly of their time and effort. I especially wish to thank the cops: Detective Jon Spear, Sergeant Tom Waterson, Lieutenant Edward Carberry, and Sylvia Romans of the Miami Police Department; Detectives Ronnie Young and Buddy Barber of the Chesapeake Police Department; Detective Joe Gross, Metro-Dade Police Department; and Special Agent Steve Emerson of the Florida Department of Law Enforcement. Thanks also to Dr. Charles

Wetli of the Dade County Medical Examiner's Department, an entertaining and enthusiastic teacher who patiently instructed me in watching autopsies. And thanks to George Slattery, Jr., and Ed Dubois, both fine polygraphists, for their assistance and insight regarding the delicate art of polygraph examination.

In my research, I met several fine lawyers, great raconteurs who were immensely helpful and generous with their time despite crushing professional schedules. My thanks to the dynamic defense team of Alan Ross and Bob Amsel, and to the hardworking (and underpaid) prosecutors: Kevin DiGregory, John Kastrenakes, Paul Mendelson, and David Waksman of the Dade County state attorney's office, and Ben Daniels.

During the trial I was fortunate to meet Joan Fleischman, Patrick May, and Christine Evans, talented *Miami Herald* reporters who supplied advice, encouragement, and camaraderie. The excellent work of these reporters and others, especially Edna Buchanan, contributed immeasurably to my research. Although it wasn't possible to credit their work in the text of this book, I am indebted to them for their invaluable assistance, which I gratefully acknowledge here.

I am grateful to friends and relatives of the principals in this story, many of whom helped me enormously despite the sad memories which my questions recalled. Special thanks to Anne and Marvin Sheldon, Len Levenstein, C. J. Levenstein, Richard Hays, Dr. Fred Wasserman, Ted Grossman, Lynn Wruble, Jay Rossin, Sharon Johnnides, Scott Flower, Myra Wenig, Edward Smith, Jack Jamme, Ben Abernathy, Donna Brown, Bill and Beckie McDillon, George McDillon, and, in memoriam, Beatrice Wojtanek. I am especially grateful to those who requested anonymity but helped immeasurably.

My appreciation also to the jurors who generously shared their experiences with me: Dr. Catherine Poole, Margaret Gage, James Wilbur, Kenneth Fritts, and Rodolfo Gonzalez. And thanks to my excellent typists Deanna Esquijarosa and Sherry Westbrook for their tireless assistance.

Finally, my deepest gratitude to my long-suffering family, my parents, and my friends, especially Trisha Welles and Ana Barnett, all of whom offered unflagging encouragement, love, and support during this long and often lonely endeavor. I couldn't have made it without you.